Prophets and Poets

PROPHETS AND POETS

A COMPANION TO THE PROPHETIC BOOKS OF THE OLD TESTAMENT

EDITED BY
GRACE EMMERSON

The Bible Reading Fellowship

SPCK

Published by
The Bible Reading Fellowship
Peter's Way, Sandy Lane West
Oxford OX4 5HG
ISBN 0 7459 2599 5
The Society for Promoting Christian Knowledge
Holy Trinity Church
Marylebone Road, London
ISBN 0 281 04820 7

First edition 1994

Acknowledgments

Revised Standard Version of the Bible copyright © 1946, 1952, 1971 by the Division of Christian Education of the National Council of the Churches of Christ in the USA.

New Revised Standard Version of the Bible, copyright © 1989 by the Division of Christian Education of the National Council of the Churches of Christ in the USA.

A catalogue record for this book is available from the British Library

Printed and bound in Great Britain
by J.W. Arrowsmith Ltd, Bristol

CONTENTS

A NOTE

There is a companion volume to *Prophets and Poets*. Entitled *Sowers and Reapers*, it covers the four Gospels and Acts, and is edited by John Parr, joint-editor of *Guidelines*.

CONTRIBUTORS

John Barton is Oriel and Laing Professor of the Interpretation of Holy Scripture in the University of Oxford, and an Anglican priest.

Dan Beeby, a minister of the URC, was formerly Lecturer in Old Testament studies in the Selly Oak Colleges, Birmingham, and Principal of St Andrew's Hall.

John Eaton was formerly Reader in Old Testament studies at Birmingham University.

Grace Emmerson was until recently a Visiting Lecturer in the Department of Theology in the University of Birmingham. She is an Anglican lay minister.

Eric Heaton was formerly Dean of Christ Church, Oxford.

Paul Joyce, an RC layman, is Lecturer in Old Testament studies in the University of Oxford and Fellow of St Peter's College.

Rex Mason was, until retirement, Lecturer in Old Testament and Hebrew in the University of Oxford, Fellow of Regent's Park College and Lecturer at Mansfield College, Oxford.

Enid Mellor is a specialist in Religious Education and has taught in the department of education of King's College, London.

Harry Mowvley was formerly Lecturer in Hebrew in the University of Bristol and Vice Principal of Bristol Baptist College.

Joseph Robinson is Master of the Temple and Canon Emeritus of Canterbury Cathedral.

John Rogerson is Professor of Biblical Studies in the University of Sheffield and formerly joint-editor of *Guidelines*. He is an Anglican priest.

John Sawyer is head of the Religious Studies department at the University of Newcastle.

Michael Tunnicliffe is a Methodist minster in Birmingham. He is Old Teatament tutor for Black and White Christian Partnership at Selly Oak.

GENERAL INTRODUCTION

How to use this book

This is not intended as a detailed commentary but is designed as a handy volume to keep alongside your Bible. In addition to general articles on the Old Testament, it provides an introduction to each of the Old Testament prophetic books together with notes commenting on specific passages. In the case of the major prophetic books, such as Isaiah, Jeremiah and Ezekiel, their sheer length makes it impossible to include notes on every passage, but our hope is that the essence of each prophet's message will be clarified by being set in its historical context. Ancient Israel's world was very different in many ways from ours, yet the Old Testament as holy Scripture still speaks to us today—sometimes in challenge, sometimes in comfort—if we read with open minds and believing hearts. For this reason, from time to time sections are included 'to think over', and we hope that this will help readers to relate in a practical way to their daily Christian living what are often difficult passages from that pre-Christian world.

Of the prophetic books contained in the Old Testament, Amos in the eighth century is the earliest, and Malachi in the mid-fifth century possibly the latest. Zechariah 13:2–6 indicates the disrepute into which the prophetic office eventually fell, to be replaced by a different type of literature known as 'apocalyptic' of which the book of Daniel is an early example. But long before the rise of the great eighth-century prophets (Amos, Hosea, Isaiah and Micah) there had been many other prophetic figures at work in ancient Israel.

Israel's early prophets

Abraham is the first Old Testament figure to be described as a prophet (Genesis 20:7). His role here is portrayed as intercession, a characteristic function also of later prophets. Moses, too, appears as a prophetic figure, a mediator between God and his people, conveying the Lord's word to Israel, and representing the people before the Lord. The promise in Deuteronomy 18:15 of a future prophet like Moses became an important element in Israel's expectation as we see from the New Testament. Some regarded Jesus as the expected prophet, others identified him with Elijah (John 1:21) who already in Israelite tradition was regarded as having an 'eschatological' role as herald of 'the great and terrible day of the Lord' (Malachi 4:5). Thus the concluding words of the Old Testament point forward to the New Covenant.

The role of prophets in ancient Israel

One of the important things to notice immediately about the prophets is that they were involved in the whole of life, not just in what might be thought of as the 'religious' sphere. We find them involved in affairs of state and in military affairs as well as in worship and in the proclamation of God's word.

Samuel. One of the most familiar names among the early prophets is Samuel who served alongside the priest Eli in the temple of Shiloh. The account of his birth in response to his mother Hannah's prayer, and the story of his call by God, whose voice he mistook initially for that of Eli, have been a delight to many (1 Samuel 1–3). Here we come upon one of the distinguishing characteristics of all true prophets, the awareness of a specific call from God. The priesthood was hereditary; not so the prophetic ministry. Samuel's eventual role as a prophet ranged from giving advice in personal domestic matters to involvement in great affairs of state. The account of his anointing of Saul as Israel's first king in the tenth century BC (1 Samuel 9–10) illustrates various other facets of his prominence in the life of the nation. He has been sought out by Saul and his servant as a last resort in their fruitless quest for some straying domestic animals (notice that it is deemed appropriate to pay for the information and it is the servant who has the money! 9:7–8). Samuel is indeed highly respected in the community. The communal feast cannot start until he is present to 'bless the sacrifice' (9:11–13). He is also widely involved in the administration of justice (7:15–17).

Groups of prophets. Appearing in the same narrative, but in marked contrast to Samuel, is a band of prophets (1 Samuel 10:5ff). The mention of a Philistine garrison (10:5) suggests that these prophets may have been patriotic figures resisting the foreign domination of the time. The reference to their use of musical instruments is significant. We find the prophet Elisha, in a later century, calling for music in order to facilitate his prophesying (2 Kings 3:15). The story of Saul's encounter with this band of prophets seems to imply that, for Saul at least, prophesying was an involuntary, ecstatic experience: 'the spirit of the Lord came mightily upon him'. An even stranger episode is recounted in 1 Samuel 19:20–24 where first Saul's messengers, then Saul himself, are frustrated in their attempt to capture David, of whom Saul has by that time become jealous, by being immobilized through a similarly ecstatic, indeed irrational, experience. Saul's behaviour here is a far cry from the dignified figure of Samuel, though it must not be overlooked that Samuel is portrayed in 19:20 as head of this same band of prophets.

Nathan. We move on now to the time of King David, and to the famous prophet Nathan, another illustration of prophetic activity. Though associated closely with the royal court, he is not afraid to stand apart from the establishment and to criticize the king for his adultery with Bathsheba and his infamous plot to annihilate her husband Uriah. Nathan's words to David exemplify not only the function of a prophet in bringing God's word and will to bear on a situation, but the dramatic means by which a message might be presented. His poignant little story about the poor man's ewe lamb (2 Samuel 12:1–6) arouses the king's anger. Caught up in the story David's emotion spills over and he pronounces summary judgment on the guilty: 'As the Lord lives, the man who has done this deserves to die; and he shall restore the lamb fourfold, because he did this thing, and because he had no pity.' Nathan's words fall like a thunderclap: 'You are the man', two simple words in Hebrew (*'atta ha'ish*). The sequel is significant. The prophet is clearly a man to be respected even by the monarch. David's immediate response is not anger against the prophet but a stark acknowledgment of sin (v.13).

Ahijah and Shemaiah. In the turmoil following Solomon's death two prophets take centre stage. Ahijah is portrayed as taking the initiative which leads ultimately to the division of the kingdom. Meeting Jeroboam, already marked out as a leader by Solomon, he performs a dramatic symbolic action. Tearing Jeroboam's garment into twelve pieces, he signifies the break up of the kingdom, over ten of whose tribes Jeroboam is destined to become king (1 Kings 11:29–32). The other prophet, Shemaiah, acts as a restraint on Solomon's successor, Rehoboam, dissuading him from attempting to recover the allegiance of the northern tribes by force. These narratives illustrate not only the significant influence of prophets on national affairs but the use of symbolic actions so characteristic of some of the later prophets (particularly Jeremiah and Ezekiel). The divine word, uttered by God's messengers the prophets, was held to have inherent power both in its destructive aspect (Jeremiah 23:29; Hosea 6:5) and in salvation (Isaiah 55:10–11). But along with the spoken message often went symbolic actions, not simply as illustrations, but with the power of the acted as well as the spoken word.

Elijah and Elisha. To the ninth century belong these familiar names, Elijah and Elisha, the former a towering figure concerned with the meaning of true commitment to the Lord, and with social justice, even where it meant opposition to the powerful monarch, Ahab, and his still more ruthless queen, Jezebel. The element of personal danger which the prophetic ministry entailed for some at least is evident in the Elijah story. Fleeing for his life from Jezebel's anger, he falls prey to depression and to loneliness (1 Kings 19:3–4, 10). The prophets were thoroughly human, and the prophetic ministry was a costly one. The best known of the Elijah stories are his confrontation with the prophets of Baal on Mount Carmel (1 Kings 18:16–44), and his support of Naboth whose vineyard the king coveted for a vegetable garden (1 Kings 21). The inalienable right of an individual to his ancestral land (sadly still an issue in today's world) found a champion in Elijah.

Elisha, to a greater degree than Elijah, is seen as a wonder-worker, credited with miracles of healing, the most famous of these being the story of Naaman, the Syrian general. But his role, too, was a varied one, involving wider responsibilities for the nation's well-being. He was valued as an adviser to the king in conflict with Syria (2 Kings 6:9–12), to such an extent that at his death the king bewailed him as the defence of Israel, 'my father, the chariots of Israel and the horsemen thereof' (2 Kings 13:14).

Women in a prophetic role. To be a prophet was not simply a male preserve. Although few women prophets appear in the pages of the Old Testament, some clearly had considerable status in the community. One such was Huldah, contemporary with Jeremiah, to whom King Josiah turned when the law scroll (the nucleus probably of the present book of Deuteronomy) was discovered in the temple. In his consternation at how far the nation's religious life had been a denial of God's will, he consulted Huldah whose outspoken response is described in 2 Kings 22:14–20. Yet, respected though she was even by the king, it is noteworthy that no collection of her sayings was transmitted in writing in contrast to the extensive volume associated with her contemporary Jeremiah.

The two most famous of the women prophets are Miriam, sister of Moses and Aaron (Exodus 15:20), and Deborah (Judges 4:4), a woman of courage in the fight against a foreign oppressor in Judges 4 and 5. The prophetess of Isaiah 8:3 is generally considered to have been given this title as wife of the prophet Isaiah.

We find also a passing reference to a prophetess, Noadiah by name, who was numbered among Nehemiah's opponents when, in the middle of the fifth century BC, he sought to rebuild the walls of Jerusalem and to safeguard the identity of the little struggling community after the exile (Nehemiah 6:14).

Relations between prophets and rulers

Over the years the relationship between prophet and monarch changed. David responded immediately to Nathan's judgment on his adulterous and murderous action; Jeroboam (soon to be king) and Rehoboam paid heed to the words of Ahijah and Shemaiah respectively. By Jeremiah's time (seventh century BC), however, respect for the prophet had diminished. Not only did King Jehoiakim systematically destroy Jeremiah's words by public burning of the scroll (Jeremiah 36:21–24), but, under Zedekiah, the prophet was thrown into a muddy underground cistern to await certain death from hunger, had not an Ethiopian eunuch protested to the king (Jeremiah 38:4–13).

A costly ministry. It is easy to gain the impression that powerful prophets such as Amos were solitary figures, uttering their stern proclamations of judgment in splendid isolation. Yet even in the book of Amos there is more than a hint of opposition; the influential priest of Bethel tries to expel him from Israel, the northern kingdom, and drive him back to his homeland in Judah. Above all in the book of Jeremiah we encounter the sufferings of a prophet both from external hostility and from inward despondency. For here we read of false prophets who deride his message, contradicting his challenging, soul-searching words with a message of easy comfort ('peace, peace, when there is no peace'), ignoring both the realities of the situation and God's demand for repentance. In this connection Jeremiah chapters 27–28 (and chapter 23 too) make interesting reading. Hananiah, one of the false prophets, is seen in confrontation with Jeremiah. Like Jeremiah, Hananiah introduces his message with the traditional prophetic formula 'thus saith the Lord' (28:2). Like Jeremiah, too, he performs a symbolic action. But there the similarities end; the messages are incompatible. Jeremiah wears a yoke to symbolize the people's forthcoming enslavement in Babylon: Hananiah dramatically tears apart the yoke to proclaim a message of deliverance. Similar prophetic opposition can also be seen at an earlier period in the story of Micaiah, standing out as one true prophet in the face of four hundred who give a message the king wants to hear (1 Kings 22:14ff).

Preachers not writers. With the possible exception of Ezekiel, the prophets were preachers not writers. When, why and by whom their words were eventually written down we cannot say for certain. But the fact that a prophetic message was sometimes expanded to meet new circumstances is a reminder to us that these words were written, not merely to record what belonged to the past, but to bring God's word, whether of judgment or salvation, to bear on the present and the future.

ISRAEL'S PROPHETS IN THEIR HISTORICAL CONTEXT

In some instances scholars differ as to the precise dates, but the following chart gives a general outline of the chronology.

c. 1020	Saul anointed king by Samuel
c. 1000	David anointed king by Samuel
	Nathan
922	death of Solomon—division of the kingdom
	Ahijah and Shemaiah

Judah—southern kingdom		**Israel—northern kingdom**	
		c. 760	Amos
		c. 745–725	Hosea
c. 742–701	Isaiah		
725–690	Micah		
		722/1	fall of the northern kingdom
627–585	Jeremiah		
630–625	Zephaniah		
625–600	Habakkuk		
612–610	Nahum		

Exile in Babylon (587–538)

593–560	Ezekiel
550–539	Second Isaiah (ch. 40–55)

Return from exile under Cyrus (538)

c. 538–c. 515	Third Isaiah (ch. 56–66) ?
520	Haggai
520–518	Zechariah
	Obadiah ?
500–450	Joel ?
c. 450	Malachi
c. 425	Jonah ?
166–165	Daniel

THE PROPHETS AS POETS

We start with life on a housing estate—about 580BC, in the hot river-valley of Iraq (ancient Babylon). People would sit in the shade of their mud-brick walls or stand in the doorways, and eagerly pass on the word to gather shortly to hear a new message from their prophet. They looked forward to it with pleasure, as though they were going to sit at the feet of a fine singer of love-songs, skilful also with the lyre. The comparison of the prophet to a singer here in Ezekiel 33:30–33 has probably arisen because prophets expressed their message in poetry, and hence in chanting voice, and sometimes used musical instruments (1 Chronicles 25:1–3).

In our culture we know 'poets' as people who use language in attractive rhythm and measure and are skilled with rhymes and other plays of sound and sense. We expect them to express rare insights, being gifted with direct, intense awareness that sees beyond the normal. So they have great resources of imagery. Devoted to the truth, they clash with popular falsehood and lies of corrupt regimes. We speak of their 'inspiration' and they themselves feel that their insights are 'given' to them.

All these features appear also in the Hebrew prophets. Rhythm and measure are commonly present, though used with freedom (notice the large proportion of the prophetic books which are printed in poetic lines in modern translations). Can you feel, even in translation, the pulsing beat of the following lines: 2 + 2 + 2?

Heár O heávens,
give eár O eárth,
for the Lórd has spóken.

This continues with three beats in each line:

Chíldren I raísed and reáred,
but théy have rebélled agaínst me.
The óx his ówner knóws,

and the áss his máster's críb;
Ísrael doés not knów,
my peóple has nó understánding.

Isaiah 1:2–3

A beat of 3 + 2 is sometimes used for pathetic effect, as in dirges:

Fállen, no móre to ríse,
is Maíden Ísrael;
próstrate ón her lánd,
with nóne to raíse her.

Amos 5:2

These examples of rhythm also show the great feature of Hebrew poetry that has been called 'parallelism'. Things are said twice over in different words, or at least there is a balance of one statement with another. If the second statement does not repeat the preceding thought, it may take it up and add a little, or it may offer a contrast, or it may just balance it rhythmically. Skilful patterns of thought are thus developed, which (thankfully) even translations can mirror. Various effects are achieved—emphasis, climax, suspense, terror, joy, beauty. We might say that, rather than rhyming the last words of lines (this is not common in Hebrew), they 'rhymed' thoughts.

They were sensitive to the sounds of particular words and often built up effect with repetition of consonants or vowels within the lines. *Hoy ha-hokakeem ḥokakay awen*, cried Isaiah (10:1)—'Ha, you enactors of enactments of iniquity!' There was awe for words—they seemed to carry a destiny waiting to be unfolded by the inspired prophet. Thus Amos brought out the doom deeply appropriate to Gilgal: *hag-gilgal galo yigleh*, 'Gilgal shall surely go into exile' (Amos 5:5). Similarly from 'Gaza' was disclosed the Hebrew word 'forsaken', from 'Ashdod' 'plundered', and from 'Ekron' 'uprooted' (Zephaniah 2:4).

A prophet would look at some object and see deep down to a message in it, or such an object might return before his inner eye in a moment of inspiration. The steam and flames blown by a north wind from a cauldron over a fire in the open brought to Jeremiah a vision of invaders sweeping down from the north, cities in flames and streams of refugees (Jeremiah 1:13–14). Locusts, forest-fire and a sagging wall became to Amos signs of judgment threatening his people, and a basket of fruit at summer's end (*kayits*) became the tragic sign of the end (*kayts*) decreed for that society (Amos 7:1–6; 8:1–2). The imagery that fills the poetry of the prophets gives power to their words, as though Nature itself, God's handiwork, were adding its voice to the prophet's cry for weal or woe (e.g. Jeremiah 4:23–28; 5:8; Hosea 14:4–8; Joel 2:31).

The Hebrew prophets, like modern poets, could incur the wrath of the government, while the general public might also turn on them. The distress of finding hostility everywhere, and even in God, is expressed in a series of poems in Jeremiah. These illustrate how poetry was the medium of solemn prayer and how a response of God might also be heard in poetic form (Jeremiah 12:1–4). The climax of these poems comes in Jeremiah 20:7–18, ending with a passage where all the lights of the soul have virtually gone out, and God can no longer be addressed, nor his name spoken. But even this poetry was still a cry to heaven. And the sequel shows that it was heard, and Jeremiah lived yet many years to serve God faithfully.

Although the most attractive poetry from the prophets is that of Isaiah 40–55—song-like, exciting—the most brilliant poet of all is probably the less familiar Nahum. He depicts the defeat of the world tyrant Assyria in vivid scenes, but it is likely he does so *in advance* of events. His poetry is then his weapon, given by God, all the more effective for its concentrated brilliance. The truth of God's action appears in advance in the poem; it is reality coming to birth, and subsequently fills out into a great event of world history.

In their poetry then, as in their symbolic actions, the Hebrew prophets had to be instruments of God. All could be only by inspiration. It seemed to them that the hand of the Lord fell upon them (Ezekiel 3:22), he put his burning word in their bones (Jeremiah 20:9), they became in their very selves signs, living messages of God (Isaiah 8:18; Ezekiel 12:6, 11). Ezekiel (see 33:32) would say to us as to his contemporaries, 'Do not read our poetry for pleasure in its eloquence, but hear its message, and act upon it!'

THE PROPHETS AND THE NEW TESTAMENT

'To him all the prophets bear witness' declares Peter of Christ (Acts 10:43). For the early Christians the coming of Jesus was a new and stupendous event, but not unheralded. The words of the prophets enabled them to make sense of the story—they 'read' the prophets in the light of the events of Jesus' life, and they interpreted that life through the sayings of the prophets. The ancient Hebrew texts and the recent events of history illuminated each other. At first in spoken sermons and later in the writings of the New Testament, Christians set about 'making connections'. By direct quotation, and also by indirect allusion, the New Testament authors turned for support to the prophetic books. It should be noted, however, that different parts of the New Testament utilize the prophets in different ways.

Gospels and Acts

In these narratives the emphasis is upon fulfilment. The story of Jesus and of the early Church is portrayed as the confirmation of the Old Testament promises. So for instance the following passages are cited:

Jesus' birth	Isaiah 7:14; 9:6; 11:1; Micah 5:2
John the Baptist	Isaiah 40:3; Malachi 3:1; 4:1
Jesus' parables	Isaiah 6:9–10
Palm Sunday	Zechariah 9:9
Jesus' suffering and death	Zechariah 11:12; Isaiah 50:6; 52:13—53:12; Jonah 1:17
Resurrection and ascension	Daniel 7:13–14
Day of Pentecost	Joel 2:28–29
Mission to the Gentiles	Isaiah 42:6–7; 49:6; Amos 9:11–12

Words from the prophetic books are related to these events with phrases like 'thus was fulfilled what had been spoken through the prophet' (Matthew 2:17). Such a process was not confined to the Christian church. Interpretation and re-interpretation of prophecy was also a feature of Judaism in that period. So, for instance, the authors of The Dead Sea Scrolls wrote commentaries on books such as Habakkuk and Nahum applying the ancient words to their own historical situation.

Here then the stress is on *prophecy as prediction*.

The Letters

The use of the Old Testament in the Epistles is somewhat different, but phrases like 'as Scripture says', 'as it is written', 'according to the Scriptures', are common. Paul and the other New Testament letter writers were concerned with establishing right doctrine and right conduct in the churches. The ancient texts were quarried in order to confirm and support the new Christian world-view, for as it is noted in 2 Timothy 3:16, Scripture 'is useful for teaching, for reproof, for correction and for training in righteousness'. Thus in central Pauline letters such as Romans and Galatians the apostle calls upon the text of Habukkuk 2:4, 'the righteous shall live by his faithfulness' in setting out his understanding of 'justification by faith' (Romans 1:17, Galatians 3:11). He seeks to show how his crucial doctrine is not 'new fangled' but deeply embedded within Scripture.

Christian writers sought answers not only to the question 'Who was Jesus?' but also 'who are we?'. They needed to demonstrate that Christians (including Gentiles) were now part of the people of God living under the 'new covenant'. Thus in Hebrews 8 the words of Jeremiah 31:31–34 are extensively quoted. The death of Jesus established this new covenant, and the Christian Church was the 'new Israel'. At the same time Christian apologists had to explain why the majority of the Jewish people had not accepted Jesus as the Christ. Passages in the prophets which spoke of the stubbornness or hardness of heart of the Israelites to the prophets' preaching were now applied to the rejection of the Christian message. Isaiah 8:14, which speaks of 'a stone of stumbling', is quoted both in Romans 9:33 and 1 Peter 2:8. In Romans 9–11 a whole catalogue of 'proof texts' is cited to explain the lack of response by the Jewish people and the contrasting success of the mission to the Gentiles.

Again comparison can be made with near contemporary Jewish sources. In the codification of Jewish law known as the Mishnah, passages of Scripture are quoted to confirm the alternative 'world-view' of Rabbinic Judaism. Present doctrine and practice are bolstered by the ancient texts.

Here the stress is on *prophecy as upholding right teaching*.

The Apocalypse

The book of Revelation adapts the prophets in yet another way. The visionary nature of the work draws heavily on prophetic texts, in particular the books of Ezekiel, Joel and Zechariah, and on the apocalyptic book of Daniel. John of Patmos produces a kaleidoscope of images drawn from the visionary elements of the prophets. For instance, Revelation 5 weaves together into a new tapestry the following threads:

v. 1	Throne vision	Ezekiel 1
	Scroll vision	Ezekiel 2:9
vv. 2–4	The scroll sealed	Isaiah 29:11; Daniel 12:9
v. 5	The descendant of David	Isaiah 11:1
v. 6	The slain lamb	Isaiah 53:7
	The seven spirits of God	Zechariah 4:10
vv. 7–8	The four living creatures	Ezekiel 1:5ff
vv. 9–10	A new song	Isaiah 42:10
vv. 11–14	Worship in heaven	Daniel 7:10

This is typical of the literary genre of apocalyptic writings produced in the 200 years before and after the birth of Christ.

Here the dominant aspect is *prophecy as vision*.

The various New Testament authors therefore turn to prophecy to interpret the life of Christ (prophecy as prediction), to direct and instruct Christian churches (prophecy as upholding right teaching) and to kindle hope for what is still to come (prophecy as vision). The past life of Christ, the present existence of the churches and the future hope of glory are all undergirded by prophecy.

Other aspects

Additional features may also be noted briefly.

i) Quotations from the prophets in the New Testament writings often ignore the context in which the original words were spoken. The famous Immanuel text in Isaiah 7:14 was originally addressed as a word to King Ahaz at a particular crisis point in his reign. However, to discover the historical application or 'plain meaning' of the text does not exhaust its possibilities. Both Jewish and Christian writers in the Middle Ages spoke of at least four layers of meaning in a text—from the literal through to the mystical. Modern preachers may be warned against taking texts 'out of context' but this was not a problem for interpreters in the first century.

ii) Often quotations are run together. So Mark 1:2–3 marries Malachi 3:1 and Isaiah 40:3, and Romans 9:33 is a combination of Isaiah 8:14 and 28:16.

iii) The Old Testament was originally written in Hebrew (and some Aramaic). Later translations were made into other languages for Jews who no longer spoke Hebrew. The New Testament authors wrote in Greek and therefore often used the Greek versions, especially that known as the Septuagint, when quoting the prophets. For example, in Isaiah 7:14 the Hebrew text has a word meaning 'young woman', which the Greek Septuagint translates as 'virgin', and it is this translation which is quoted in Matthew 1:23. In 1 Corinthians 15:54–55 Paul quotes from Isaiah 25:8 and Hosea 13:14 in words which do not correspond precisely to either the Hebrew text or the Septuagint, but may reflect other translations. So we should not expect citations in the New Testament to reproduce exactly the equivalent passages in the Old Testament section of our Bibles.

Conclusions

In the New Testament we see the way in which the early Christians 'read' the Hebrew Scriptures. Some prophecies were considered already fulfilled in Christ, others still awaited completion. In their methods and assumptions Christian expositors shared many things in common with their Jewish counterparts. Where they parted company was in their interpretation of the same biblical texts in relation to Jesus of Nazareth. Faced with alternative ways of 'reading' the Hebrew Scriptures, it was important for them to demonstrate continuity with the Old Testament record and to be able to affirm, in the words of one of Peter's sermons, that 'to him all the prophets bear witness' (Acts 10:43).

READING THE PROPHETS TODAY

'Today' is an apt word; it is both a signpost and a caution. The biblical prophets wrote about the times in which they lived, and prediction was less important than warning and exhortation. They believed themselves to be commissioned and inspired by Yahweh to speak his word to their contemporaries—to point them away from their foolish and corrupt ways and to show them true religion and morality. They claimed direct inspiration: the most usual word for 'prophet' means literally 'one who is inspired by God' (2 Peter 1:21); their words carry a sense of conviction and of compulsion:

The Lord God has spoken,
Who can but prophesy?

Amos 3:8

Since tomorrow is inherent in today there was also an element of foretelling, more often than not the outcome of a realistic look at the national and international situation. When Jerusalem fell to Babylon in 587BC the calamity was only what prophets such as Isaiah, Jeremiah and Micah had predicted:

Zion shall be ploughed as a field,
Jerusalem shall become a heap of ruins.

Jeremiah 26:18

So in reading the prophets it is not helpful for us, any more than it was for the people of Israel and Judah, to look for exact dates and future events; the message for us is what it was for them—for example, that sin brings its own consequences, but that repentance brings forgiveness.

The teaching of early prophets such as Elijah and Elisha is always set in a story, which is a help in reading and remembering it. The major prophets, Isaiah, Jeremiah, Ezekiel and the twelve shorter prophets from Hosea to Malachi are more difficult. But they too have their stories, and it is worth finding out about them. The clue usually comes at the beginning where a date is put to the prophet's work by listing the kings during whose reigns he prophesied (Amos 1:1; Isaiah 1:1); with a concordance or Bible dictionary we can find out, probably from 1 and 2 Kings or 1 and 2 Chronicles, what was happening at the time, and this gives a real context to the prophecies. Later, when Israel and Judah no longer had kings of their own, the prophets gave the name of the king of the ruling power, which was Persia in the case of Haggai and Zechariah (Haggai 1:1; Zechariah 1:1). In the books of Isaiah and Jeremiah some narrative is included and this helps to illuminate their words for us. Sometimes we are not given direct information, and we have to deduce the background from clues in the text. This is always worthwhile; the message of restoration and hope in Isaiah 40 to 55, when we read it against the background of exile in Babylon, makes sense to us, as it did to the Jews to whom it was addressed.

The prophets were people, not disembodied voices, and if we look we can find out something about them. For example Amos, who prophesied to Israel, the wealthy and decadent northern kingdom, was 'a herdsman and a dresser of sycamore-fig trees' (Amos 7:14) from Tekoa (Amos 1:1) in the infertile southern kingdom, so it is not surprising that he was horrified at what he saw, and that his teaching was less than welcome. A stranger proclaiming a deeply unpopular and unfashionable message is equally unacceptable today. By contrast Isaiah of Jerusalem was a courtier, accustomed to having the ear of the king; it was shocking, then as now, when an establishment figure pronounced harsh judgment on his master (Isaiah 39).

Context and personality are helpful, but what is most important is the universal and timeless message which the prophets proclaim. Injustice, oppression, greed, hypocrisy and violence were prevalent thousands of years ago and are evident in our own society; any newspaper or television news programme will tell us as much. But equally, God has not changed. His justice, mercy, steadfast love and sovereign power are for ever. At the very end of the Old Testament he speaks through the prophet Malachi (3:6):

I the Lord do not change;
therefore you, O sons of Jacob, are not consumed.

The prophets were real people, living in real situations, and it helps to understand their message if we get to know them in their context. But paramount in reading their words is the need to be open to the relevance of their message to us and to our own times, and to apply it to our own lives.

TRANSLATING THE BIBLE

One of today's great riches is the number and variety of English translations of the Bible. We can choose traditional or modern language, formality or simplicity of style and expression, as best suits us. Yet this opportunity for personal choice is itself something of a problem, not least for those who write, and those who read, Bible study notes. Not only do the words of the various translations differ, but the division into paragraphs may vary too, and a meaning which seems clear in one translation may not be so obvious in another.

This is not the only problem. Some of us grew up in days when it was customary to learn by heart passages of the Bible, thus storing up resources for times of illness or weakness when reading becomes impossible, or for those rarer crises which befall some who are deprived of their Bible whether through the banning of its use or through their own confinement as hostages. At such times comfort comes through Scriptures stored within the memory. Unfortunately the present variety of translations has discouraged this practice. And yet there is benefit too. For those who wish seriously to study the Bible it is helpful to consult more than one translation. Fresh insights are gained. It is 'like looking through a new window at an old landscape' (A.M. Hunter). For it is possible for a passage to become over-familiar, and reading it in another translation jolts us with surprise: 'Is this really what the text means? Why did I never see that before?'

The art of translating is no easy one. Translating is not a mechanical activity, merely transferring words from one language to another. Words in different languages are rarely precise equivalents and the context will determine which one of a number of English words is appropriate as a rendering of a Hebrew word. But clearly it is at this point that every translator is, to some extent, obliged to be an interpreter. A famous example is the Hebrew word *hesed* which basically means 'steadfast loyalty' and is used to describe God's covenant relationship with his people and theirs with him and their fellow humans. It is this word which is used in Hosea 6:4, 6 and Micah 6:8 as well as frequently elsewhere. It is an interesting exercise to look up these passages in any versions of the Bible which you have and compare them. Where the New Revised Standard Version has 'love' (Hosea 6:4), and 'steadfast love' (Hosea 6:6) and 'kindness' (Micah 6:8), the New International Version has 'love', 'mercy' and 'mercy' respectively. In contrast the Revised English Bible translates as 'loyalty' in all three instances.

Reading a translation, however competent, can never be quite the same as reading the original, for there is always another consideration in the translator's mind: what kind of reader is he or she translating for? Is it to be a formal translation for public reading, or simple and more homely? And this is the reason for many of the variations between translations. These modern readers are different from those who originally listened to the ancient prophets. And yet it is a mistake, one that is commonly made, to think that for those who know the original language (Hebrew in the case of the prophets) everything becomes clear. That is not so. There are difficulties within the text, sometimes because of obscure words, sometimes through problems of interpretation. Even Jesus' original hearers did not always understand him. Part of the reason in their case was that they lacked spiritual perception. '*I believe*, therefore I understand' (Augustine).

But, you may be thinking, why can we not have a literal translation, keeping as close as possible to the original? The problem here is that Hebrew ways of saying things are not English ones, and sometimes an over-literal translation obscures the meaning. However, translations such as the Revised Standard and New International Versions reflect in general the structure and expressions of the original language, whereas the New English Bible (and its recent revision the Revised English Bible) and the Good News Bible, both very valuable translations, aim for more idiomatic modern English. In one sense, a translation takes on a life of its own. This has been particularly true of the King James version (AV) which has itself so greatly influenced the English language, contributing a number of familiar expressions of which the Biblical origins are often forgotten.

Some aspects of the original cannot be captured in translation. The prophets were poets, and sometimes they used a play on words to sharpen their message in a way which startled, and even shocked, their hearers.

An outstanding example is found in Isaiah 5:7:

[God] looked for justice [mishpat],
but behold, bloodshed [mispah];
for righteousness [tsedaqah],
but behold, a cry [tse 'aqah]!

It is not possible to represent this alliteration adequately in English. Ezekiel's famous vision of the valley of dry bones presents a similar difficulty in its repetition of one Hebrew word (*ruah*) to signify both wind, breath and spirit, and most English versions have footnotes to this effect. But it is clearly impossible in English to convey the meaning adequately without using these three different words as appropriate.

The structure of the Hebrew language itself sometimes creates a problem. A famous instance is Amos' reply to the priest of Bethel who scornfully challenged him to go back to his own country and earn his living there (Amos 7:12–15). Did Amos reply, 'I am no prophet', or did he say, 'I was no prophet . . . but it was the Lord who said to me, "Go and prophesy to my people Israel." '? The difficulty here is that the Hebrew sentence in this instance has no verb and consequently does not express the time reference. But anyway, does it matter? Yes, it is significant, for on the first alternative Amos is disclaiming any connection with those known as prophets, and by implication disapproving of them, whereas on the second alternative he is willing to be classed as a prophet (*nabi'*). Here a decision about the meaning of the text inevitably influences the translation.

Likewise it is the distinctive nature of the Hebrew alphabet which accounts in some instances for substantial differences in translation. An interesting illustration is found in Isaiah 62:5 in the difference between the Revised Standard Version and its newer revision. The Hebrew (followed by the RSV) literally means, 'your *sons* shall marry you', a surprising image even as a metaphor! In contrast, the New Revised Standard Version has 'so shall your *builder* marry you', a thought entirely consistent with the Old Testament idea of God as husband of his people. Can these two versions be translating the same text? The answer lies in the fact that the Hebrew alphabet consists only of consonants. The detailed vowel system that we have in printed Hebrew Bibles belongs to approximately the eighth century AD. It may be that occasionally the vowels, which are not part of the sacred text, have been incorrectly transmitted. In this particular example the consonants are *bnyk*; the difference lies mainly in the vowels: read as *banayik*, the meaning is 'your sons'; read as *bonek*, the meaning is 'your builder'. The latter lies behind the Good News Bible, 'He who formed you will marry you', and the Revised English Bible, 'so will you be wedded to him who rebuilds you'.

Our translations are eminently trustworthy and dependable, but translation is never a mechanical exercise. It is an art, not a science. Although, in general, the distinction between paraphrase and translation is a valid one, at times there is only a narrow dividing line between them. A translator's aim is generally to make the language of the Bible familiar to the modern reader, though more recently there have been voices raised against 'domesticating' the Scriptures. Certainly the prophets themselves were strange figures and their message was extraordinary. This is a dimension we must not lose. The Scriptures speak of God who is beyond human language and understanding.

To conclude, the transfer from one language to another is difficult but it is not impossible, as the undiminished power of the Scriptures throughout the centuries to change human lives and to bring us to God continually testifies.

Further reading

For more detailed treatment relating to both Old and New Testaments see:

G.I. Emmerson, 'Problems of Translation' in R.J. Coggins and J.L. Houlden, editors, *A Dictionary of Biblical Interpretation*, SCM Press, London, 1990

C. Hargreaves, *A Translator's Freedom: Modern English Bibles and their Language*, JSOT Press, Sheffield, 1993

ISAIAH

1–39

Almost all that we know of the prophet Isaiah is to be found in the first thirty-nine chapters of the book that goes by his name. He played a prominent part in events of the kingdom of Judah. The history of Judah is given in 2 Kings, and Isaiah is mentioned there, but most of what we learn about him there is repeated in chapters 36–39 of his book. Those chapters, an extract from 2 Kings, seem to have been added to the prophecy so that all the information about Isaiah could be available in one book. So Isaiah 1–39 is the source both of his teaching, and also of the information we know about him. The rest of the book of Isaiah, chapters 40–66, is concerned with other prophets, and relates to a much later period of history.

Yet Isaiah 1–39 is not a biography. It is made up of that part of the prophet's teaching, and such information about his life, as was remembered by disciples and collected by them to be passed on to future generations. Nor is the information contained in the book set out in chronological order. (The story of Isaiah's call by God to be a prophet is found in chapter 6 following five chapters of the teaching that he gave as a prophet.) So, to put the story into context, we need to look first at what we are told in 2 Kings of the history of the kingdom of Judah in Isaiah's lifetime, and then relate his teaching, as far as it is possible, to his life. Of course, this can only be done where the teaching arises out of, or relates to, some historical incident of which we have knowledge. Some of the teaching is quite general and could have been given at any time during his ministry. Indeed, it may have been given more than once.

So, who was Isaiah? He was a citizen of Jerusalem who lived in the eighth century BC. He was an important and influential member of the society of his time. He was consulted by kings on the great issues of the day: issues upon which the very future of the society depended, and, even when not consulted, he made his views on such matters known. So he was probably an aristocrat, and issues of state and, in particular, national security greatly concerned him. He was active as a prophet during the reigns of two kings, Ahaz (736–716BC) and Hezekiah (716–687BC).

Why was a prophet so deeply involved in secular matters? The answer is that political and religious issues were so closely interrelated in his time that they could not be kept apart. So the issues that he was involved in were political but his interest in them, and the influence he tried to exert upon them, were religious. For him the integrity, more, the very existence of his faith, was dependent upon the decisions taken on political issues.

To understand this, we must look back into the history of his people. The people of Israel had first settled in Palestine some hundreds of years before Isaiah's time. They believed that they were God's chosen people; that the land had been given to them as a gift from God, and that it was their duty and vocation to create in that land a community that lived in the pattern that God willed for all human communities. So, by their obedience to the will of God, they would set an example for others to follow. Their neighbours, the Canaanites, did not follow God's ways. They had created societies devoted to the pursuit of power and wealth at all costs. To many of the people of Israel, and to their kings in particular, they were a temptation, and almost all the prophets were concerned, as was Isaiah, to resist that temptation. To succumb to it would mean the spiritual destruction of the community, and its failure in obedience to God.

For Isaiah this general issue presented itself in a particular form. After the death of Solomon the people of Israel had separated into two kingdoms. Isaiah was a subject of the southern, smaller kingdom named Judah with its capital at Jerusalem. In his time, both Hebrew kingdoms belonged to a group of states that were spread along the eastern shore of the Mediterranean sea. As such they lay along the land route linking the two great empires of Egypt and Assyria. Assyria was an aggressive power, out for conquest, and aiming to get at Egypt by capturing, one by one, the little states that lay in its way along the Mediterranean coast. To meet the Assyrian threat the little states sought to create alliances with each other. These alliances were, of course, the political issues with which Isaiah was concerned.

But they were more than political issues. Such an alliance meant recognizing, and to some degree sharing, the religion of the other nation. Thus king Ahaz introduced an Assyrian altar into the temple at Jerusalem (2 Kings 16:10–16). To Isaiah this was apostasy. The God of Israel was so different in character from the gods of the other nations that there could be no sharing of worship without grave danger of the loss of Israel's own distinctive faith. So he stood for political isolation, a rejection of all diplomatic alliances, because only that way could the distinctive character of his people's faith and worship witness to the uniquely personal character of their God. This was a policy that involved great risk. Isolation meant weakness. Only close political alliances seemed able to guarantee any real security for the nation. But for Isaiah that was the true test of faith. Was security to be sought in political alliances that compromised the purity of Israel's faith, or in trust in God himself? If the land was God's gift to his people, could he not be relied upon to preserve them in it? Reliance on any other help but God's alone was faithlessness. Isaiah fully accepted that following his policy could, probably would, mean invasion and the suffering that such invasion would bring, but, even at the worst of times, hope need never be abandoned. For in the end, God would create a better future in which all he willed for his people would be brought about by a perfect king ruling over a perfect society.

Further reading

For the Book of Isaiah:

A.S. Herbert, *Isaiah 1–39*, Cambridge Bible Commentary

R.E. Clements, *Isaiah 1–39*, New Century Bible

For the historical background:

E.W. Heaton, *The Hebrew Kingdoms*

John Rogerson, editor, *New Atlas of the Bible*, Macdonald

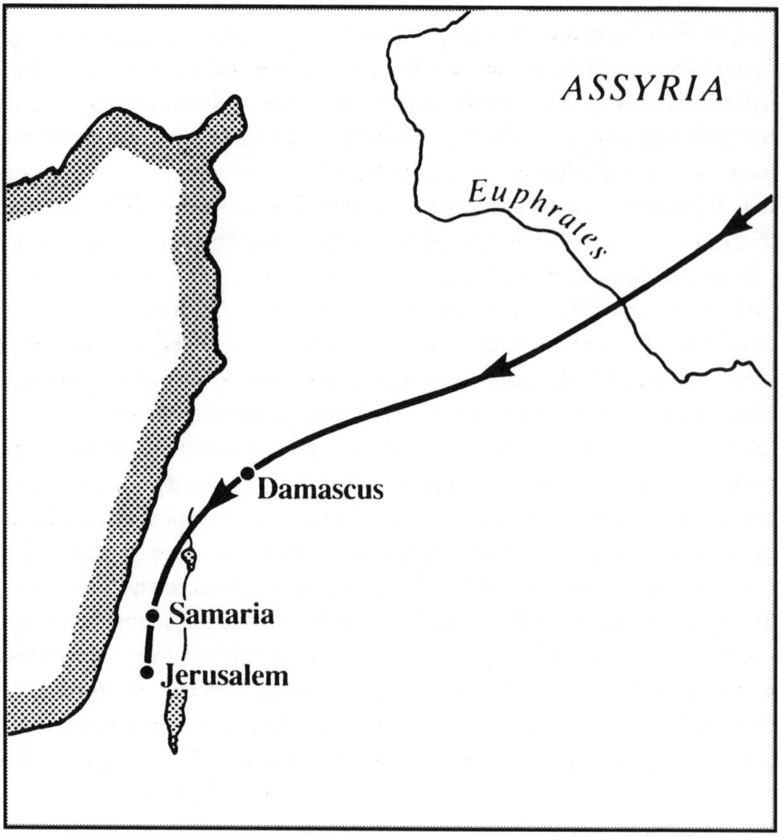

God calls Isaiah

Isaiah 6:1–4

This story describes the beginning of Isaiah's ministry and it is dated. King Uzziah died in the year 742BC. The story gives the authority for Isaiah's claim that he was God's spokesman. No one chose to be a prophet. The work was usually uncomfortable and unpopular and its authority would have been undermined if anyone seemed to be undertaking it out of personal ambition. All the prophets spoke and acted with the conviction that they were impelled by God. They could do no other.

Something happened in the temple to Isaiah that convinced him that he had been face to face with his God. No description of God is given. His presence is implied by the vision having taken place in the temple which was looked upon as God's earthly dwelling place, and the purpose of the vision was declared by the presence of the seraphim. These were mysterious winged animals which were believed to wait upon God in perpetual worship and service. One pair of wings covered the face in worship, the second covered the body in humility and the third were ready for instant service. They epitomize the service to which Isaiah had been called. The whole building was endlessly filled with a hymn of praise which declared the character of the God whose servant Isaiah was to be. He was *holy*.

Holiness. The word 'holy' was already well-known and much used. It meant 'separation' or 'otherness'. It pointed to the essential difference between the Creator and his creatures. But this 'difference' could be interpreted in different ways. It had been thought, for example, that the difference lay in power. God was all-powerful; man was comparatively powerless. One part of the value of the vision was in showing Isaiah the true nature of that difference. In earlier times the separation implied by holiness had been understood as simply physical. A holy place was a place set aside for God's use. A holy house was one in which God dwelt in much the same way as a palace was a house in which a king lived. Isaiah's response showed that holiness went far deeper than that. The separation it indicated was one of character. The Creator differed in character from his creation. The people, even Isaiah, were unclean. In this encounter the truly religious character of the word 'holy' has been established for ever.

Glory. Then too, there was the glory. Glory referred to outward splendour. It could be used of God as the Creator, or of kings as earthly rulers. But with human beings outward splendour could be a cover for inner emptiness or faithlessness. With God glory was that outward splendour that *revealed* the inner being. The creation itself spoke eloquently of the goodness, reliability and faithfulness of God. Just as important for Isaiah as the fact of meeting God was the revelation of the nature of God. It was the Lord, Israel's God, who was calling him.

We repeat the words of the seraphim at Communion services, 'Holy, Holy, Holy is the Lord of Hosts' (Isaiah 6:3). They should recall to our minds that holiness to which we are called, and the direct link between worship and life which they imply.

Send me *Isaiah 6:5–8*

Isaiah's honest response to his sense of the holiness of God established a real separation between himself and his God. He was unclean and therefore unworthy of the office to which God was calling him. More than unworthy, he was not capable of being and doing what God would have him be and do. The revelation of the holiness of God seemed to have created an impasse that could not be bridged. Then God took the initiative to recreate in Isaiah the capacity to serve. The image of the altar-fire suggests both cleansing and energizing. Once God had removed the impediment, Isaiah responded with obedience. It is the combination of the initiative of God and the obedience of a human being which creates a servant of God.

The message *Isaiah 6:9–13*

Isaiah found that he had a very unpalatable message to declare. The message summarized the experience he would have as a prophet from that day on to the last day of his ministry. He, for his part, must speak the word that God had given him to speak. The people might hear the words physically but they would be incapable of understanding and appropriating them. They could not change, as God demanded that they should, because they were not willing to change. 'There are none so deaf as those who will not hear.' The NEB softens the meaning of the Hebrew in verse 9. Compare the RSV or the JB where the full harshness of the Hebrew is brought out in the translation. Far from restoring the people to God in repentance and faith, the word of the prophet seemed to do no more than lay a further layer of insulation on their lives, isolating them even more from God and making any change that much more difficult. It seemed that this could only continue and increase until the suffering and destruction which is the fruit of sin came upon them.

Obedience. The prophet's obedience seemed to lead inevitably to suffering. In his suffering he would be at one with the people who had brought suffering upon themselves by their sin. So there is a first hint here that it would be by suffering rather than by words that reconciliation would be brought about. The temple ritual itself taught that the only way for the unholy to approach the holy was through sacrifice.

> *The call to be God's mouthpiece comes only to the few but it has lessons for us all. God has work for every one of us who is willing to be his servant. We discover what our work is through obedience.*

True and false worship

Isaiah 1:1–17

So far we have followed the story of Isaiah's call. We shall look now at representative passages from his teaching which illustrate further what Isaiah had to tell the people.

This passage contains a typical comment of Isaiah on the worship that the people offered. They thronged the temple. They were assiduous in the performance of what they considered to be their religious duties. Isaiah told them that their religious practices meant nothing to God to whom they were directed. This must have puzzled the people. What more could they do that they had not done already? The answer was, 'Nothing'. The problem lay not in what they did, but in the spirit in which they offered their worship. They were failing to distinguish between the true and false meaning of holiness. Their worship was being offered as a substitute for lives that were other than God would have them be. True worship was an offering that represented a life lived in the service of God. Hands that had shed the blood of some other child of God could not be raised acceptably in prayer. One true test of a life that was acceptable to God was concern shown for those in society who were underprivileged and had not the power or influence to obtain what was due to them. In Israelite society, such were the oppressed, the orphan and the widow. Holy living was demonstrated by care for such persons. Assiduous attendance at temple worship and indifference to the fate of such persons meant that the worship was insincere and unholy. Worship cannot be divorced from life.

One people?

Isaiah 5:8–23

The people had lost all real sense of community. They were meant to be one people, God's own people, but they were no more than a collection of groups and classes with different ideas and conflicting interests, held together simply by living in the same geographical area.

The sense of being one people had been lost through the possession of land. Ownership of land had opened up the possibilities of wealth and power to the strong and unscrupulous. The rich used even the structures of society to further their own interest. The law that was meant to protect the weak could be perverted by bribes or threats. The lifestyle of the rich was filled with selfish extravagance and drunkenness.

The complete lack of any sense of the proper relationship between worship and life had eroded all sense of common interest. There was no sense of responsibility for each other and to God. The land had been presented to them originally as God's gift in which they should live as his people. It was being treated as the possession of those who had been strong enough to capture it for themselves. They intended to hold it against all comers by all means.

God's vineyard *Isaiah 5:1–7*

This parable sums up Isaiah's teaching to the people on the subject of holiness. This is pre-eminently the teaching to which they will listen but will not understand. When the vineyard did not produce grapes of the quality to be expected every possible explanation would have been sought other than that the vines themselves were defective. Every possible solution would have been tried other than the obvious one of replacing the vines with new stock. The image of Israel as a vine planted by God was a favourite one. Jeremiah used it in the same sense (Jeremiah 2:21), and Ezekiel seems to have known this parable (Ezekiel 15:1–8). The Psalmist also uses the image (Psalm 80:8–18). The image of Israel as God's vine was clearly well-known. It must have come into use after Israel's possession of the land of Canaan. It implied that the land was a good gift from God to be used to the full.

This view had not always been held. There had been a time when Israel was suspicious of the land as an alien element in her heritage. Many of the devout thought that it should be treated with reserve and used only sparingly because its fruits were a possible source of corruption. The best known of such groups were the Rechabites (see Jeremiah chapter 35), who made a particular point of avoiding the vine and its fruit. Isaiah took a different view but he was as aware as any Rechabite of the temptations that the land offered.

Notice how the prophet draws in his audience to share in judgment on the unfaithful vineyard (v. 3) only to find themselves accused (v. 7). Compare with this Nathan's parable against David's sin in 2 Samuel 12.

We discover material possessions are a gift from God. No one has a freehold on life: we are all leaseholders. We need then to accept responsibility to God for everything we possess.

A threat to Judah *Isaiah 7:1–9*

Here we see Isaiah acting as a statesman. He offers advice to the king on a matter that threatens the very existence of the nation. The year was 735BC. The Assyrians had undertaken one of their campaigns to subdue the little kingdoms that lay in the way of their access to Egypt. Two of these kingdoms, Judah's northern neighbours, had determined to create a military alliance to oppose the advance of Assyria. One was Israel, with Samaria as its capital, The other was Aram (Syria) whose capital was Damascus. Isaiah advised King Ahaz not to join the coalition. His advice was a mixture of political wisdom and religious conviction. In his view the coalition had not the strength to succeed. It would be destroyed by the Assyrians. Also the coalition had not the strength to compel Judah to join. Jerusalem was a very powerful fortress that could hold out indefinitely. Finally, these military and political adventures were bound to fail because God wished to preserve the independence of Judah. The significance of this last point lay in the fact that only political independence ensured purity of religious worship. One of the consequences of an alliance with another state was that the gods of the other state were accepted as objects of worship. Israel had always been committed since Moses' time to the exclusive worship of the Lord God. So any military alliance also involved religious issues. To join the alliance, as Ahaz considered doing, would destroy the nation spiritually. To remain isolated, as Isaiah counselled, would preserve the nation spiritually, and physically too, if Isaiah's reading of events was correct.

A sign from God *Isaiah 7:10–17*

Ahaz would not accept Isaiah's word so the prophet suggested that the matter should be settled by a direct approach to God. This is what was meant by a sign. Some test should be arranged, perhaps within the temple, whose result could only be controlled by God. So the result could be taken to declare God's will. The king had not sufficient confidence in his own decision to subject it to such a test.

The birth of a child. Isaiah then replied that God would supply his own sign. It would be the birth of a child. In Israelite tradition God was believed to have indicated new initiatives by the birth of a special child who had grown up to become an outstanding servant of God. Isaac's birth had been seen in this way (Genesis 17:16–19), as was Samson's and Samuel's. The sign here was to be the birth of a new child in this succession; that it *was* a sign would be shown by the special name given to the child, Immanuel, God with us.

Centuries later the birth of Jesus was acknowledged by the first Christians as being in this succession. Indeed they claimed that Jesus was the greatest of all the special servants of God. For them he was the 'Immanuel', far more than the child to whom Isaiah had first given the name.

Blessing or curse? It is not clear whether the birth was to inaugurate a period of special blessing or disastrous judgment. 'Eating curds and honey' has been understood to mean blessing: curds and honey was a kind of ambrosia, the food of the gods. On the other hand it is also the natural food of the nomad and as such can be seen to point to a time of poverty and deprivation. In the circumstances the second interpretation seems the more likely. God's sign is offered to convict the king of faithlessness.

Disaster *Isaiah 7:18–25*

This passage resolves the ambiguity noted above in reference to 'curds and honey'. It describes a time in the near future when the people would suffer terrible disaster. Many interpreters have judged it to be a passage added to the original book by a disciple of the prophet whose purpose was to settle the ambiguity. Evil times did fall upon Judah after 735BC and the disciple was keen to show that Isaiah had seen that they were coming. The actual words used here may have been spoken by Isaiah. The work of the disciple would have been to collect them and place them at this point in the book, so that they come to have a particular reference to the Immanuel prophecy.

Humiliation. Both the great powers, Assyria and Egypt, would descend on Judah like plagues of flies and bees. Shaving the hair from head and body was a mark of humiliation and the NEB masks the full horror of the Hebrew, which gives not 'body' but 'feet'—a euphemism for the genitals. Within the lifetime of Isaiah every part of the land of Judah with the exception of the city of Jerusalem had suffered such an extreme of humiliation.

A prophetic symbol *Isaiah 8:1–4*

The birth of Isaiah's son was a prophetic symbol. The prophets declared God's will to the people not only in words but also in symbolic actions. Such actions were believed to have great power. They indicated God's will as clearly and decisively as any words. That is the reason why the child's mother was referred to as the prophetess. The birth of the child was itself a prophecy.

The conception and birth of this child is clearly related to the Immanuel prophecy. Perhaps Ahaz ignored that prophecy and this was a second attempt to gain his attention. The name given to the child was a part of the symbol. It was not meant for the king alone: the intention was that the name should be known to the general public. The name, though in itself full of threat ('speed-spoil-hasten-plunder' NEB) was meant as a sign of blessing. The threat was directed against the two kings of Aram and Israel who were threatening Judah. Within a very short time they would be defeated by the Assyrians and cease to trouble Judah.

If 7:18–25 is the work of a disciple, who added other prophecies of Isaiah to the original writing, these words would originally have followed directly after the Immanuel prophecy. They may then have been meant to show its fulfilment. The alliance of the two kings did fail but the long-term result of this was not blessing for Judah. Because of the policies of Ahaz and his successor the disasters spoken about in 7:18–25 also happened.

The waters of Shiloah *Isaiah 8:5–10*

This passage is made up of two sections which were probably originally independent, 6–8a and 8b–10. They were likely to have been first spoken on different occasions. They have been joined together here because they are both seen to relate to the occasion when the prophet met king Ahaz 'at the end of the Conduit by the Upper Pool'.

Waters of menace. The first prophecy (6–8a) is one of judgment and uses the imagery of water. Jerusalem received its water supply from a spring, and a conduit had been made to channel the water from the spring to a pool so that the water could be stored. The prophet contrasted the water gently flowing along the conduit with the great river Euphrates. Jerusalem lived by the water that was directed to it along the conduit (Shiloah means 'directed'). God had sent his prophet to be a conduit of the Spirit. His words were the water of the Spirit, sustaining life, but they had been rejected. Since the people would not accept that water they would receive the rough, turbulent and destructive waters of the Euphrates—the Assyrians.

Waters of hope. The second prophecy (8b–10) is a hymn of faith and hope, perhaps added here to modify the gloom of the first prophecy. The basis of hope is Immanuel. Humanly speaking, the future might look black and full of menace, as the first prophecy stated, but in the end all things and all people were in the hand of God. Israel had concrete experience in their past of God's love and care. What he had done in the past, he would do again in the future. So the one sure basis for faith and hope was the character of God.

Hardship — *Isaiah 8:11–18*

Here we reach the conclusion of the incident with King Ahaz. Ahaz did not accept Isaiah's word. He sought for a solution to his problem by asking for help from the Assyrians. The result was that he became their vassal and had to compromise the purity of his faith by accepting Assyrian idols into the temple. Isaiah was told to maintain his loyalty to God even though that loyalty would involve him in hardship. King Ahaz's solution would lead the people to face a different hardship. They would become more and more alienated from their God.

The remnant. Part of the hardship that faced Isaiah was the need to be silent. The policy that Ahaz had decided to follow was to Isaiah so totally contrary to God's will that any word of his that was loyal to God must appear to be treason to the king. The word of God to Isaiah at 6:9 had come to very bitter fulfilment. But witness was possible even in silence. The prophet and his disciples, 'the sons whom the Lord has given me', lived on quietly in Jerusalem. They lived faithful to God and so were themselves signs ready to be active again for God when circumstances should permit.

The problem of discipleship is not so much recognizing God's signs, as knowing how to interpret them. That special maturity which possession of the Holy Spirit gives is surely seen in the capacity to find the true interpretation of the signs that God sends. Silent witness can be more effective in some circumstances than words, but it involves the agony of deciding when to speak and when to be silent.

The day of doom

Isaiah 2:6–22

After the death of Ahaz, and Hezekiah's succession to the throne, Isaiah broke his silence. Once again he was God's spokesman declaring to the people God's attitude towards their activities. It is impossible to be certain of the date of many of the passages that have been collected in chapters 1–39. They could have been spoken either in Ahaz's time or Hezekiah's. What Isaiah said fits the situation in the reign of both kings. For this reason they may have been spoken more than once, in which case they are summaries of the prophet's attitude to this aspect of the life of his people. One basic element in the situation was that the upper classes of Judaean society had become wealthy. The wealth came both from ownership of land and also from trade. Trading implied friendly relationships with neighbouring nations, and, in the conditions of those times, a friendly attitude to the religious practices of those neighbours. The distinctive elements in the Hebrew religion and way of life were being eroded. Reliance upon God was being replaced by reliance upon wealth. The people were not abandoning religious practice but, by their growing conformity to the practices and values of other nations, the distinctive qualities of their own religion were disappearing.

A time would come when all this would be put to the test and the truth about the situation would be made clear. Natural disasters would happen which would make the people realize that wealth could offer no lasting security, and that the gods of the neighbouring nations were powerless idols, without meaning or value. This would be God's 'day of doom'.

It is not difficult, looking at our world, to believe that the day of judgment must be a day of doom. There is so much suffering around us, and so many prophecies of coming disaster from nuclear bombs, ecological breakdown, and other perils, that it is only too easy to expect approaching doom. But the New Testament tells us that Good Friday was the day of God's judgment, and, if that is so, then hope always lies beyond disaster.

Society in decay

Isaiah 3:1–15

The coming time of disaster would be so fierce that the whole fabric of society would crumble. All those who exercised any kind of leadership in society would have their authority undermined. The basis on which they had built their society had proved to be useless. Youth would take over the leadership since their elders had proved to be failures. But youth was without knowledge or experience, and simply made matters worse. Any person who had managed to preserve a few possessions would be turned to for leadership, but would shrink away from what had become an impossible task. The prophet draws a graphic picture of a society in total disintegration.

Whose responsibility? What is the value of this description? Is it anything more than a crude attempt to frighten people into change? For Isaiah the issue was responsibility. When the disaster came it would not be mere bad luck. It would not be a matter of the people being swept up in a disaster whose origins lay outside their own control. The situation would be the consequence of the people's misuse of the land that God had given to them. The leaders would bear the greatest responsibility, but the whole people were involved. All had willingly acquiesced in the corruption of society.

The Assyrian rod

Isaiah 10:5–11

How would God bring about his 'day of doom'? Isaiah's answer was that since God is in control of the whole universe, he uses his creatures to fulfil his will. Here the dreaded Assyrian would be the weapon that God would use. The baldness and simplicity of Isaiah's words raise a problem of great perplexity. Are we to think of a righteous God as using a cruel and unrighteous empire as his instrument? There is a problem for religion in this, but faith has to begin with the facts of experience. Life itself provides the material with which faith must deal and if faith tries to ignore life then it becomes itself a very pale and sickly creature.

The facts. Isaiah has clear evidence to hand. The Assyrian empire had become a real threat to the future of Judah. At the time that Isaiah was speaking these words the Assyrians had already conquered all the countries to the north of Judah. Samaria, the capital city of the state of Israel, had fallen. Judah was the next country in the line of Assyria's advance towards Egypt. There was no human reason to believe that Judah would not be destroyed as all the other countries had been. So with an Assyrian threat to Judah imminent, what was to be said of the situation? For Isaiah it did not mean, as it probably did for other religious teachers, that God had lost control of events. Rather God was in control of all events. Nor had God changed his attitude towards his people. His purpose was still their well-being. It was their stupidity and faithlessness which had brought the Assyrian army on the scene. Once that army had appeared it too could be God's instrument.

God's use of people *Isaiah 10:12–19*

Can the holy God use an unholy people as his instrument? Isaiah clearly thought so, but he did not take the simplistic view that persons and nations are helpless automata, unknowing pawns being pushed about on the chessboard of history. The Assyrian was a free agent, making his own plans, furthering by his actions his own ambitions and aspirations. In his own eyes he was a completely free agent, doing what he alone wanted to do.

Isaiah accepted all this as true. It would be immoral to punish the Assyrian for deeds for which he was not responsible. Yet, at the same time, there was a higher level at which the Assyrian's actions were the instruments of God's purpose. To the eye of faith, life was an interrelationship of personal forces, so that, at one and the same time, the actions of the Assyrian could be both his own free act and also the instrument of the will of God. God was in complete control of his universe.

Three deductions follow from this. First, the Assyrian like all other people is responsible for his actions and must accept this responsibility before God. Secondly, the Assyrian like all other people may succeed in what he sets out to do and thus believe that he has imposed his will on events; but to the eye of faith God uses the Assyrian to impose his own will. So in events which may seem black and bitter, faith still looks for the will of God. Thirdly, since God, not the Assyrian, is in ultimate control, faith can, even in the darkest moments, hold on to the certainty that there is a good future yet to be revealed.

The interrelationship between God's design and human free will causes us many doubts and much heartache, but in the end we must affirm both.

A remnant shall return *Isaiah 10:20–23*

We have already noticed one occasion on which Isaiah gave his son a name that was meant as a prophetic symbol (8:3). Isaiah had another son who had gone with him to meet King Ahaz (7:3). That son also bore a symbolic name. His name 'Shear-jashub' means 'a remnant shall return', and can be interpreted either as a prophecy of doom or of hope. By the first interpretation its meaning is, 'only a remnant shall return'. The majority of the people will be lost. The alternative is to understand it as meaning that though most will be lost yet God will not be left without some faithful servants, a remnant *shall* return.

The future. Here again the same words are used. The Assyrian was a rod. His blows upon the people would be real and severe. But he was an instrument of God and that would be made plain in that 'a remnant shall return'. The future to which the people must look forward is both threatening and also hopeful. The hope comes through the acceptance of the threat and what lies beyond it. Isaiah sees no easy time ahead for his people, and he offers no easy words of false and deceitful comfort. Faith is no shield behind which to cower until the storm is past. Rather it is a rock against to lean so as not to be blown away in the storm.

The stock of Jesse *Isaiah 11:1–9*

Isaiah's faith forced him to see all that happened as a part of God's will. It never allowed him to ignore the unpleasant things in life. Yet by the same token, it would not allow him to see those things, here suffering and defeat for his people, as the final things in life. God is good, therefore all things must in the end work together for good. God is faithful, and so the promises he has made to his people will be fulfilled.

David's seed. Long before Isaiah's time Jerusalem had been captured by David and made the capital city of his kingdom. One aspect of God's promise to his people was a promise made to King David that his descendants would always reign in Jerusalem (2 Samuel 7:12–16). It seemed in the light of events in Isaiah's day that this promise had been rash. Most of the descendants of David had used their reigns to turn the kingdom away from God and towards the ways of their pagan neighbours. So the Assyrian had been sent as God's rod. Yet beyond that Isaiah looked for a good future. He visualized it as an ideal kingdom ruled over by a descendant of David who would be filled with the Spirit of God. He would be full of insight and judgment to plan the right things, and full of energy to put them into operation. The harmony and perfect fellowship created by such a king would spill over into nature itself so that the whole creation would reflect the being of the God who had made it.

In our world where human knowledge and responsibility have increased so greatly, we need to remind ourselves, even more frequently, that it is only in response to God that the universe will become the harmonious creation God wills it to be.

Hard lessons to be learned *Isaiah 28:1–13*

Historical background. In 705BC the Assyrian emperor Sargon II died, and in the period of confusion that followed, when several pretenders were trying to gain power, most of the little countries who were Judah's neighbours rebelled and declared their independence. Egypt encouraged them and Hezekiah threw in his lot with them. Retribution followed swiftly and fiercely. The new emperor,

Sennacherib, led his armies to bring the rebels to heel. He invaded and occupied the whole of Judah. Only the city of Jerusalem held out against him, but Hezekiah was trapped in it and in the end had to make peace on humiliating terms. Chapters 36–37, copied from 2 Kings, tell the story of this time. The teaching collected together in chapters 28–33 was probably given during this time when the destruction of Jerusalem seemed very near.

Ephraim's future. The first part of this passage, verses 1–6, was originally spoken during the early years of Isaiah's ministry. It refers to the kingdom of Israel, here called Ephraim, one of the enemies of Judah, in 735BC. That kingdom was captured by the Assyrians and its capital city, Samaria, destroyed in 721BC. The current situation seems to have reminded Isaiah of the words he spoke about Samaria. He saw a comparison between the situation of Samaria and Jerusalem. By quoting words originally spoken years before about Ephraim (Israel) he is implying that Judah is following along the same path that Israel has already trod, and heading for the same fate. From verse 7 onwards he speaks directly of Jerusalem. As with Samaria the leaders of Jerusalem have attempted to drown their despair in drink. Isaiah had tried to teach them how to respond to the Assyrian threat but they would not listen; now they would have to learn their lesson from the Assyrians.

The servant of God must be completely realistic about the human situation, and yet not despairing.

The servant of God must be totally attached to God: only so can he or she see clearly.

The servant of God must be equally attached to people: only so can he or she feel fully. The resultant tension creates a cross.

The holy city

Isaiah 29:1–8

Ariel was a name given to Jerusalem. It meant 'altar-stone', and emphasized the significance of Jerusalem as the place that contained God's temple. In the first part of this teaching, verses 1–4, Isaiah emphasized the evil times that were about to befall Jerusalem. How could God idly stand by while the city which contained his house was under threat of destruction from the armies of a pagan king? The answer was that the army that would besiege the city was 'my army', God's army. This is the same teaching that Isaiah had given earlier when he had called Assyria God's rod (10:5). The Assyrian besiegers were not a sign that God was impotent but that he was holy. The Assyrian army was God's purifying fire.

Jerusalem's future. Fire was associated with the temple altar. It was meant for purification, not for destruction. The latter part of the passage, verse 5 onwards, claims that Jerusalem would not be destroyed. The siege would be lifted. Isaiah's firm faith that God had promised to preserve Jerusalem and David's dynasty, and that he would keep that promise, would not allow him to contemplate the destruction of Jerusalem. He had just as firm a faith in the descendants of David. They were capable of being led astray but they would never in the end reject their God.

Events seemed to confirm the truth of Isaiah's word. Jerusalem was not taken. But there were disastrous longer-term consequences. The rallying cry, 'God will not allow Jerusalem to be destroyed', created, in later years, false confidence. It was to be a great hindrance to the prophet Jeremiah a century later when he had to confront the people of Jerusalem with the consequences of their wickedness.

God or chaos? *Isaiah 30:6–11*

The thought moves away from the plight of Jerusalem itself to the stupidity and bad decisions on the part of the rulers of Judah that had provoked the Assyrians into their invasion. They had allowed themselves to be seduced by the Egyptians who were concerned only with blocking the Assyrian route to Egypt. Their interest was the safety of Egypt, not Judah, and the Egyptians were so weak that they could not even control the direct route along the sea coast between Egypt and Judah. Communications had to be maintained by the dangerous route through the eastern desert. This was clear evidence of the impotence of Egypt as a military ally.

In the story commonly used to explain the creation of the world, it was told that the creation had resulted from a fight between a god and a monster who was the symbol of evil, worthlessness and chaos. That monster was named Rahab—a name not to be confused with Rahab in Joshua 2:1; the second consonant and the vowels are different, and can be represented in English as Răhăb (the chaos monster) and Rāchāb (the woman of Jericho). The prophet here pictures Egypt as such a defeated and impotent monster. The full stupidity and wickedness of the Judaean rulers is to be seen in that they have preferred to trust in the monster who brings chaos rather than in God who is the author of creation. The decision is so outrageous that it ought to be remembered for ever.

True security *Isaiah 30:15–18*

These words give the prophet's own solution to the dilemma that Judah was in. The security of the nation, he believed, did not lie in any alliance. Rather Judah ought to pursue a policy of quiet independence. Isaiah's judgment was made up of two elements, the one political, the other religious.

The political element lay in Isaiah's estimate that Judah was so insignificant militarily and economically, and also so difficult to conquer because of her geographical position, that the great nations would leave it in peace so long as it made no attempt to interfere in their activities. The religious element was based on the view that a small, independent Judah would be free to pursue its own religion without the need to make room for religious practices forced upon it by powerful neighbours. Their common life would then be lived as God wanted.

The refusal of the leaders to accept this policy was both a political and a spiritual disaster. It was the capacity of Isaiah to hold together political and religious issues, and to point out that Judah's response to events had consequences on each of these levels, that has led to him being seen as both a statesman and a prophet.

Flesh and spirit *Isaiah 31:1–5*

Here the contrast between the two alternative policies is put in its starkest terms. On the one hand there is reliance upon the Egyptians with their large and powerful army. Isaiah has already made plain that on the human level he personally has no confidence in Egypt; but that is not the point here. Those in Judah who had sought an Egyptian alliance did have confidence in Egypt. The point Isaiah is making here is that their judgment is at fault, not because Egypt cannot provide the help for which they were looking, but because they were looking for the wrong kind of help. They were looking for a solution in terms of human power and strength. What they ought to have been seeking was a solution that would involve spiritual qualities and preserve spiritual values. That is what was meant by the 'staying quiet' solution referred to at 30:15.

The advice that Isaiah offered—avoid political involvements with other nations—came out of the particular circumstances of his own time. His words ought not to be taken out of context and used as a moral absolute to be applied to all similar circumstances. What does come from his teaching as absolute is that spiritual values should always be treated as supreme. Political judgments should aim to support and not ignore, much less deny, such values.

Future perfection *Isaiah 32:1–8*

The aim of all political and diplomatic activity should be the establishment of a society which not only is governed by just rulers but also exhibits justice in every part of its life and activity. Such a society would be a true reflection of the God who had created it. Its whole existence at all times, and in every aspect of its being, would be true worship because it would be completely fulfilling the purposes of God. One great contrast between such a society and the one in which Isaiah lived in Jerusalem would be that in the perfect society every action would be clearly evaluated according to its true moral and spiritual worth, and the inner nature of every human being would be transparent for all to see. Actions would reveal character, not hide it.

Isaiah believed that God could and would bring such a society into being. He saw it as the perfected Judah of the future. His confidence that this would be so lay in his faith in God, and the strength of that confidence was demonstrated by the way in which he involved himself in the day-to-day life and activities of his people. Most of what he saw around him could have led him to pessimism and despair. It certainly led him to speak fierce words of judgment against Judah and its rulers. Yet realism never led him to despair, because, in the end, the whole of his life was based on deep faith in God. 'Here am I, send me,' he had replied to the call from God (Isaiah 6:8). That confidence in God and willingness to serve him then became, and always remained, the touchstone of Isaiah's life.

All my hope on God is founded;
He doth still my trust renew,
Me through change and chance he guideth
Only good and only true.
God unknown,
He alone
Calls my heart to be his own.

Isaiah's faith and ours.

ISAIAH

40–55

The names Israel and Judah

The name Israel has two distinct uses in the Old Testament. It has a geographical sense and a theological one. After the division of the kingdom following the death of Solomon in about 922BC, the name Israel refers in a geographical sense to the northern kingdom (sometimes called Ephraim) with Samaria as its capital and its main sanctuaries at Dan and Bethel, in contrast to Judah with its capital and temple at Jerusalem. It is, however, used in a religious sense to refer to the people of God, and thus, after the fall of the northern kingdom to the Assyrians in 721BC, it is applied to Judah. These two meanings need to be distinguished.

The historical setting

Chapters 40–55 all relate to one particular situation in the life of Israel between the years 550 and 539BC. The people addressed by the prophet are in Babylonia, to which they (or their families) had been exiled after the Babylonians had captured Jerusalem in 587BC (2 Kings 25). They thought that their God had deserted them or simply been defeated by the more powerful gods of Babylon. They were in the grip of despair. And yet they had good grounds for hope. Babylon was itself being threatened by a Persian military genius called Cyrus. Beginning as the king of the vassal state of Anshan, since 550BC a series of conquests had brought him an empire that spread from Asia Minor in the west to the borders of India in the east. He had sealed the fate of

Babylon by subjugating Mesopotamia and in 539BC was to occupy the city of Babylon without a struggle. This final conquest held out the hope of release for the Jewish exiles, and the prophet exultantly declares it to be imminent (see 41:2–4, 25; 44:28; 45:1–6; 46:11; 48:14–15).

The prophet

The author of these chapters is commonly referred to as 'Second Isaiah' or 'Isaiah of Babylon', simply because we do not know his name. He was clearly a member of the exilic community in Babylon and his message exposed him not only to ridicule and rejection by his fellow-Jews but also to death at the hands of the Babylonian authorities. It is likely that he is the 'suffering servant' of the four poems known as the 'Servant Songs' (42:1; 49:1–6; 50:9; 52:13—53:12) which, in Christian interpretation, have taken on deeper meaning with reference to the sufferings and death of Christ.

The message

'Second Isaiah' rings the changes on six bold assertions:

1. The Jews in Babylon are still God's chosen people.

2. Their suffering in the exile is not evidence of God's weakness but of his justice and power.

3. Punishment is now at an end. Their deliverance from Babylon and return to Jerusalem are imminent.

4. Cyrus will be the agent of this deliverance, as he has been called by God himself to conquer Babylon.

5. This reversal of Israel's fortunes will certainly happen because its God (unlike the bogus gods of Babylon) is the one real God, sovereign over all the nations and the Creator and sustainer of all that is.

6. The return of Israel to its homeland and the restoration of the city of Jerusalem will be steps towards the inauguration of the kingdom of God.

Facts and faith

The actual events were not as wonderful as the prophet suggested. Cyrus did conquer Babylon; he did allow the exiles to return. But it was no triumphant 'Second Exodus'. Many Jews chose to remain in Babylon rather than face the uncertainties of life in Jerusalem. Those who returned still remained subject to the Persian empire and the other nations showed no signs of acknowledging the sovereignty of Israel's God. There was no immediate realization of the prophet's vision.

If we were to judge him by his accuracy in predicting the future, we would of necessity declare Isaiah a failure. But he was no professional soothsayer. He was a *prophet*, and the business of a prophet was not to foretell the future but, rather, to shape it. He wanted his hearers to become aware of God's will. In this way he *did* shape the future, for the exiles overcame their feeling of rejection and came to share his faith that, despite everything, they were still the people of God.

For the recurrent message is about faith—a faith which faces up to the realities of the world and at the same time soars above and beyond them. He switches constantly between the interpretation of present historical events and the declaration of future possibilities which baffle our understanding. Like a dancer, he rarely has more than one foot on the ground.

Further reading

R.N. Whybray, *The Second Isaiah*, Old Testament Guides, Sheffield, 1983

R.N. Whybray, *Isaiah 40–66*, New Century Bible, 1975

C.R. North, *Isaiah 40–55*, Torch Commentary

God is on the move

Isaiah 40:1–11

These verses form the prologue to the work of Second Isaiah and include his call to be a prophet. First, we are to imagine God presiding over a meeting of his council in heaven. He makes an announcement of momentous significance: Israel's bondage in Babylon is about to end and the exiles will be brought back to Jerusalem. As earlier prophets had spoken of God's judgment on the nation, it was easy to see the exile as a punishment. Now, however, the punishment is a thing of the past. Forgiveness has begun.

A second exodus. We next have the order for the building of a highway from Babylon to Jerusalem. True, the journey would cross rough, undulating, sometimes mountainous desert but a few thousand returning exiles would hardly need a change in the geography to be able to reach home. The prophet's exuberant language means that this journey, like the exodus from Egypt at the beginning of Israel's history, will demonstrate to 'all flesh' the majestic sovereignty—the 'glory'—of Israel's God.

Call of the prophet. But—'All flesh is grass'. The world is an unreliable transient place. How can our anonymous prophet proclaim his message of salvation with such confidence? What is the evidence?

There is no evidence! Being a prophet means proclaiming something simply because it is God's promise, trustworthy and enduring. When he accepts this, he has begun his prophetic work.

But the announcement made in heaven must now be proclaimed on earth. The good news is about the coming of God. It is easy to think of God as conqueror and king (see v. 10), but now he is presented in a different guise—that of a gentle shepherd.

President—engineer—ruler—shepherd. All these images crowd upon each other in this short passage.

Doubts dispelled *Isaiah 40:12–31*

Second Isaiah's proclamation of deliverance from Babylon was by no means well-received by the exiles. It was hard for them to believe any longer that God had either the power or the will to help them. The prophet's task, therefore, was to rekindle their conviction. He attacks their negative view of God in a form of argument which is made up partly of questions and partly of affirmations drawn from the Psalms.

There are, in fact, four separate examples of such a 'disputation' in this section. The exiles' complaint is either implied or explicitly stated.

1. The grandeur of God (vv. 12–17). Whether you look at the world of nature or the world of politics, what to man is immense, to God is infinitesimal. He holds the seas in the hollow of his hand and the nations (even Babylon) are to him like from a drop from a bucket. In his infinite grandeur, Israel's God is in a class by himself.

2. The uniqueness of God (vv. 18–24). They are not to compare God to any other gods, nor, of course, represent him by images. Israel's God is none other than the creator of the world and all its inhabitants. His people have nothing to fear from any earthly power.

3. The authority of God (vv. 25–26). The gods of Babylon were identified with the sun, the moon and the stars. These were regarded as exercising ultimate control over events on earth—and the exiles were tempted to believe it. No, says the prophet; the heavenly bodies were created by Israel's God; he can order them about as a king does his troops on parade.

4. The grace of God (vv. 27–31). The final disputation rebuts the complaint that God is indifferent to the exiles' plight. God is not like a majestic monolith, coldly indifferent to his creation; he is a God who is very much concerned.

'Wait for God' (as in the Psalms) here means looking to him with confident expectation and trust. Those who 'wait for him' in this way not only wonder at his power, but also find in it the basis of their own strength.

God's action in history — *Isaiah 41:1–20*

Israel's faith looked to public historical events and not private mystical experience for evidence of God's presence. In the four sections of this passage, the prophet claims that God's action is manifest in the present (vv. 1–5), was manifest in the past (vv. 8–13) and will be manifest in the imminent future (vv. 14–16, 17–20).

To understand the first section (vv. 1–5) we must imagine a judicial enquiry in court. The nations are assembled to consider who is responsible for the victorious conquests of Cyrus. The prophet (who is writing before the conquest of Babylon but believes it to be imminent) claims that God is using Cyrus as his agent in bringing about Israel's liberation. So this is the answer to the 'enquiry': it is the God of Israel who is responsible because he is the first . . . and to the last—the *only* God. (41:6–7 about the making of idols should be read as a continuation of 40:19–20; see above.)

Next, we have an oracle spoken by God promising salvation to the fearful and despairing exiles. Again, the ground of their confidence is God's action in history—the action by which, beginning with Abraham, he called Israel to be his chosen people (vv. 8–13).

Another oracle of salvation, with its characteristic 'Fear not', follows (vv. 14–16). Israel seem to be complaining that they are a mere worm or a poor louse!—but the significant fact is that God is their *redeemer*. This is the first occurrence in Isaiah 40–55 of one of the prophet's most important terms. In the Old Testament, 'redeemer' means next-of-kin, whose duty it is to help and protect a distressed member of his family (see Leviticus 25:47–49; Ruth 3:11–13; 4:1–6). Therefore, when God is called the redeemer of Israel, he is thought of as acting as their kinsman and restoring the fortunes of the family.

With God's strength the exiles will overcome the mountain of obstacles which beset them. The little louse will pulverize all opposition.

Finally, the people are complaining that the heat and drought of the desert which separates them from Jerusalem prevent them from returning home (vv. 17–20). God will do a great miracle, as he did at the first 'exodus' (Exodus 17:1–7): he will bring forth water for their thirst and trees to give them shade. But not just for their sake: every time God acts to save his own people, there is a demonstration of his power and love which all may 'consider and understand'.

The appeal to events *Isaiah 41:21–29*

In our own time, syncretistic religions, compounded of vague idealism and oriental mysticism, are threatening to become fashionable cults of spiritual escape. By contrast, the Bible speaks of a God who has disclosed his nature and purpose in and through historical events. The difference is crucial.

Second Isaiah made a most notable contribution to this understanding of life. Here the scene is once again the divine law-court. The gods of Babylon are on trial and are challenged to present their case (v. 21). What have they to say about events in the past and about their outcome? What do they know of the future? The answer is nothing. They know nothing and are nothing (vv. 22–24, 29). The God of Israel, on the other hand, is able to foretell the future, because he knows and controls the inner workings of history.

Second Isaiah does not hesitate to put his conviction to the test. As he wrote, Cyrus, King of Persia, was advancing with his victorious armies towards Babylon.

The outcome of this conquest was to be the release of the Jews in exile there, but, even before it happened, here was the prophet affirming that it was the God of Israel who had called Cyrus from the north-east and that it was in his name that Cyrus was making his conquests (v. 25). The dumb idols of Babylon knew nothing of the significance of what was happening (v. 26), but the one true God did!

To the prophets of Israel, history was meaningful, because it was getting somewhere; it was getting somewhere, because it was being taken somewhere, and Christians have a similar conviction, as God 'in these last days . . . has spoken to us by a Son' (Hebrews 1:2).

God's agents *Isaiah 42:1–9*

A passage like this reminds biblical scholars of the need for humility: no amount of learning can guarantee that any one exposition of its meaning is correct. There is little doubt, however, that it is made up of two independent sections: verses 1–4 and verses 5–9.

The mission of the prophet. In verses 1–4, God presents his 'servant' as a prophet; especially chosen, endowed with God's Spirit, commissioned to establish divine order among the nations. Whilst Second Isaiah often uses the term 'servant' to describe Israel these verses seem to describe an individual. Is this individual the prophet himself? If so (and it is quite probable), these verses may have been added later by another writer, as a kind of 'letter of introduction' for Second Isaiah.

Second Isaiah's ministry to his contemporaries in exile was a quiet one. They were battered, fragile people, and needed sensitive handling—how different from the earlier prophets' doom-laden protests! Did he also believe that he had a mission to convert 'the nations'—that is, pagans as well as Jews (vv. 1 and 4)? Some scholars believe so. But one thing is missing: any possibility that a *free* response could be elicited from the Gentiles—and how could any religious mission be authentic if it did not leave its hearers free to respond either for or against?

The mission of Cyrus. The meaning of the second section of this passage is problematic. It speaks of one who has been called by God and commissioned to deliver captives out of prison and to be a light to the nations. The personal language favours an individual (rather than Israel) and the task suggests again Cyrus' conquest of Babylon. Cyrus could be thought of as 'a light to the nations' in the sense that his victories came to them as an 'eyeopener': for the first time they became aware of the glory of God. The prophet had foretold Cyrus' victories; so the exiles could now see them as manifesting, not just a pagan general's might, but the glory of God.

The end of Israel's punishment *Isaiah 42:10–25*

Second Isaiah was soaked in the liturgical language of the Psalms and the introductory verses of this passage echo the Psalter's hymns of praise (vv. 10–11; see Psalms 96 and 98). Praise is the most spontaneous and least ambiguous expression of faith; and here the prophet invites the whole world to sing a new song in the acknowledgment of the new act the Creator is about to perform. He means, of course, God's triumph over Babylon, which will liberate his exiled people. As in the first exodus, so also in the second exodus: God is a mighty man of war (v. 13; compare Exodus 15:3).

War of liberation. God is now represented as describing his strategy for the exiles' deliverance (vv. 14–17). It is his answer to their complaint that he had done nothing for too long (see Isaiah 64:12; Psalm 89:46).

With that astonishing boldness which characterizes Hebrew poetry, God is compared to a woman in labour, suffering, as it were, the birth-pangs of the glorious new events now imminent. Already the prophet had announced God's promise to his people that he would turn 'the dry land into springs of water'; now he reverses the image to symbolize God's conquest of Babylon: rivers will become desert wastes (v. 15). After that, by contrast, the exiles' journey home will be miraculously easy (v. 16).

Convicted of their past sinfulness, yet saved by God's love. This is how the prophet saw his contemporaries. But it is also a parable of our own relationship to God through Christ.

Suffering for sin. The last section of this passage (vv. 18–25) is in a muddle because it has been clumsily expanded by a later writer (it is best to disregard verses 19b, 21, and 24b). The prophet's original intention was, it seems, to counter the exiles' argument that it was useless to look for help from a God who had done nothing about the misery they were suffering in Babylon (v. 22). The answer was brutally direct: God had, indeed, done something about their misery—he had brought it about. It was a punishment for their sin (vv. 18, 24). If God could punish, he could also redeem; he it was who gave them into the hands of the Babylonians and he it is who is now about to deliver them.

If we spend five minutes trying to think only of God, how many distinct images shall we come up with? We shall find how poor our religious imagination is compared with the prophet's. How many images has he crowded into a single chapter?—king, warrior, shepherd, judge, Creator, woman in travail . . .

We must follow the prophet in holding together two more truths about God—that he is totally other, infinitely great, the Creator of all; and yet that he is infinitely concerned with every single one of his creatures.

The prophet's ability to see the hand of God in the victories of a pagan ruler (Cyrus) was astounding in its time. Even now, do we not too readily assume that God is on the side of the 'Christian' nations?

Bold promises and bold claims *Isaiah 43:1–13*

The passion with which the prophet affirms that the Israelite exiles were God's very own people, uniquely honoured and loved, is an indication of their reluctance to believe any such thing. For a people as for an individual, to acknowledge that one has a special role in God's purpose is an act of faith, and involves facing risks; and the exiles had reached such a depth of despair that they simply wanted to be left alone and not think about the future.

This passage falls into three parts. Two oracles of salvation (vv. 1–4 and 5–7) offering reassurance—'Have no fear'—are followed by a 'court scene' in which Israel is a witness, while God asserts his primacy and incomparable power (vv. 8–13).

In the first oracle of salvation (v. 1) Israel is 'ransomed' by God. It is as if Cyrus, through his victories, now holds Israel prisoner; and to free his people God will pay a 'ransom'—Egypt, Ethiopia and Seba. These are countries of which God, the Lord of all, is the real 'owner'; by allowing Cyrus to occupy them he is imagined as 'ransoming' Israel.

(In verse 4 the New English Bible includes two further peoples in the ransom price: the Edomites and the Leummim—for whom see Genesis 25:3. But this is a reading of the Hebrew text which is not generally accepted. The RSV reads, 'I give men in return for you, peoples in exchange for your life'.)

The second oracle of salvation promises the gathering of the exiles from the four corners of the earth in a great family reunion of God's children. Despite the personal intimacy of the language ('my sons and daughters'), the prophet takes the view that it is not merely for his people's sake that God is acting, but for his own glory in the eyes of the world.

We who are taught not to boast or seek public acclaim find it disconcerting when (as in verses 8–13) God is represented as doing just that. All the nations are assembled in court to have it proved to them that there is nothing to be said for their gods, which did not predict and cannot interpret the conquests of Cyrus (v. 9). The Israelites, on the other hand, despite their blindness and deafness are expert witnesses to their own God's utter uniqueness; they are so because he has chosen them as his people for this very purpose: 'to know me and put your faith in me and understand that I am He' (43:10). The assertion 'I am He' is one of Second Isaiah's characteristic phrases for expressing his fundamental conviction that the God of Israel is God in the absolute sense—the only God (see 41:4; 46:4; 48:12).

'I am He'. Writing in remote Babylon, hundreds of miles from Jerusalem where the God of Israel had been worshipped, our prophet nevertheless proclaimed the absolute uniqueness and sovereignty of God. Can we ensure that our own vision of God is not confined to our own time and place, but takes account of the sheer greatness of the world's Creator?

Manifold and great mercies

Isaiah 43:14–28

Second Isaiah communicates in this passage the intense excitement with which he looks forward to the imminent deliverance of Israel from their captivity in Babylon. It is more than the exiles escaping from the Chaldaeans (another term to describe the Babylonians) (v. 14); it surpasses even that great founding event—the miraculous deliverance of Israel from their captivity in Egypt and the crossing of the Red Sea (vv. 16–17; see Exodus 14–15). Now, even now, the God of the exodus is about to do a *new* thing (v. 19); grateful remembrance, therefore, must give place to eager expectation (v. 18). This second exodus will be such as to consummate the Creator's purpose. The barren wilderness will cooperate by providing water for his chosen people and the taming of its wild beasts will symbolize the dawning of the new age (vv. 20–21; compare Isaiah 11:6–9).

In verses 22–28, the prophet's exuberance is suddenly quenched in an unexpected indictment of Israel—a passage which is far from easy to interpret. Again using the form of a trial (v. 26), the prophet represents God as summoning his people to court, in order to defend himself against their charge. They accuse him of having punished them unjustly: he has destroyed their kingdoms and sent them into exile (v. 28), despite their enthusiastic service of worship and sacrifices.

God's reply is a counter-accusation: Israel may have offered sacrifices in plenty, but they were of no concern to him. What *did* concern him was their sinfulness (v. 24). Israel could present no case which would establish their innocence before the divine court; indeed, they had been in rebellion against God from the beginning of their history (vv. 27–28; for the sin of Jacob, see Hosea 12:3). Nevertheless, their acquittal was assured, since God their judge was also their redeemer. Israel's salvation depended not on their own righteousness, but on God's manifold and great mercies.

A question of confidence *Isaiah 44:1–8, 21–23*

The oracle of salvation with which this passage begins (vv. 1–5) once again seeks to restore the exiles' confidence. God has created Israel and chosen them to be the servant of his purpose; they are 'Jeshurun'—a rare name for Israel, which means, perhaps, 'the righteous one' (see Deuteronomy 32:15). Thus favoured, the exiles have no fear. Their blessings will be so great and so obvious that they will attract people from outside Israel, who will come and enrol as members of God's privileged community. That foreigners should be attracted to Israel as individual proselytes is a theme which occurs again—see 56:3. But this is not the same as a direct and deliberate mission to convert the Gentiles, for which, in the Old Testament, there is very little evidence.

To read the second unit of this passage (vv. 8 and 21, 22), we must omit the satire on idols (vv. 9–20, see below), which is a later addition. Our unit begins with a miniature trial scene, in which God calls on the pagan deities to justify their claim to be 'gods'.

What is a 'god'? Here, it is simply a being who can predict the future. Babylonian religion was obsessed with ways of divining the future. But their gods, unlike the God of Israel, were incapable of yielding this knowledge—they are judged to be incompetent impostors.

Perhaps Second Isaiah, in his anxiety to boost the morale of the exiles, was treading on dangerous ground here. The great prophets believed in God's sovereignty; only the popular prophets claimed, rather dubiously, that God gave them foreknowledge. Foretelling the future has no place in true religion.

Further encouragement is offered by the concluding verses of this section (vv. 21–22). There is now nothing to prevent the fulfilment of God's promise.

A brief hymn of praise concludes the passage (v. 23). All creation is invited to celebrate the coming deliverance of Israel; for this decisive event the perfect tense is used ('the Lord *has ransomed* Jacob'): it may be counted on as a certainty!

The absurdity of idols *Isaiah 44:9–20*

It is generally agreed that this satire on the making and worship of idols was interpolated into the work of Second Isaiah and not written by him. The style is cruder than that of the prophet; it is not even certain whether it is prose or poetry. More significantly, the writer fails to draw the contrast between these false objects of worship and the true God, which was one of Second Isaiah's favourite themes (compare 40:19–20; 41:6–7; 46:6–7). The passage reads like a conventional tract against idol-making.

The writer's mockery is based on the assumption that there is no distinction to be drawn between a god and its representation: idols have no corresponding reality and are simply shams, human concoctions. The Roman satirist Horace provides a striking parallel when he represents a log as saying, 'Once I was a fig-tree, good-for-nothing wood, when the craftsman, after hesitating a while whether to make me a stool or a Priapus [the god of gardens], decided for the god.'

Modern idolatry. Very few Christians are tempted to manufacture and worship idols of wood and metal, but we are still exposed to the more subtle temptation to make idols of words and ideas. We may easily find that we are upholding theological doctrines rather than responding to the living God. A particularly damaging kind of idolatry takes place when we confine God to the *residue* of human existence—when we let him in only to that part of our life which we cannot account for and cope with on our own: 'Then what is left of the wood he makes into a god'. Bonhoeffer wrote in one of his letters from prison that we must think of God as not on the borders of life but at its centre. Our faith is not merely a last resort when all else has failed, but the mainspring of everything we think and do.

'Idolatry' has a different meaning in every age. Is there some 'idol' today which we put in place of the true God?

Extraordinary claims *Isaiah 44:24–45:7*

Of all the prophets, Second Isaiah is the one who makes the strongest claim to know the truth about the nature of God. This passage once more directs the exiles' attention to the unique sovereignty of the God of Israel. The prophet's whole faith hinges on the conviction that the one and only God is in a special sense the God of Israel.

Poems which sound like self-congratulation seem unattractive to us; but they were a feature of religious literature in the ancient Near East, and so in verses 24–28 the prophet is following an established convention. The God of Israel, as Creator of all that is, exercises complete control over individuals and events. On the one hand, he makes fools of the diviners and wise men of Babylon. On the other hand, he fulfils the predictions of his own Israelite prophets—in particular those concerning the rebuilding of Jerusalem and the cities of Judah. (It is uncertain what particular manifestation of God's power is meant in v. 27; the saying appears to be out of place.)

The key to God's intention to bring about the return of the exiles to a rebuilt Jerusalem is the Persian King Cyrus, whose irresistible conquests are promised in 45:1–3. More audacious even than these promises is the way the prophet describes Cyrus' special status in relation to God's purpose: he is both his 'shepherd' and his 'anointed'. Both these titles normally belonged to Israelite kings. In fact, the royal terms used in these verses may well reflect the ceremony which was enacted at the accession of Israelite kings (see Psalms 2 and 110). But now these royal prerogatives are transferred to a foreign king; and this signals a profound change in the religion of Israel. God and monarchy no longer belong together. It is becoming possible to think of God's people in a way which makes political power irrelevant.

Meanwhile, military conquest continues to be accounted evidence of divine activity. Although Cyrus himself was unaware of God as the source of his strength, paradoxically his function was to awaken such an awareness throughout the world: 'so that men from the rising and the setting sun may know that there is none but I' (v. 6). Second Isaiah is not the man to retreat from the logic of his uncompromising monotheism; if there is only one God, he must be the author of both good and evil (v. 7). Here he raises issues which are for philosophers rather than prophets.

God's hand is to be found in history, but not always just where we expect to find it. If the prophet could find it in the victories of a pagan (Cyrus), we too have to be ready to see that he may not always be (as we tend to think) 'on our side'.

The Creator's universal rule *Isaiah 45:8–25*

Once again, the prophet interprets the meaning of contemporary political events in the light of God's purpose as Creator. The horizons are as wide as the world and as extended as time itself, but the clue to it all is the redemption of Israel. In its primary meaning, this 'redemption' is an event of history: the deliverance of the Jewish exiles in Babylon by the conquest of Cyrus, the Persian king. Ultimately, however, this event means for the prophet nothing less than the inauguration of the new and final age—the consummation of all things.

It is hardly surprising that the exiles found it difficult to focus so vast a vision on the person of the Gentile Cyrus (v. 11). In reply to their scepticism, the prophet employs a neat (if dangerous) argument. Can the creature question the Creator, the pot the potter, the child his parents (vv. 9–10)? The God of creation is the God of history and Cyrus is conquering in response to his call (vv. 12–13). Moreover, Cyrus is only the first of a long procession: all the nations will come to acknowledge God's redemptive work for his people and confess that, although hitherto hidden, he has now disclosed himself in history as the Saviour of Israel (vv. 15–17).

Characteristically, Second Isaiah adds that the Saviour of Israel is indeed the true and only God—both the God of creation who overcame chaos that men and women might live in the world, and the God of revelation who spoke openly by his servants the prophets that men and women in the world might live according to his purpose (vv. 18–19; Amos 3:7). Second Isaiah's intention here is to mock the Babylonian practice of divination ('I do not speak in secret, in realms of darkness') and to claim authenticity for his own prophetic message.

The final section of this passage (vv. 20–25) depicts the 'survivors of the nations' on trial for failing to recognize that the God of Israel (as foretold by the prophets) was indeed inaugurating his universal rule. Here, non-Jews are included in God's saving purpose (v. 2). This is not to deny that Israel is a privileged nation. On the contrary, it is a way of showing how great this privilege is. The God who chose Israel had (and has) the whole world at his disposal. Nothing could give more significance than that to the fact that he has nevertheless chosen and called *one* people: Israel.

God will accomplish his purpose *Isaiah 46:1–13*

The Old Testament seems to be addressed almost exclusively to Jews, and to have a message only for them.

Christianity is a world religion with a universal message.

How can the one be a preparation for the other?

It is a mistake to hunt high and low in the Old Testament for 'broad-minded' references to non-Jews. The universal significance of the Old Testament is not to be found in scattered passages which are generous to Gentiles, but in the fact that it bears witness to the purpose in history of the one true God.

The early Church immediately undertook a mission outside the Jewish world to the Gentiles. This was a new phase of God's same purpose in the world, a purpose that was first unfolded in the life of Israel.

Why did God choose Israel in the first place? The answer must be sought in the New Testament, where the original purpose finds a new fulfilment.

Or put it another way. God has revealed himself to us, not by proclaiming 'truths' about himself, but by his deeds. We can perceive, from what he *did* for his chosen people, what we may hope he intends for the Gentiles. The Bible is held together, not because it always proclaims the same ideas, but because it recounts a continuous history. It shows us different phases of God's purpose. The record of these phases is what reveals to us the nature of God.

That God knows and directs the course of history is the fundamental conviction of this passage (vv. 9–10). This belief had arisen from the prophet's knowledge of God's dealings with his people. God had cared for Israel as a father cares for his son and, the prophet promises, his love would never cease (vv. 3–4). Whereas the gold-plated gods of the Babylonians had to be carried about by their worshippers (vv. 1–2, 6–7), the experience of the Israelites was that the true God carries them (v. 4). Bel was another name of Marduk, the principal god of Babylon; Nebo was the Babylonian god of writing.

It is their historical experience of redemption that the prophet bids the exiles remember (vv. 8–9). When they do so, they ought to recognize that the phenomenal advance of Cyrus on Babylon is similarly a part of God's saving purpose (v. 11). But they are unresponsive and stubborn (v. 12; cf. v. 8). Nevertheless God will not be deflected from his declared intention and his deliverance of his people is imminent.

Proud Babylon's fall *Isaiah 47:1–15*

This chapter is a splendidly vigorous poem in six stanzas mocking Babylon on her imminent and inescapable downfall. It is improbable that this song could ever have been intended to inspire terror among the inhabitants of Babylon. Its purpose must have been to inspire confidence among the Jewish exiles there. That accounts for its rabble-rousing tone and almost gloating vituperation.

The first stanza depicts Babylon as a queen toppled from her throne and reduced to the life of a slave. To menial tasks is added the supreme humiliation of sexual exploitation (vv. 1–3). The second stanza (vv. 5–7) is an indictment of Babylon's cruelty. It is God who is speaking. He takes full responsibility for sending his people into exile as a punishment. But their captors showed no mercy and offended against basic human rights.

Pride before a fall is the theme of the third (vv. 8–9) and fourth (vv. 10–11) stanzas. Babylon's repeated claim 'I am, and who but I'? is almost identical with that which Second Isaiah characteristically ascribes to God (45:5–6, 18, 22; 46:9) and so we are to understand that national arrogance has escalated to nothing less than blasphemy. Not even use of magic can save Babylon from utter ruin—a disaster like that suffered by a wife and mother who loses both her husband and her children on one day. The fifth (vv. 12–13) and sixth (vv. 14–15) stanzas expose the futility of magicians and astrologers with contemptuous sarcasm. So far from being able to save their city from destruction, they will simply go up in flames. As the New English Bible makes clear, verse 15 refers to magicians and not foreign merchants: 'So much for your magicians with whom you have trafficked all your life.'

Former things and new things *Isaiah 48:1–11*

It is generally agreed that an original oracle of Second Isaiah about the imminent 'new things' of Babylon's fall and Israel's deliverance (v. 6) has been revised in order to produce a passage which administers a severe rebuke to a quite different Jewish community. Since its members are said to call themselves 'citizens of a holy city' (v. 2) we may surmise that they are inhabitants of the newly built Jerusalem after the exile. The later additions to the text make up a formidable indictment. This community is dishonest and insincere (v. 1), obstinate (v. 4), actively idolatrous (v. 5), arrogant (v. 7) and untrustworthy from its very beginnings (v. 8). It was not in such terms that Second Isaiah addressed his despondent countrymen in exile.

The core of the original oracle was the contrast between prophecies of God's earlier deeds ('the former things') and the present announcement of this brand new, unprecedented deed by which Israel will be liberated from bondage.

The idea in verse 9 that God restrained himself from destroying his people simply because his own reputation was at stake (it being inseparable from their fortunes) occurs characteristically in the thought of Ezekiel (see Ezekiel 20:8–9, 22; 36:21–23). The action which God undertakes in verse 11 (again for his own honour) could be either the testing of Israel during the exile ('the furnace of affliction' of verse 10), or their imminent deliverance from exile.

Despite the difficulties of this passage, it communicates Second Isaiah's conviction that the imminent deliverance of Israel was in a class by itself: 'hidden things which you did not know before. They were not created long ago, but in this very hour' (v. 7). For him the 'new things' for Israel marked the inauguration of a new age for the world.

The nature of Israel's calling *Isaiah 48:12–22*

Second Isaiah's tremendous grasp of the relationship between nature and history, God's creation of the world and his covenant with Israel, is one of his major contributions to the pattern of biblical faith. In this passage, he affirms the Bible's fundamental and most daring conviction that the ultimate God has made himself intimately known.

Israel belongs to God; they are his 'called ones', called for his service and called by his name, and that name is no less than 'the first and the last' (v. 12). The God who called Israel to be his people is none other than the Creator who called into being and still commands the earth and the heavens (v. 13). The owner of Israel is the owner of the world. The events of history from first to last are under his sole sovereignty. It may be said, therefore, that as King of kings it is he who has called Cyrus (v. 15) to destroy Babylon and thus deliver Israel from bondage (v. 14). Although God's sovereignty is absolute, it is by no means distant; Cyrus may also be described as 'he whom I love' (v. 14). The Lord's love for Cyrus was part of his providential care for Israel. He has openly disclosed himself to his people by the prophets 'from the beginning' (v. 16); they have enjoyed not only his revelation but also his living presence—'I have been there' (v. 16).

In verses 17–19, a later writer has interpolated lines which represent God as being deeply moved by his people's rejection of his leadership and by their consequent loss of the prosperity promised to Abraham (v. 19, see Genesis 22:17).

The allusion to the 'father' of Israel (51:2) is followed by a brief section recalling the deliverance which most Old Testament writers celebrate as the time of the nation's birth—the exodus from Egypt and the sojourn in the wilderness (v. 21: see Exodus 17:1–7). This, however, is no mere nostalgic remembrance. The prophet is urging the exiles to trust once more in the God who brought them out of Egypt and to make a second exodus from bondage—their bondage in Babylon (v. 20; compare 41:17–20; 43:19–21). Now is the time for loud songs of triumph.

The servant and his mission *Isaiah 49:1–13*

Verses 1–6 are the second in a series of four 'songs' about the Servant of the Lord (42:1–4; 49:1–6; 50:4–9; 52:13—53:12). These are usually thought to have been originally separate compositions.

Who is this 'Servant'? In v. 3, 'my servant' seems to be a way of describing 'Israel'; but in verses 5–6 he is a person commissioned to restore Israel's fortunes. It is perhaps best to regard verse 3 as a later addition; we can then identify the Servant with Second Isaiah himself.

These verses are then readily intelligible as the account of a prophet's experience: called (vv. 1–3), opposed (v. 4) and recommissioned (verses 5–6).

A second question (also long debated by scholars) is raised by verse 6: 'a light to the nations'. Did Second Isaiah believe that the Gentiles were to share the privileges enjoyed by the Jews as the people of God? Certainly he often imagined them as being brought to acknowledge the superiority of Israel and the indisputable sovereignty of their God: 'Kings shall be your foster-fathers and their princesses shall be your nurses. They shall bow to the earth before you and lick the dust from your feet' (49:23; compare 43:3–4; 45:14; 49:7). Passages such as this show that the prophet was taking a 'world view' of God's sovereignty; but they fall far short of suggesting that God actually *cared* for the nations as much as he cared for Israel.

His attitude, therefore still sounds to us somewhat nationalistic. But perhaps he saw further. Perhaps he became aware of a task which may properly be described as a *mission* to the Gentiles. In any case, his words were borrowed by Simeon to describe the infant Jesus; and then they are certainly understood to offer salvation not to Israel only but to all humankind (Luke 2:29–32).

The good shepherd. The second unit of this passage (vv. 8–13) is another oracle of promise and reassurance to the exiles. They will be led like a flock of sheep from Babylon to their restored homeland by their loving God himself (vv. 9–11), and they will be joined by dispersed Israelites from all the corners of the earth. Syene is the southern district of Egypt now known as Assouan (v. 12).

Unfounded fears *Isaiah 49:14–26*

The exiles are complaining: 'The Lord has forsaken me; my God has forgotten me' (v. 14), and 'Can the captive be rescued from the ruthless'? (v. 24). In other words: is God willing, and is God able, to deliver them from Babylon? This passage is built around God's reply to these two complaints.

The prophet answers the first charge in personal metaphors. God's love for Zion transcends the love of a mother for her child (v. 15); the architect's plans for the rebuilding of the city are engraved on his hands (v. 16). Miraculously, the restorers are quicker at the job than the destroyers were and the citizens of Zion are already flocking back (vv. 17–18). Although she thought of herself as bereaved and barren, Zion will soon be adorning herself like a bride, the jewels being her children now on their way home from exile in overwhelming numbers (vv. 18–21). An order goes out to the nations that they must ensure the Israelites' safe return, their kings and queens to act as the slaves of their former prisoners (verses 22, 23).

God's reply to the second charge—that he lacked the power to save his people—is equally emphatic and equally harsh in its attitude towards the non-Jewish world (vv. 24–26). So thoroughly will the oppressors of Israel be crushed that they will be reduced to cannibalism and all the world will hear about it (v. 26). This kind of presentation of the special role and privilege of Israel seems deeply repulsive. There is, however, no support in the Bible for the view that the purpose of God could have been easily achieved in the world by broadcasting as widely as possible a few simple religious truths. When God chose to reveal himself in the history of a human community, the risk of a kind of 'chauvinism' was there from the start.

It is often said that it is only by reading the Old Testament that Christians are prevented from becoming an inward-looking sect, only concerned with their own salvation. Second Isaiah is an outstanding example of a prophet who teaches us to perceive the nature of God through events in the wider world.

What sort of God is it who is revealed in history? A sovereign God, certainly. But also a loving God, intimately concerned with each one of his human creatures.

History always has to be told from some vantage point. The vantage point of the Old Testament is the Jewish people, and the history of God's purpose for the world is told from their angle. Can we do better ourselves? Our vantage point is the 'Christian' West. For centuries we have assumed (as Israel did) that the other 'nations' (Africa and Asia, for example) would come to see God through us. If we have been made aware of the apparently nationalistic limitations of Second Isaiah, can we now learn something about ourselves?

Confidence in God *Isaiah 50:1—51:8*

Has God abandoned his people? Is he unable to redeem them?

As so often in Second Isaiah, these questions are treated as if they were charges in court, and God has to defend himself.

The answer to the first charge (v. 1) is puzzling: it appears to say that the 'wife' was not formally divorced, the 'children' not sold into slavery. But—it was their own fault if they were!

In verse 2 the scene is still the court room, but the accusers have failed to appear—or at least they have nothing to say for themselves! As for the charge that God lacked the power to redeem his people, it was enough to recall that the God of Israel was the Creator of the world (v. 3).

The next section (vv. 4–9), which is the third of the so-called Servant Songs (see comment on 49:1–13), describes an intensely personal experience. There can be little doubt that the prophet is speaking about himself. His call to be a prophet was like the training of a teacher—the language is that of the school room. But then the scene darkens. His calling resulted in physical punishment and (what was worse in that culture) public humiliation. Jeremiah, who had a similar experience, rebelled against it (11:18–20; 15:15–18). Second Isaiah accepts his lot without complaint, confident that God will vindicate him.

The two verses following the poem about the prophet (vv. 10–11) were probably interpolated by a rigorist Jew after the exile, with the purpose of making a distinction between two classes of Jew—the righteous God-fearers and the wicked (see Malachi 3:16–18; Zephaniah 3:11–13).

The last section of the passage offers encouragement to the exiles (51:1–6). There is no need to worry about the smallness of their community; they are the children of Abraham and heirs to his promise that they will become a great nation (Genesis 12:1–3). Stricken Jerusalem will be transformed into a garden of Eden—a veritable *Paradise Regained* (v. 3). The coming deliverance is described in verses 4–6 in terms borrowed from the first so-called Servant Song (42:1–4); whether or not the nations are expected to share God's blessing of Israel, they are certainly subject to his sovereign rule.

The final two verses of the passage (vv. 7–8) are intended for the encouragement of God-fearers in the Jewish community and may have originated in the same circles as 50:10–11.

An appeal to God *Isaiah 51:9—52:6*

Here and there in the Bible can be found traces of a 'myth' of creation: Rahab and the dragon were monsters who inhabited 'the sea and the great deep'. They symbolized the chaos which God had to overcome before he could bring creation into being. The same ideas were also used to describe God's acts in history; and so here (in v. 10) the 'sea' comes to mean the waters which God divided to deliver the Israelites from their bondage in Egypt.

The passage begins with the impassioned and despairing appeal to God, who had conquered the powers of chaos at the creation, but who was also the exiles' own God, the God of exodus. Would he accomplish a comparable victory for his people now?

God's immediate reply is given in verses 12–16. Israel need have no fear: their maker is the maker of all things, and what he has made is within his power both to comfort and control (vv. 12–13). There are tremendous implications in being the chosen people of the Creator of the universe (vv. 15–16). God has revealed himself in a unique way to Israel: but he has also made them his agent in a purpose of which the final goal is no less than a new heaven and a new earth. The prophetic teaching of the Bible will never for one moment allow the people of God to sink into cosy parochialism.

An appeal to Jerusalem. 'Awake, awake': this second call is addressed to Jerusalem to rouse herself from her helplessness and hopelessness (vv. 17–20). The time has now come for God to intervene and remove from his people the cup of his wrath and give it instead to their barbaric oppressors (vv. 21–23).

'Awake, awake': a third call invites Jerusalem to get ready for her restoration (verses 1–2). Babylon had been depicted as a queen reduced to a slave girl (see 47:1–15); Zion the slave girl will now be freed to become a queen. Never again will she be defiled by her Babylonian conquerors.

The final verses of the passage (vv. 3–6) consist of miscellaneous additions in prose by a later hand.

The end of the exile *Isaiah 52:7–15*

The first oracle of this passage is a hymn celebrating the good news of Jerusalem's deliverance (vv. 7–10). It is brought by a messenger and received in triumph by the watchmen of the city. Faith that the Lord is king, as celebrated in many a Psalm (e.g. 97, 99), was now to be confirmed in a particular act of royal compassion: 'for the Lord has taken pity on his people'. The tense of the verbs is perfect, because, although the event still lies in the future, it is imminent and sure—as good as done. The deliverance and restoration of Jerusalem will demonstrate before the whole world the power of Israel's God.

The new exodus. The second oracle (vv. 11–12) urges the exiles to leave Babylon and make their way home. They should bring with them the sacred vessels which the Babylonians years ago had stolen from the temple at Jerusalem (2 Kings 25:13–15); for this task they must keep themselves ritually clean. Unlike the old exodus from Egypt, this new exodus from Babylon will not be in 'urgent haste' (Exodus 12:11; Deuteronomy 16:3). But, as before, God will lead them from the front and protect them from the rear (compare Exodus 13:21, 'And all the time the Lord went before them, by day a pillar of cloud to guide them on their journey, by night a pillar of fire to give them light').

Things unheard of. 'Behold, my servant . . .' Verses 13–15 seems to begin the fourth and most famous of the so-called Servant Songs, which occupies the whole of chapter 53. But verse 14, which describes a disfigured individual, is generally thought to have belonged originally to the end of 53:2. If we take this away, we are left with a passage which reads best as another brief independent promise by God to the exiles that they were about to be restored—'lifted up, exalted to the heights' (v. 13). In which case the Servant here is not the prophet, but Israel.

The main thrust of the oracle is clearer in the translation of the Revised Standard Version than in that of the New English Bible. As the nations used to be aghast at Israel's wretched plight, so now they will be startled and rendered speechless on witnessing its sudden recovery.

The Servant's obedience and triumph *Isaiah 53:1–12*

This poem is so deeply woven into the texture of the New Testament that it is difficult to read it as it would have appeared to a Jew when it was first written in the sixth century BC. C.H. Dodd has observed: 'Of the twelve verses there is only one which does not reappear, as a whole or in part, somewhere in the New Testament. No one author quotes the chapter extensively; it is rarely that two or more writers quote the same verse; only one writer quotes as many as two successive verses—quoting them, however, in a way which shows that he had the whole chapter before him (Acts 8:26–40). But one sentence or another from the chapter is quoted, or unmistakably echoed, in all four Gospels, in Acts, Romans, Philippians, Hebrews and 1 Peter. This surely means that the writers of the New Testament, while one of them might choose one sentence for quotation and one another, all considered this chapter, taken as a whole, to have outstanding significance for the understanding of the Gospel' (*The Old Testament in the New*, page 9).

Self-sacrifice and obedience. The chapter as a whole is the story of an individual who voluntarily submits himself to humiliation and suffering for the sake of others, accepts without complaint the consequences of the sins of others, is put (it seems) to an ignominious death and only then is recognized and rewarded by God. What emerges is a model of personal self-sacrifice springing from total *obedience* to God: and this is why it seemed a divinely intended prefigurement of the self-sacrificial obedience of Christ.

In detail, the text of the poem is in places obscure, and may originally have had a somewhat different meaning. It is even possible that the Servant was not put to death at all, but, rather, was put into a Babylonian prison. But the general line of thought is clear.

Thanksgiving for the prophet. The poem takes the form of a thanksgiving by the friends of Second Isaiah—it may well have been they who composed it. It begins with an expression of their astonishment at his deliverance by God (v. 1; see also v. 11). The prophet was physically unattractive, he was tormented and despised (vv. 2–3). They had supposed that his intense suffering showed how gravely he must have sinned; now they recognized that they themselves were the cause of it. He was suffering *for them* (which does not mean *instead of them*) and it was they who were benefiting from his steadfast obedience to his prophetic calling (vv. 4–6).

Vindication. The prophet silently accepted ill-treatment at the hands of the Babylonians, which culminated in his being 'cut off from the world of the living' (v. 8, REB). Either he was literally put to death, or (possibly) he was 'as good as dead' in prison—the Hebrew text is too obscure for either meaning to be certain. If he was really put to death, verses 10–13 can only mean that God raised him from the dead—which would be the first time that a belief in the possibility of resurrection was expressed in Israel. If he was merely imprisoned, these verses would describe his release. Either way, God would have acted, against all expectation, to vindicate him.

Home Again

Isaiah 54:1–17

Like other prophets before him (notably Hosea), Second Isaiah uses the analogy of marriage to describe the relationship between God and Israel. Jerusalem had been barren during her separation from her husband for the period of the exile in Babylon (v. 1), but now, with the coming deliverance from bondage, she must prepare to house unexpected hosts of children (vv. 2–3). The sin which led to disaster and divorce will be forgotten, for her husband is about to redeem her and restore her to the affectionate relationship she enjoyed as a young bride (verses 4–6). On the scale of the 'everlasting love' of God, Israel's judgment—the exile—would be seen as no more than a 'moment' (verses 7–8); God's compassion is infinitely greater than his chastisement.

Restoration. The prophet's immediate concern is the return from exile; but in this poem it is already clear that the restoration of the exiles is merging in his mind with his ultimate concern, which is the 'restoration' of all things. The new age will be founded on a new promise. God has 'sworn'; and his 'oath' is as permanent as the 'everlasting covenant' which God made with Noah and of which every rainbow is the sign (vv. 9–10; Genesis 9:8–17). There is probably another reason why 'these days recall the days of Noah' (v. 9): the covenant with Noah was as all-embracing as the Flood itself, and established God's peace throughout all creation.

The new Jerusalem. The second half of the passage (verses 11–17) celebrates the glory of the new Jerusalem and its security from all harm. The city will glitter with a brilliance far surpassing unaided human skill, and this will put the pride of Babylon to shame. Again, we find the prophet moving on from his immediate expectation. He has a vision of the consummation of all things—for which, indeed, his language was used by later writers (see Revelation 21:18–21).

Verses 14–17 expound the total security of the new Jerusalem. Before the exile it had been believed that the royal sanctuary of Zion enjoyed complete immunity from attack. The doctrine had been strenuously denied by prophets like Micah and Jeremiah, and was shown to be utterly false by the fall of the city to Babylon. Second Isaiah, however, is in too euphoric a mood to speak with any caution on the subject: indeed he has a theological reason for his confidence. God is the Creator of all the makers and all the users of all weapons. He has everything under his control, and can guarantee Jerusalem's safety.

The new covenant *Isaiah 55:1–13*

This triumphant conclusion of the poems of Second Isaiah announces to Israel that they stands on the threshold of fulfilment and the inauguration of the new age. Its blessings are freely available to the hungry and thirsty and everyone is invited (v. 1). What is offered is the spiritual nourishment of the kingdom of God; and so it is not surprising to find that the prophet's words (verses 2–3) are echoed in John's Gospel: 'Do not labour for the food which perishes, but for the food which endures to eternal life . . .' (6:27); 'Jesus said to them, "I am the bread of life; he who comes to me shall not hunger, and he who believes in me shall never thirst" ' (6:35; see also 4:14).

The universal kingdom. God is about to make with his people the new and everlasting covenant which he promised to David their king (v. 3; see 2 Samuel 7:8–16). As David was a 'witness to all races . . . and instructor of peoples', so now the people of Israel as a whole will bring the nations to acknowledge the sovereignty of their God (verses 4–5).

The ministry of Jesus opened with a proclamation of the coming of the kingdom and a call to repentance: 'The time is fulfilled, and the kingdom of God is at hand; repent, and believe in the gospel' (Mark 1:15). So here, in the epilogue to his book, the prophet calls upon Israel to 'return to the Lord' in penitence; for, incredible as it may seem, God's superiority to man is to be found in his willingness and desire to offer free forgiveness (vv. 6–9).

Israel may or may not be able to comprehend their imminent redemption; but it is purposed by God and will surely be performed. There is no uncertainty between the word and the deed; when God speaks, it is done.

The new creation. Second Isaiah concludes his book with a lyrical description of the redemption of Israel in terms of a second and final exodus from bondage. Unlike the first exodus, when Israel 'came out of the land of Egypt in hurried flight' (Deuteronomy 16:3), the redeemed people of God will be 'led forth in peace' and nature will respond with exuberant joy. For this is no mere return of exiles, but the consummation of the Creator's purpose.

These last chapters have developed already familiar themes, though with a heightened sense of confident expectations.

But an entirely new note has been introduced by the fourth Suffering Servant Song (chapter 53). We may read this again and again, finding in it a startling anticipation of the Passion of Christ, and using it, as the early Christians did, to deepen our own understanding of how the suffering of one could, by the providence of God, be for the healing and salvation of all.

ISAIAH

56–66

These eleven chapters make up the third and last major part of the book of Isaiah. They are generally believed to come from the period of the restoration of the Jews to their homeland after the exile in Babylon, which took place in the sixth century BC, between 597 and 538. In the Babylonian conquest, which ushered in the exile, the people of Judah had lost all that they held most dear: land, city, temple, king—some even thought that the God of Israel had himself been defeated by more powerful gods. The faith of the nation was tested to breaking point. Amazingly, a believing community survived: in 539, the Persians defeated the Babylonians and in the following year they permitted the Jews to return home. Some (though by no means all) took this opportunity. But when they arrived home, they were in for a disappointment: the story of these years is one of division (for example, between those who had returned and those who had never been exiled) and also of disillusion (as hard social and economic realities took the shine off the bold hopes for a new future). For a generation, opportunities to rebuild the temple were wasted, until the prophets Haggai and Zechariah goaded the people into getting on with the task, which was in fact completed in 516BC. Our text reflects all the tensions of this unsettled period at the end of the sixth century.

Although they are relatively late, chapters 56–66 continue a style reminiscent of the original prophet Isaiah, who lived in the eighth century (his words are found in the first part of the book). But they are even closer in style to chapters 40–55, generally attributed to an anonymous exilic prophet, usually called Second Isaiah (Deutero-Isaiah). By the way of deliberate contrast, the term Third Isaiah (Trito-Isaiah) is often used in connection with Isaiah 56–66, either simply as a label to identify these chapters, or sometimes as a name for the main prophetic figure responsible for them.

One of the most fascinating things about these last eleven chapters is the way in which, through subtle shifts of language, the inherited vocabulary of the Isaiah tradition is adjusted to meet new circumstances. The unconditional promises of Second Isaiah tend to become dependent on right behaviour in Third Isaiah; hopes that are for all in Isaiah 40–55 are generally reserved for a narrower group of faithful in chapters 56–66. All of this reflects an attempt to cope with the non-fulfilment—or perhaps the delayed fulfilment—of much that had been hoped for.

A very positive fruit of the renewed emphasis on right behaviour in these chapters is that they give us some of the great biblical passages about social justice. One thinks of 58:6ff: 'Is this not the fast that I choose: to loose the bonds of wickedness, to undo the thongs of the yoke, to let the oppressed go free . . .?', or, again, of the words from chapter 61 read by Jesus in the Nazareth synagogue: 'The Spirit of the Lord God is upon me, because the Lord has anointed me to bring tidings to the afflicted; he has sent me to bind up the brokenhearted, to proclaim liberty to the captives . . .' (61:1ff; see Luke 4:16–30).

Another important feature of our chapters is that we find, in phrases like 'Behold, I create new heavens and a new earth' (65:17), hints of the style known as apocalyptic, which was to become increasingly characteristic of the later Bible, in books like Daniel and Revelation. Indeed, some have argued that we can observe here a vital stage in the development of this genre: one way of coping with the failure of reality to live up to the grand hopes of the returning exiles may have been to project these hopes into the future, when God would intervene dramatically to vindicate his faithful ones.

The notes are based on the Revised Standard Version.

Suggested further reading

P.R. Ackroyd, *Israel under Babylon and Persia*, New Clarendon Bible, Oxford University Press, 1970

G.I. Emmerson, *Isaiah 56–66*, Old Testament Guides, JSOT Press, Sheffield, 1992

C.R. Seitz, editor, *Reading and Preaching the Book of Isaiah*, Fortress Press, Philadelphia, 1988

J.D.W. Watts, *Isaiah 34–66*, Word Bible Commentary, 25, Word Books, Waco, Texas, 1987

C. Westermann, *Isaiah 40–66*, Old Testament Library, SCM Press, London and Westminster Press, Philadelphia, 1969

R.N. Whybray, *Isaiah 40–66*, New Century Bible, Oliphants, London, 1975 and Eerdmans, Grand Rapids, Michigan, 1981

Salvation for the obedient *Isaiah 56:1–8*

'Keep justice, and do righteousness'—our text begins with words very reminiscent of the moral challenge of the original Isaiah himself. And yet we are soon made aware that we are in a different world, in which the people long for the realization of disappointed hopes. The assurance is given that 'soon my salvation will come'; the great promises of a glorious restoration offered by Second Isaiah had come to little, but now they can still come to pass. The reason for the delay is the people's failure to obey.

What are the demands of God which must be obeyed? The people must observe the sabbath (which, like circumcision, had in the exile grown in importance as a badge of identity for the Jews) and they must keep their hands from doing evil.

Typical of the uncertain early days of the return were questions of who was to be included in the community and who excluded. The answer here is liberal and generous: eunuchs and foreigners should be included. Eunuchs are explicitly excluded from the community in Deuteronomy (23:1). The inability to have descendants to continue one's name was felt to be a tragic disability; but here moral obedience is more important than any physical limitation: the faithful eunuch is promised 'a monument and a name better than sons or daughters'.

Foreigners have a special place in the words of Second Isaiah (for example, Isaiah 49:6 speaks of the servant of the Lord as a light to the nations, bringing salvation to the end of the earth). This positive attitude is picked up here; though in order to share in the blessing of Israel the nations must take on the obligations of Israel, including observing the sabbath and offering sacrifices. The theme is summed up here in the beautiful words, 'My house shall be called a house of prayer for all people.' In the Gospel of Mark (11:17) Jesus is presented as quoting the words of our passage as he cleanses the temple of money-changers.

How good are we at including and welcoming the poor and the foreigner? And how often must it be on our terms? Must the outsider conform to our ways before we let him or her in?

The wicked rebuked

Isaiah 56:9—57:21

In this passage we find a sharp contrast between the arrogant wicked and those of a contrite and humble spirit.

First, in a dramatic image, the beasts of the field are called upon to come and devour the 'blind watchmen'—perhaps false prophets, or bad leaders in general. The wicked are also called 'shepherds without understanding', as in Ezekiel's tirade against the shepherds of Israel who are only concerned to feed themselves (see Ezekiel 34).

The criticism of the wicked is picked up in verse 3 of chapter 57. In what sounds like a formula summoning defendants to court, 'draw near hither!', the wicked are called upon to give an account of themselves. Very strong language is used, 'sons of the sorceress, offspring of the adulterer and the harlot', evidence perhaps of sharp divisions in the community during the years following the restoration from exile. The charges made seem to include sexual debauchery (vv. 5, 8); but it may be that sexual licence is used (as often in the Old Testament) as a symbol of false worship, especially if this involved the fertility rites of Canaanite religion. Certainly the practices of false religion are the main object of attack: 'slaying your children in the valleys' (v. 5)—child sacrifice had never entirely been suppressed; 'journeying to Molech with oil' (v. 9)—worship of a pagan god; 'sending down even to Sheol' (v. 9)—dabbling in spiritualism.

Blessings for the humble. Half-way through verse 13 the tone begins to turn to the positive theme of the second half of the chapter. 'He who takes refuge in me shall possess the land, and shall inherit my holy mountain.' The final verses of the chapter continue this theme of assurance with a striking contrast between God—high, lofty and holy—and the person of contrite and humble spirit. During and after the experience of exile, the Jews increasingly thought of their God as holy and remote and yet here we have a marvellous declaration of faith that he also makes himself present 'to revive the spirit of the humble, and to revive the heart of the contrite'—words which have much to say to the Christian, not least as we meditate on the incarnation, God's presence among us in the humblest of settings.

Self-indulgent fasting! *Isaiah 58:1–14*

'Why have we fasted and thou seest it not?' This is the question asked by the people of Judah; it may even be a quotation from an actual lament, the words of a people disappointed with the restoration and unable to understand why God's promises have only been partly fulfilled. They imagine that they are pious and righteous, but they are fooling themselves, for they even bicker and fight as they claim to worship God. Their worship is in fact a form of self-indulgence (v. 3).

Do our religious observances serve our own ends more than those of God and our neighbour?

True self-sacrifice. A redefinition of proper worship is called for and is now offered in a great passage: 'Is not this the fast that I choose?'—not self-centred fasting, but behaviour which is compassionate and loving. The practice of fasting itself may not be rejected altogether here; but the word 'fast' is made a symbol for a deeper kind of self-sacrifice—generous care for the oppressed, the hungry, the homeless, the naked. How one treats such people is the measure of true worship; we are reminded of Jesus' words in the parable of the sheep and the goats in Matthew 25: ' "Lord, when did we see thee hungry and feed thee, or thirsty and give thee drink?" . . . "Truly, I say to you, as you did it to one of the least of these my brethren, you did it to me." '

If the conditions of justice are met, then Israel may indeed look forward to a fulfilment of the promises of God; the Lord will answer, 'Here I am' (vv. 8–10). As so often in these chapters, these promises are recalled in words very reminiscent of those of Second Isaiah (see, for example, Isaiah 52:12). 'Your ancient ruins shall be rebuilt; you shall raise up the foundations of many generations'—words probably spoken soon after the initial return of exiles to their ruined city in 538BC.

As in chapter 56, so at the end of this chapter, the importance of observance of the sabbath is emphasized—not as a hollow routine, but as a source of joy: 'call the Sabbath a delight; and the holy day of the Lord honourable'. We are reminded of Jesus' positive and humane teaching on the Sabbath: 'The Sabbath was made for man, not man for the Sabbath' (Mark 2:27).

Do we need a redefinition of our worship (as of fasting in Isaiah 58), a turning away from self-centred practice to that which is genuinely loving and compassionate?

Separated by sin

Isaiah 59:1–21

'The Lord's hand is not shortened, that it cannot save'—again we encounter the problem of the apparent failure of promises. In exile, the Jews had doubted that God could save them (compare Isaiah 50:2); now they have returned to their homeland, but they still doubt the promise of a full restoration. This is a situation which is all too familiar to us: how often we take for granted all that God has done for us in the past, and feel sorry for ourselves and resentful towards God! It is stressed in the present passage that the failure of the promises to materialize is not because of any shortcoming on God's part but rather because of the sins of his people: 'Your iniquities have made a separation between you and your God.'

The sins of the people are outlined: 'Your hands are defiled with blood'—we are reminded of the charges levelled by the original Isaiah at the community of his own day (see Isaiah 1:15). There is, moreover, manipulation of the law ('No one enters suit justly, no one goes to law honestly')—one of the most consistent forms of oppression by the powerful through the ages.

How often do we blame God for failing to make himself present to us when it is in fact we who are shutting him out?

A public confession. At verse 9 the tone changes—we seem to move from judgment upon the people to confession by the people. This is one of a number of passages in our text which may have a basis in the public worship of the Jews. 'For our transgressions are multiplied before thee, and our sins testify against us'—rarely is guilt admitted quite so explicitly, even in the laments of the Psalter (compare Psalm 51:3)! Verse 14 contains a particularly striking image: 'truth has fallen in the public square'—one cannot help thinking of the distortion of truth which has become so much part of our contemporary public life, whether in politics or in the media.

God intervenes. Half-way through verse 15, we have another dramatic change of tone: 'The Lord saw it, and it displeased him that there was no justice'. An assurance of divine intervention is given and vindication by God is now described in the vivid picture of a warrior preparing for battle. Such imagery is not unusual in the Bible; it may seem at times primitive and even repugnant, but remember that the overriding theme here is that of a God for whom justice and righteousness are of absolutely central importance.

The final verse of the chapter, which seems to be an independent footnote, contains a beautiful assurance of God's permanent presence and blessing.

A light to the nations *Isaiah 60:1–22*

'Arise, shine, for your light has come, and the glory of the Lord has risen upon you.' Light is one of the recurrent images of our chapters, a powerful symbol of the God who pierces the darkness of our human condition with his life-giving presence.

The concern with foreigners which we found in chapter 56 is again prominent here, and is associated with the dominant theme of light: 'And nations shall come to your light, and kings to the brightness of your rising.' The inclusion of the nations in the salvation of God is one of the unifying themes of the whole Isaiah tradition (see, for example, Isaiah 2:2–4 and 49:1–6), a marvellous anticipation of the taking of the gospel of Christ to the Gentiles by St Paul. Here in Isaiah 60 the nations help with the return of the Jews to their homeland, and so themselves become agents in the saving work of God. The 'nations' of verse 6 and 7 are various regions of Arabia; Tarshish (v. 9) seems to have been a Phoenician colony as far afield as Spain!

Nationalism? However, we must not allow ourselves to be swept away altogether by the romance of this universal vision, for it is not without an element of nationalism. Not only the nations but also their wealth will come to Zion (see, for example, v. 5)—and woe betide any nation that does not cooperate (see v. 12)! Verse 11 looks forward to foreign kings being led captive and verse 14 to old scores being settled. Such hopes are perhaps understandable, given that the Jews had suffered so much at foreign hands. We do well though to remind ourselves that the primary thrust of the chapter is that of the glorious light of God which will draw all, even the nations, to him. 'They shall bring gold and frankincense, and shall proclaim the praise of the Lord' (Isaiah 60:6)—surely Matthew must have had this verse in mind as he described the wise men bringing their gifts from foreign nations to the Christ child!

Good news for the afflicted *Isaiah 61:1—62:12*

We come now to one of the truly great passages of the Old Testament, one indeed which the Gospel of Luke presents Jesus as using in his 'keynote speech' in the synagogue at Nazareth at the start of his ministry (see Luke 4:16–30).

The opening words of chapter 61 seem to recount the call of a prophet, perhaps the leader of the community from which our chapters come. The author may be modelling his own mission on that of the Servant spoken of in Second Isaiah, seeing his task as being to help bring the old promises to fulfilment. The first Christians clearly read this passage (and indeed the Servant passages of Isaiah 40–55 themselves) in the light of their knowledge of Jesus, and it is very proper that we should do the same, seeing in Jesus a perfect acting out of the role here.

Anointed by God. It is clear that the prophet who speaks in Isaiah 61 is called to a very special office indeed. He is both inspired by the Spirit of God and also anointed for service.

Anointing is only very rarely used of prophets in the Old Testament and was rather the normal way of inaugurating the reign of a king in ancient Israel. But 'the anointed one' is the meaning of the familiar term 'Messiah', the figure whom many came to expect as the agent of God's blessings upon Israel; the present passage may reflect such hopes.

The task of the prophet is to 'bring good tidings to the afflicted'; with this we may compare the promises to the person of a 'contrite and humble spirit', the righteous one who patiently awaits the fulfilment of the word of God (see 57:15). The prophet is also sent to 'proclaim liberty to the captives', that is to say he is to perform the true 'fast' described in chapter 58, letting the oppressed go free and breaking every yoke.

Verse 8 roots all of these hopes in the nature of God: 'For I the Lord love justice, I hate robbery and wrong.' It is because it is the will of God whom we worship that we must struggle for justice in the world.

Chapter 62 declares God's blessing on Zion, or Jerusalem, the holy city established as the capital by King David. Zion is one of the unifying themes of the great book of Isaiah, which tells of judgment upon and then deliverance for the city, which symbolizes the nation Israel as a whole. As we have seen, chapters 56–66 emerge from the period of the restoration of the Jews to their homeland after the exile and yet they reflect many divisions, frustrations and disappointments; chapter 62 is a very upbeat chapter though, echoing some of the themes and languages of the optimistic chapters 40–55 (see, for example, verse 10). Vindication, salvation and glory are promised in verses 1–2, and moreover this turn of affairs is to be witnessed by the nations (a recurrent theme in the Prophets). It is striking that this chapter promises deliverance without making explicit references to conditions or demands (which tend to characterize Isaiah 56–66, as we have seen).

Verse 2 introduces a motif which is to run right through the chapter, the giving of new names. The giving of special names, symbolizing new realities, is a characteristic feature of much of the Old Testament (compare Isaiah 1:26; Jeremiah 33:16; Ezekiel 48:35). Zion shall no longer be called 'Forsaken' and 'Desolate', but rather 'My delight is in her' and 'Married' (v. 4); her inhabitants shall be dubbed 'The holy people', 'The redeemed of the LORD'; Zion will be known as 'Sought out, a city not forsaken' (v. 12). Verse 5 reads rather oddly; it may be that we should amend to 'your builder' (in other words God) rather than 'your sons'. Verses 6–7 introduce the theme of watchmen; the reference here may be to heavenly watchmen, guardian angels—God has seen to it that he should be reminded to keep to his promise of fully restoring Jerusalem! Verses 8–9 express the coming salvation in ways typical of the down-to-earth practicality of the Old Testament, and characteristic especially of covenant passages such as Deuteronomy 30:9ff and Ezekiel 36:28ff—food and drink are to be assured, both for domestic consumption and also for use in religious ceremonies. The rousing declaration of verse 11 could be taken as a summary of this whole chapter: 'Say to the daughter of Zion, "Behold, your salvation comes" '.

The God of vengeance *Isaiah 63:1—64:19*

'Who is this that comes from Edom . . .?' God the bloodstained warrior returning from the slaughter—what a chilling image! In Isaiah 59:16–17, where God is described as putting on his armour, the vanquishing seems primarily to be of enemies within the community; here, it is exclusively foreign nations which God the avenger treads down in his anger. Edom was a territory to the south-east of Palestine, and Bozrah was one of its major cities. Edom had taken advantage of Judah's misfortune during the exile and was hated with particular intensity, though here it seems to represent all the enemies of Judah.

We may wonder what we should make of such violent and even vindictive language. Before we condemn too quickly, let us remember that Judah had suffered cruelly at the hands of the nations throughout the sixth century, and let us acknowledge also that the wish for retribution is there in us all. The Old Testament is often uncomfortably honest about raw human emotions—and maybe that is part of its value to us, in that it helps keep our religion realistic about the feelings we human beings have.

The saving God. With verse 7 a fresh section begins and continues to the end of chapter 64. Here, in a style very close to that of Psalms, the community laments its fate, confesses its sins, and appeals to God to relieve its situation and bring a full restoration of normal life. As in many of the laments of the Psalter, an important place is given to the recalling of the mighty acts with which God has favoured Israel in the past, in spite of their sins: God has acted to save before; why should he not do so again? The appeal is expressed in the most dramatic terms at 64:1, 'O that thou wouldst rend the heavens and come down, that the mountains might quake at thy presence'; the prophet cries out to God to come to his people in judgment and in salvation.

The Christmas story tells of the coming of God in a rather different way, as a baby in a manager, but in its own way this is itself a 'rending of the heavens', a bringing together of heaven and earth.

A community divided

Isaiah 65:1–25

This chapter opens with one of the clearest statements of the saving initiative of God to be found in the Old Testament: 'I was ready to be sought by those who did not ask for me; I was ready to be found by those who did not seek me.' There is an ironic contrast between the end of chapter 64, where the people ask whether God will keep silent regardless of their prayers, and the start of this chapter, where God affirms that he has sought his people in spite of their ignoring him. A distinction seems to emerge in this passage between the wicked and those who are described as the 'servant' or the 'chosen' of God (see vv. 8–9). This is sharpest in verses 13 and 14, with their contrast between 'my servants', who are to be blessed, and 'you', who are to be punished. This language may reflect a profound division within the community in and around Jerusalem during the restoration years, almost a schism between rival groups. In any case, one of the ways of coping with the disappointment of the hopes of a glorious restoration (such as those which had been voiced by so-called Second Isaiah) was to express those hopes in a more selective and conditional way: the promises will indeed be fulfilled—but *only* for the obedient 'servants' of God.

New heavens and a new earth. 'For behold, I create new heavens and a new earth' (65:17): God promises a dramatic new intervention. In these very last chapters of Isaiah we have much that seems to point forward to the language of apocalyptic, a style of writing which we find in books such as Daniel and Revelation. These books speak of God breaking into history to judge the wicked and to save the faithful. The very last verse of the chapter borrows words from near the start of Isaiah (see Isaiah 11:6–9) to express a vision which we would do well to wish on our war-torn world today.

Can we free ourselves to be surprised by the newness of God? Can we face the judgment of God with honesty and also open our hands to receive the fulness of his promises?

The temple challenged

Isaiah 66:1–24

One of the major symbols of Judah's new beginning after the exile was the rebuilding of the Jerusalem temple. Our chapters contain a number of positive references to the temple (see, for example, 56:7; 60:7; 62:9). It comes as quite a shock then to find that the final chapter of the book opens with words that seem to question the whole idea of rebuilding the temple: 'Heaven is my throne and the earth is my footstool; what is the house which you would build for me, and what is the place of my rest?' Some spoke of the temple as God's 'footstool' (compare Ezekiel 43:7; Isaiah 60:13); and yet here God's 'footstool' is not the temple but the earth. At the very least this is a serious challenge to the rebuilders of the temple: God created all things and is not to be contained in a mere man-made building! Indeed, the present verses may go further, and actually oppose the rebuilding of the temple. This would be quite the opposite of what the prophets Haggai and Zechariah were saying at this very time; but we ought not to be surprised if different views were being expressed about this very important topic—think of the range of opinions on any religious issue today.

Do we try to contain God in our rituals and doctrines, when all the time he is bigger than any of them?

God as mother. Verses 7–12, as other parts of our text, picture Zion as a woman; moreover, verse 13 even extends the feminine imagery to God, in the lovely words, 'As one whom his mother comforts, so I will comfort you.' Maybe this is one of the specific ways in which our religious assumptions need to be challenged. We still hesitate over using language in our worship which fully includes women as well as men, and yet here the Bible itself rushes on to talk of God as *mother*.

Can we be open to fresh ways of perceiving and speaking of God? And do we really take seriously the fact that God lies above and beyond any particular words and images we may use?

The judgment of God. Like parts of chapter 65, much of chapter 66 is rather like the apocalyptic writings in tone. We may well feel unable to make positive use of all this material (many will find the last verse of the book a particularly difficult one). Nevertheless, we are today perhaps too ready to play down the element of judgment in our biblical tradition; it may be that much of this language can provide a sobering challenge to many of our modern assumptions.

JEREMIAH

Anyone who has tried to read the book of Jeremiah straight through without any reference to a commentary or explanatory notes will know what a bewildering experience it is. The book starts easily enough, with the call of the prophet in chapter 1; but there then follow many chapters of exquisite poetry which are occasionally interrupted by prose narratives. While the imagery and passion of the poetry are astonishing, it is far from easy to understand what the poems are referring to; and the prose narratives do not add up to a complete story, but give uncoordinated glimpses into the life of Jeremiah. From chapter 25, the material is mostly prose narrative, and the story begins to emerge of Jeremiah's imprisonment during the siege of Jerusalem by the Babylonians in 588–587BC, and of what happened to him after the destruction of Jerusalem. Even so, the story is left incomplete, with Jeremiah being taken to Egypt against his will. Chapters 46–51 contain the prophecies against the surrounding nations that are typical of the major prophetic books of the Old Testament.

The content of Jeremiah, then, is almost impossible to understand without reference to commentaries; unfortunately, the commentaries differ considerably in how they approach the book! At one extreme are commentaries that try to date each saying with precision in the life of Jeremiah, and at the other extreme is the view that we can know little, if anything, about the words and works of the historical Jeremiah and that the book reflects an attempt to come to terms with the destruction of Jerusalem on the part of the post-exilic community, using the figure of Jeremiah as the focus for that attempt.

Ordinary readers of the Bible will be impatient with this state of affairs, which they will regard as typical of arcane discussions among scholars who, they will imagine, know nothing of the real world. While this is an understandable reaction, it is not a fair one. There is undoubtedly much truth in the view that the book of Jeremiah was put into the form in which we have it by a community that had survived the destruction of their country, their capital and their temple, the latter being the focus of their religious faith. This calamity, which has been repeated many times in the real world since, and which is not unknown today, inflicted deep social and psychological wounds upon the community, whose healing was assisted by the composition and use of the material we call the Book of Jeremiah.

At the same time, those scholars are correct who assert that, in the character of the prophet Jeremiah in his book, we have access to a real person who lived through, and experienced with his people, the traumas of the years leading up to the destruction of Jerusalem and its aftermath. In my view, the basic reliability of what we learn about Jeremiah in his book is confirmed by recent archaeological discoveries, such as the bullae published by Avigad and Shiloh in 1986 which name 'Berakhayu son of Neriah the scribe' (see Jeremiah 36:4) and 'Gemariah son of Shapan' (see Jeremiah 36:10). However, we must never forget that our access to the past has always to be put in the form of a narrative, and that every narrative is written from a particular point of view. This is as true of books of the Bible as of any other writings; and the standpoint of the Book of Jeremiah is that of a shattered community coming to terms with a new self-understanding.

In view of what I have just written, readers of these notes may be surprised that I have approached them more from the perspective of the historical Jeremiah than of the post-exilic community. This is a strategic choice governed by the need to try to make complex material as understandable as possible whilst being restrained by the limits of space available. These notes are best considered as a way into Jeremiah. For those who wish to go deeper, there are suggestions for further reading.

However we approach Jeremiah, one thing is clear: that discipleship is costly. This is true whether we consider things from Jeremiah's individual angle, or from the angle of the community that told his story. Jeremiah (who can also stand for his community) was subjected to ridicule, rejection and imprisonment. He was accused of being a traitor. In his anguish he accused God of deceiving him. He may well have died without seeing any vindication of the truth of what he proclaimed. On the face of it, this is a dark and hopeless book. But its seeming darkness arises from the fact of God's involvement with a human race that believes that it knows best and wants to go its own way. To seek to win it back to himself God becomes involved in its sufferings, which are the more acute when viewed from the perspective of love. Anyone, individual or community, called by God to share in the divine mission knows something of the fellowship of those sufferings, and learns what it means to trust and hope. Details of Jeremiah's life and times are given in the notes. The following themes are covered:

1. Jeremiah's call and early prophecies (627–622BC)
2. The gathering storm clouds (609–597BC)
3. Jeremiah's 'cross' and inner anguish
4. Prophecies against the nations
5. Jeremiah and the fall of Jerusalem
6. Prophecies of hope.

Further reading

The bullae referred to above were published by Y. Shiloh in *Israel Exploration Journal*, 36, 1986, and by N. Avigad, *Hebrew Bullae from the Time of Jeremiah: Remnants of a Burnt Archive*, Jerusalem, 1986.

An excellent introduction to Jeremiah, its study and relevant commentaries is by R.P. Carroll, *Jeremiah*, Old Testament Guides, Sheffield, 1989.

For some of the social background to Jeremiah see J. Rogerson and Philip Davies, *The Old Testament World*, Cambridge, 1989, pages 50–51. There is also an excellent treatment of Jeremiah, as well as the general theme of doubt in R. Davidson's *The Courage to Doubt*, London, 1983.

— CALL AND EARLY PROPHECIES —

Background and date *Jeremiah 1:1–3*

According to the opening verses, Jeremiah's work as a prophet covered forty years, from Josiah's thirteenth year (627BC) to

Zedekiah's eleventh (587BC). In fact chapters 40 to 45 take the account of Jeremiah's life and words to a time later than 587BC. They relate that after the fall of Jerusalem Jeremiah lived at Mizpah under the governorship of Gedaliah, until the latter was murdered, and the people fled to Egypt taking with them an unwilling Jeremiah. How long after 587BC these events happened we do not know. It is possible that the deportation mentioned in Jeremiah 52:30, which took place in 582BC, was a reprisal for Gedaliah's murder. In this case, five more years must be added to the length of Jeremiah's ministry.

Two important points are mentioned about Jeremiah's background. The first is that he came from a priestly family. 1 Kings 2:26–27 records that Solomon banished the priest Abiathar to Anathoth for supporting Adonijah's claim to succeed David as king. Jeremiah may thus have come from a family of priests who remembered that they had once been ousted from Jerusalem. The second point is that Anathoth was in the land of Benjamin. The border between Judah and Benjamin was such that although Anathoth is only some four miles north-east of Jerusalem, it was in a different tribal area. By the time that Jeremiah began his work, Judah and Benjamin had together made up the southern kingdom of Judah for three hundred years; but people have long memories about boundaries! The tribe of Benjamin had provided Israel's first king, Saul, and it had also provided a rebel against the rule of David (2 Samuel 20). Now, for three hundred years, Benjamin had been very much the minor partner in a kingdom dominated by David's tribe and city.

It may be that the scathing denunciations that Jeremiah was to utter against Jerusalem owed something to his place of birth, and to a certain hostility that people from Benjamin felt towards Jerusalem. Of course, there was much more than simple local rivalry behind Jeremiah's words. He would not have spoken as he did if God had not moved him. On the other hand, God takes people as they are, and he works through all the things that contribute to their make-up, if they will let him.

Jeremiah's call to be a prophet *Jeremiah 1:4–10*

The account of Jeremiah's call to be a prophet shares many features with the calls of others in the Old Testament. Like Moses (Exodus

4:10) Jeremiah tries to excuse himself because he is not a good speaker. Like Isaiah (Isaiah 6:7) his mouth is touched, and like Ezekiel (Ezekiel 3:1–3) he is given God's words. If people are to express in words their inner feelings and experiences they need the help of ready-made phrases or patterns. This seems to have been true of attempts in the Old Testament to describe how people had been called.

Although it shares something with other accounts, Jeremiah's is quite distinct. In particular we are not told when or where he was called, whereas we know when and where Moses, Isaiah and Ezekiel were called. The lack of mention of when and where may indicate that Jeremiah's conviction grew gradually, and could not be pinpointed. As we shall see, he certainly had cause to doubt his calling and message.

If Jeremiah's sense of being called was something gradual and continuous, this may help us to understand the reference to his being designated as a prophet before he was born. It seems unfair and monstrous that God should single out an individual before his birth to undergo the suffering and anguish that Jeremiah experienced. It appears less monstrous if we can see it in this way. As his work progressed and his doubts increased, it was important that Jeremiah should have a degree of certainty that he really was speaking God's words. The surest way in which he could have that certainty was by being assured that his prophetic office went back to before his birth. God had been watching over him from before birth, and in all the uncertainties that he faced would continue to be with him. The designation to be a prophet before he was born was a promise of assistance, not a monstrous imposition upon the free will of an individual.

Nevertheless, when Jeremiah was first moved to become God's servant, he wanted to draw back from the task. How right he was. If he could have seen what lay ahead he would never have dared to begin. The same would be true of many since, and many today. But God's service, whatever hardships it may bring, is not an imposition upon individual freedom. It is the discovery of life, in company with the Lord of life.

To Jeremiah the cost of discipleship was:

- *no wife or family*
- *loss of credibility in the eyes of others*
- *anguish at what was to happen to the people.*

It is possible that the two visions related here marked the beginning of Jeremiah's prophetic work. In both cases, everyday things that anyone could see took on a deeper significance, as God moved Jeremiah to see them as signs of his work in the world.

The almond tree begins to bud in January, ahead of other trees. Jeremiah may have seen in this a sign of activity when everything else seemed to be lifeless. He was reminded also of the similarity in Hebrew of the words 'almond' (*shaqed*) and 'watching' (*shoqed*), and was thus assured that, contrary to appearances, God had been watching over his word. Which word was this? It was not a particular word or utterance (the Hebrew can also mean 'thing' or 'matter') so much as God's purpose in general, his promises and his warnings to Israel of the consequence of disobedience.

The meaning of the first vision. If we assume that Jeremiah saw the almond tree in the first year of his work (627BC), this would have been a reassuring vision. For much of the century Judah had not been independent, but had been subject to the rule of Assyria. The preceding years had seen a resurgence of evil religious practices, including child sacrifice (2 Kings 21:1–6). When Manasseh, in whose reign the abuses happened, died in 642BC, his son was assassinated after a reign of less than two years, and the boy king Josiah was placed on the throne (2 Kings 21:19—22:2). Under Josiah the first steps were taken towards restoring true faith in the God of Israel. Also, the power of Assyria was declining, and in 626BC the Babylonians freed themselves from Assyrian rule. It would be possible to see in the almond tree a pointer to these events. The long winter of seeming inactivity was over. God had been watching over his people all through the dark period that was now ending. Now his activity would be clearly seen.

The second vision. But if the vision of the almond tree suggested hope, this hope was rudely shattered by the second vision, that of the boiling pot whose steam was blowing from the north. A time of the declining power of the old enemy, and of the renewal of national hopes, was not the best time to suggest that God was going to bring judgment upon Jerusalem in the shape of an enemy from the north.

From the outset of his career, Jeremiah was going to find himself in conflict with what everyone else wanted to believe and hope.

Israel the bride of God *Jeremiah 2:1–13*

You do not need to have been married or to have had a family to know what it is like to be rejected by someone that you love. There are many relationships outside marriage and the family where rejection can be experienced. Jeremiah was not married (Jeremiah 16:2) but this did not stop him drawing on what were probably his own experiences to describe how Israel had rejected God.

In verse 2 Jeremiah pictures the original relationship between God and Israel in terms of love at its youngest and most tender, in the honeymoon period of the wilderness wanderings. Then, Israel was totally dependent upon the gifts that God so willingly showered upon his people. The wilderness traditions themselves (Exodus 16—Numbers 36) give a different view. There Israel is pictured as complaining and discontented (compare Exodus 16:3). Perhaps Jeremiah did not know the wilderness traditions in the form that we now have them, or perhaps he is using poetic licence in order to emphasize his main point, that after being dependent on God in the wilderness the people turned from him as soon as they were settled in their own land.

Many parents and youth leaders have experienced the anguish of seeing their young people going their own way, fascinated by new friends and new ideas, apparently totally forgetful of all that they owe to parents or leaders. The anguish will be worse if these new friends and ways seem to be bad. In Israel it was not only the common people but their leaders (v. 9) who were fascinated by the culture of the land of Canaan. No doubt they thought that they were in tune with the demands of their new situation when they made unjust laws or prophesied in the name of the fertility god Baal.

In fact, they had changed their god. Jeremiah draws a contrast between other peoples who are faithful to their principles and Israel who is unfaithful to God (vv. 11–12). He ends with a striking illustration full of meaning to anyone living in a land like ancient Israel with scarce water resources. There is no comparison between a spring that constantly gives water, and a cistern that catches rain, *if it rains*. When it came to the things of God, the people preferred broken cisterns!

The foe from the north *Jeremiah 4:5–8, 13–31*

The coming of the foe from the north which was indicated in the vision of the boiling pot is now described in detail. A trumpet call warns the people to leave their villages and go to the fortified cities, which will be the only secure places (v. 5). Preparations must be made to carry out mourning rites for the loss of life and property (v. 8). The enemy is described as 'gathering storm clouds' and 'swift eagles' (v. 13; the Hebrew properly means 'vultures') and then the scene changes to that of a series of watchmen whose warnings chart the advance of the foe towards Jerusalem. First, Dan in the farthest north utters the warning, then it is taken up in the heartland of the former northern kingdom of Israel (v. 15). The warning is intended for Benjamin (reading in v. 16 'warn Benjamin that he is coming') and Jerusalem.

In verses 19–28 the prophet speaks as though the events are already happening, and that he is personally witnessing them. Of course, this is poetry, and the poet depicts the future events as a present reality. However, in receiving God's words, Jeremiah was caught between the certainty that the events would happen, and the anguish that he felt for the people, of whom he was one, upon whom the tragedy would fall. His heart is beating wildly; he would prefer to remain silent but must speak (v. 19). He seems to hear the very sound of battle (v. 21) and then surveys the devastation on the morning after (vv. 23–26). Men and even birds have vanished and the once fruitful land looks like a desert. The quaking of the heavens and hills is a sign that not just human armies, but that God himself has been at work (compare Judges 5:4–5).

Did the events so vividly seen and described by Jeremiah take place? The foe may have been the Scythian hordes who, according to the historian Herodotus (490–424BC) swept down from the Caucasus in Russia through Syria and as far as Egypt around 625BC. Whether the account of Herodotus can be trusted is a matter of dispute among experts. The view taken here is that Jeremiah's foe did not appear immediately—not for another twenty-five years! If this is correct, the effectiveness of Jeremiah's ministry from 627–622BC can be compared to that of a weather forecaster predicting snow in Jerusalem in mid-August (it simply does not snow then). If Jeremiah's early prophecies were thoroughly discredited this made things difficult for him when he began to prophesy the fall of Jerusalem many years later. It will also have caused him much suffering and inward doubts.

The reason for the disaster *Jeremiah 5:1–31*

The material in this chapter can be seen as giving the reason why the catastrophe described in chapter 4 will come upon the people. The prophet is told to search in the streets of Jerusalem to see if he can find anyone who lives truthfully and justly (vv. 1–2). Finding none, he turns to the leaders, but they, too, have turned from truth and justice (vv. 4–5). What is worse, the people have allied themselves to false gods (v. 7) and have convinced themselves that if they ignore God he will do nothing about it (vv. 12–13).

But the God of Israel is the Creator of the world. He has set up barriers which the seas dare not cross (v. 22). Do the rulers think that they can ignore the moral norms that God has set (v. 5)? If the people could only see and hear (v. 21) they would realize the futility of rebellion against the Creator, who will always speak the final word.

An unholy alliance has been formed against faithfulness to God. It is led by prophets and priests who act, not in the name of God, but in their own interests; and the people love to have it so (vv. 30–31). Only by a combination of judgment and mercy, in the course of which God's servants such as Jeremiah will suffer greatly, can God deal with such a people.

Does God call only a few to costly discipleship or does he call us all? Do we keep so silent about the cost of discipleship today, that those outside the Church despise Christian faith because they think that it is trivial?

— GATHERING STORM CLOUDS —

Jeremiah's temple 'sermon' *Jeremiah 7:1–11; 26:1–9*

Chapters 7 and 26 of Jeremiah deal with the same event, a speech delivered by the prophet in the temple at the beginning of Jehoiakim's reign (c. 608BC). The two accounts present different aspects of the occasion. Chapter 7 gives a fuller account of what was said, but does not date the speech. Chapter 26 describes how, at the conclusion of the address, Jeremiah was threatened with death, and how he escaped only because it was remembered that Micah had prophesied against Jerusalem over a century earlier (Jeremiah 26:16–19).

The date of the incident is important. If it is correct to place chapters 1–6 at the beginning of Jeremiah's ministry, then there was an interval of some eighteen years between the end of chapter 6 and the beginning of chapter 7. If we assume that Jeremiah said nothing during those years, we can suggest several reasons for the silence. In 622BC, following the discovery of 'the book of the law' in the temple, Josiah began a thorough purge of the religion of his people (2 Kings 22–23). This included suppressing the local shrines other than Jerusalem (2 Kings 23:8–9). Jeremiah may have been affected in several ways by the reform. He may have seen in it a turning back to God that would postpone or remove completely the threat of punishment. He and his family may have been affected by the restrictions placed upon priestly activity at local shrines. He may have become so discredited openly, and so filled with doubts inwardly, that he was able to say nothing.

Josiah's reign ended tragically in 609BC, when he was killed while trying to stop Necho II of Egypt going north to assist Assyria in the battle of Haran (2 Kings 23:29–30). Under his successor, Jehoiakim, the old religious abuses began to reappear. The reform may have started from the top, but it was only skin deep. In this situation Jeremiah spoke in the temple in terms that shocked the people who had gathered for a great festival. He proclaimed that God would destroy the temple just as the temple at Shiloh had been destroyed (Shiloh had been destroyed by the Philistines, although this is nowhere stated in the Bible). Further, his assertion (v. 6) that God would make Jerusalem a curse for all the nations directly contradicted the 'Zion theology' according to which Jerusalem would be the centre of a renewed earth (Isaiah 2:2–4, whatever its date, expresses this sort of hope). In the parallel account in 7:11 the phrase occurs which is taken up in the Gospels in the account of the cleansing of the temple by Jesus (Matthew 21:13 and parallels).

Does the Church today act properly as the people of God in the world?

Wisdom, might and riches *Jeremiah 9:23–24*

These two verses are a gem of a passage. They can be used, and often have been used, without any reference to the context in which they appear. Taken in context, however, they gain in meaning. The verses are part of a series of oracles of judgment, and their purpose is to warn against trusting in human achievements.

These is nothing wrong with wisdom or might or riches. The nation depended upon the skill of the wise to guide its affairs, especially in its dealings with foreign nations. The mighty provided military leadership necessary for the country's defence. The creators of wealth were vital for its material prosperity. What is condemned is the act of glorifying in these things.

To glory in wisdom, might and riches is to turn them into gods, whose worship is a form of self-worship. It is to disregard God as the sovereign Lord and to deny his place in the ordering of things. Many of Israel's troubles stemmed from the self-glorification of the strong, and the fact that they ruled over the nation for their own advantage and not for the benefit of its people.

Against the trio of wisdom, might and riches are put grace, justice and righteousness. They are not exact opposites. The pair that come closest to being opposites is might and justice, for justice was often denied to the weak by the mighty (compare Jeremiah 7:6). Grace (Hebrew *hesed*) means God's unfailing love towards his people, while righteousness means that he puts things right—a process that involves judgment and punishment of what is wrong.

To glory in these things means that a person is truly wise, truly rich and has hope in the might of the sovereign Lord. It is the opposite of self-worship, because an experience of God's faithful love brings a recognition of human inconsistency, and his justice and righteousness demand that other people should be properly respected. A nation that knows these things is truly fortunate. One that does not can only hope for God's mercy.

The waistcloth and the wine jars *Jeremiah 13:1–14*

The waistcloth. It was not unusual for people to accompany their word with symbolic actions. One of the most spectacular of such actions was that of Ahijah, who tore a new garment into twelve pieces, of which he gave ten to Jeroboam, symbolizing the division of the kingdom into Israel (ten pieces) and Judah (two pieces) at the death of Solomon (1 Kings 11:29–33). Jeremiah was ordered to buy a waist-cloth and to wear it. Then he was to hide it in a crevice of rock at the Euphrates (v. 4). Euphrates is the name of a river in what is today Iraq, many hundreds of miles from Israel. Unless all this happened in a vision, Jeremiah can hardly have travelled there and back twice, as the story demands! Possibly, a local stream with a name similar to that of Euphrates was meant, and a copyist's error produced the name Euphrates. What is quite clear is that when Jeremiah retrieved the waistcloth (v. 7) it was useless. We must presume that the crevice was damp or under water, and that the garment rotted.

The meaning of the symbolic action is spelled out in verse 11. A waistcloth is intended to be worn, not to be left in or by a stream. If it is treated thus, it will become useless. Similarly, the people of God are intended to stay close to God and to serve him. If they do not, they become useless. This is what has happened (vv. 8–10). Judah and Jerusalem have ceased to cling to God and have gone after other gods.

How are we to judge claims that are sometimes made today that God has rejected the mainstream churches and is fashioning a new people for his service?

The wine jars. The parable of the wine jars takes the forecast of disaster a step further. Several slightly different images are brought together. The drunkenness which God will bring upon the people, including the king, will make them feel secure, and unaware of the impending judgment. In drunken behaviour, wine jars are thrown to the ground and smashed. The people and their king will be like wine jars. They will be smashed and become useless.

These scenes remind us of the saying of Jesus that if salt becomes tasteless it will be thrown away (Matthew 5:13). Here, the words 'thrown away' have real and frightening consequences for Judah and Jerusalem.

The drought

Jeremiah 14:1–11

There are many references in the Bible to drought and famine. In the time of Elijah a drought lasted for over three years (see 1 Kings 17) and the family of Naomi left its Bethlehem home because of famine (Ruth 1:1–2). We are not told the date of the drought mentioned in Jeremiah 14. Many scholars place it in the early period of Jeremiah's ministry (627–622BC). Even if this is right, the compilers of the book placed this passage with material dealing with a later period, and the subject matter fits well with the theme of God's total rejection of Judah and Jerusalem.

The land of Israel is dependent for water upon springs and rains. The rains come between October and March, and fill cisterns that can be used during the dry summer. If there is little rain for several years cisterns dry out, and even springs begin to run low. Jeremiah's picture of the drought is full of pathos. It is not difficult to imagine how the nobles would express their frustration at being thirsty by taking it out on the servant who had searched for water in vain (v. 3). The animals present a heartbreaking sight, with the abandoned newly-born hind calf, and the wild asses panting for water.

Faced with such heartbreaking scenes, who could avoid praying urgently to God to do something to relieve the suffering? The prayers are recorded in verses 7–9. They end with an appeal in words which are familiar from the Order of Compline: 'Thou, O Lord, art in the midst of us . . .'

But the harshness of God's judgment to come is indicated by the fact that he will not heed these prayers. Jeremiah is ordered not to pray for the people (v. 11). Is this too harsh? Or would Judah, once the prayers were answered, return swiftly to the other gods, having used God to satisfy immediate needs? Will only the harshest treatment fulfil God's purpose?

The potter *Jeremiah 18:1–12*

In chapter 1, Jeremiah saw the almond tree and the boiling pot in passing, as it were. Here, he is commanded to go to the potter's house, where he will hear God's word (v. 2). The potter's wheel was propelled by the feet, leaving the hands free to shape the clay. Even an expert potter might need more than one attempt to make the intended vessel, and indeed Jeremiah sees the potter spoil his attempt, at which he destroys what he was making and starts again.

The main message of the scene is that God is free, not bound. The potter is not obliged to complete any vessel he has begun to make. He is a free agent. So is God. If God threatens evil against a nation and it repents, he is not bound to punish it (v. 8; and compare the Book of Jonah). On the other hand, God is not bound to his past promises to do good to a nation, if it consistently acts in an evil fashion. This is bad news for Judah and Jerusalem. Had not God bound himself to his people by way of a covenant, and had he not promised to be gracious to them for the sake of their forefathers? But these things will count as nothing: God is free to act as he will.

But there is a second meaning from the action of the potter. The potter shapes a new vessel out of the one that had gone wrong. Will God do this to his people? We are not told so; but if we can fairly see this in the passage, then there is hope as well as a threat. The old must be destroyed, and this will involve suffering and anguish if a new people is to be born that will faithfully serve God as his people. The alternative is to suppose that, in the long run, human obstinacy and self-interest can defeat the purposes of God. There is little hope in this.

Is God obliged to stand by the Church if it ceases to serve him?

The foe from the north appears *Jeremiah 22:24–30*

Jehoiachin (here called Coniah), the grandson of Josiah, succeeded to the throne in 597BC. The reign of his father Jehoiakim had seen the growth of the power of Babylon. After the final defeat of Assyria at the battle of Haran in 609BC, the Babylonians had defeated Egypt in 605BC at the battle of Carchemish. Although Egypt gained a temporary success in 602, Babylon was firmly established as the major power in the region. It was only a matter of time before the Babylonians came down upon Judah and Jerusalem. Jeremiah's foe from the north had at last appeared!

These events not only form the background to the foregoing passages, they are also the backcloth to the awesome words spoken in chapter 22 to the occupant of the throne of David.

A signet ring was a symbol of authority. To cast it off would be a radical act amounting to the abandonment of authority. Jehoichin is told that even if he were God's signet ring, this would not save him from the fate in store for him. God would not hesitate to cast him off.

The image may derive from a word-play in Hebrew between the word translated 'tear you off' and the name Coniah. The king is threatened with exile to a far land where he will die (v. 26).

In verse 28, Jeremiah seems to protest against this sentence. Jehoiachin was only eighteen when he became king (2 Kings 24:8), and his reign was to last for only three months before he submitted to Nebuchadnezzar and exile. Why, asks Jeremiah, will these things happen to him? The answer is even harsher than the original sentence: Jehoiachin will have no heir upon the throne. This is the extent of the measures that God must take to punish his people.

Prophecies such as these cost Jeremiah dearly. He did not speak his words in the spirit of a kill-joy who was only happy at the thought of the misery of others. We have seen glimpses of the anguish that he felt, of the prayers that he uttered, and the objections that he raised. The next section will explore those inner sufferings.

JEREMIAH'S 'CROSS' AND INNER ANGUISH

Opposition from Anathoth *Jeremiah 11:18–23*

It is not difficult to imagine the authorities in Jerusalem deciding to silence Jeremiah by putting pressure on those who lived in Anathoth with him. This would be a neat solution, away from the limelight. Jeremiah would have an accident, or would be struck down by an unidentifiable person. No tears would be shed in Jerusalem when the news arrived. Perhaps even the people of Anathoth needed no prompting from Jerusalem, and disliked as much as anyone what Jeremiah was saying.

Jeremiah was innocent of what was being plotted. Just as the lamb that is taken off to be slaughtered does not know what is going to happen to it (v. 19), so Jeremiah was unaware of the threat to his life until God made it known (v. 18). We can suppose that Jeremiah now confronted his neighbours openly (v. 21), and that they were equally frank. 'If you continue to prophesy in the name of the Lord,' they said, 'we will kill you'.

Jeremiah's prayer that he would see vengeance upon his neighbours will strike many readers as a less-than-Christian thought, out of keeping with the command to love our enemies. But Jeremiah does not seek satisfaction for himself. He wants the vengeance of God (v. 20: 'let me see *thy* vengeance upon them') and this does not mean revenge so much as justice. Jeremiah's own neighbours have plotted to kill him when he was totally innocent. They, perhaps threatened from Jerusalem, wanted to deny to him the chance to speak in God's name because what he said was objectionable. Jeremiah's plea is a plea that God will defend his servant and the message that God has given him to speak.

Jeremiah now finds himself with another unpleasant task, that of speaking judgment against his own neighbours (vv. 22–23). He has known the inner anguish of discovering that people whom he trusted and whom he had known for many years had banded together to kill him. Now he has to declare to them their fate!

Why do the wicked prosper? *Jeremiah 12:1–6*

This passage may consist of two different types of material; a continuation of Jeremiah's confrontation with his neighbours in Anathoth (v. 6) and Jeremiah's questioning of God on the occasion of a drought. The opening question in verses 1 and 2 is one commonly asked in the Old Testament. Why do the wicked prosper (compare Psalm 73)? In Jeremiah's case, he is not just concerned with the general problem. He has been speaking the most dreadful words against Judah, Jerusalem and the house of David, and yet from the outward point of view, the wickedness which is to be punished by the coming judgment seems to pay off in worldly terms. Jeremiah is indignant, on the other hand, that even though the wicked may thrive, and may cushion themselves against the effects of a drought, the innocent suffer. Jeremiah believes that the drought is God's action in response to wickedness—but the wrong people are suffering! The beasts and birds are innocent victims (v. 4) and even the grass and the ground are personified, as though gasping for water. Why is God so inconsistent when he is righteous in himself (v. 1)?

The answer in verse 5 is harsh and unexpected. Jeremiah has only just begun to suffer the hardship of his involvement with the people. If he cannot cope with this, how will he fare when the going gets harder? If he has not done well when racing other people on foot, how will he get on when he has to compete with horses? If he has stumbled in his own village, what will he be like in the jungle that flanks the banks of the river Jordan?

There now comes a verse which many scholars transpose to follow line 1 of 11:18. In its present position, verse 6 spells out part of the implication of verse 5. It is bad enough that Jeremiah's own household has joined the plot against him; but this is only the beginning. Jeremiah has only just begun to carry his 'cross'. He has yet to be nailed to it.

Cursed be the day of my birth *Jeremiah 15:10–12, 15–21*

In this passage, the tension between what God said would happen to Jeremiah (1:17–19) and what is actually happening has driven the prophet to breaking point. Cornered by doubts and suffering, he regrets having been born (v. 10). All that his mother brought into the world was someone destined to be a source of strife and contention for the whole land. Is the reference to his mother a rejection of what was said in chapter 1, that it was God who called him to be a prophet before his birth?

Verse 11 is difficult to translate, and by a small correction of the Hebrew text may be translated as a reassurance: 'I will make you impregnable; I will stand by you against the enemy in the time of trouble . . .' If this is correct, then verse 12 continues the reassurance by referring back to 1:18, where it is promised to Jeremiah that he will be an iron pillar and bronze walls. On this view, verse 12 is saying that no one will be able to break down what God has set up in Jerusalem.

But it is one thing to be told this, and quite another to live it out! As far as he can tell, Jeremiah has done all the right things. God's word became his delight. He did not seek the company of the merrymakers, but in solitude pondered the meaning of God's words. Why does he now feel as though he has an incurable wound, and pain that will not stop? Has God deceived him, as when someone who is thirsty goes to a known stream, only to find that it has dried up?

God's answer repeats the assurances of 1:18 and 15:12. Jeremiah will be a bronze wall against which the people will fight and not prevail. The condition is that Jeremiah does not let doubt overcome him, but that he returns to God and keeps close to him. The stakes are too high for God to abandon his servant. They will involve nothing less than the exile and restoration of his people.

Do we do enough to confront the world in general with the fact that people have religious experiences, and that these people sometimes alter the course of world history?

Threatened by the rulers *Jeremiah 18:18–23*

In the previous passage Jeremiah was close to breaking point. In the present passage and the one to follow, he seems to have broken down completely. Whether or not the Jerusalem authorities were behind the plot of the people of Anathoth, they have now banded together against Jeremiah. They are confident that they know what they are doing, and that Jeremiah is not only a nuisance, but a threat to the national life. The official priests, prophets and wise administrators are in control and Jeremiah must either be ignored or silenced.

In the face of such concerted opposition (it is not said how the decision of the rulers was conveyed to Jeremiah) the prophet breaks into a cry for vengeance upon them. The bitterness of his prayer is indicated by the fact that it is not only for vengeance on his immediate opponents, but for vengeance upon their wives and children also. The prophet who previously complained to God that the innocent were being hurt by God's judgment is now himself requesting vengeance upon the innocent. Previously he was told not to pray for the people in their need (14:11). Now he is praying that God will not forgive them.

It is easy for us to condemn all this as less-than-Christian; to say that Jeremiah lived under the old covenant and did not have our advantage of the teaching and example of Jesus. But we have to ask ourselves whether we would do any better than Jeremiah if we were in similar circumstances. As his experience so vividly shows, it is one thing to know what we ought to do and quite another thing to do it. It is easy to be morally superior by quoting the words and example of Jesus, but how far do we measure up to him? It was Jesus who said, 'Judge not, that you be not judged' (Matthew 7:1). Jeremiah's bitter cry should not be an invitation to us to consider how much more enlightened we are; it should move us to compassion and thanks for these sufferings of a servant of our God.

How does the cost of discipleship to Jeremiah compare with the cost of discipleship to ourselves?

Jeremiah's moods

In this passage we meet the most moving of what have been called Jeremiah's 'confessions'. It is a complex and highly artistic piece. Most noticeable is the abrupt change of mood introduced by verse 13. Jeremiah's prayer that he will see vengeance upon his enemies breaks into a hymn of thanksgiving for deliverance from his persecutors, only to be followed by the cursing of the day on which he was born. It is, of course, possible that originally separate units of material have been brought together to form the poem. Even if the abrupt change of mood is the result of an accidental or careless method of composition (and there is no evidence that this is so), it can be taken to show the various moods through which Jeremiah passed, with praise succeeding uncertainty, and bitterness succeeding joy. In verses 7–10 there is a strong irony. His enemies are waiting for Jeremiah to be deceived. Presumably they mean that they hope that Jeremiah will think that he is speaking God's words when he is in fact only speaking his own words. Jeremiah's complaint is that he has *already* been deceived by God (see vv. 10 and 7: 'deceived' is the same Hebrew verb in both cases). The 'deception' however, does not lead to Jeremiah's downfall, but rather to his vindication, because his 'deception' by God is in fact a confirmation of his calling as a prophet.

What comes over powerfully is that Jeremiah speaks unwillingly. He speaks unwillingly for three reasons. First, because his message warns of the destruction of his own people; secondly, because it makes him a laughing-stock in public; thirdly, because if he tries to remain silent the pain is worse than physical torment. Somehow, God has overpowered him and forced him to speak a message whose origin owes everything to God and nothing to Jeremiah.

The cursing passage of verses 14–18 takes us back again to Jeremiah's call (1:5). The only possible release that there could be would be for the prophet never to have been born; but even here he had no choice, because God had called him from before his birth.

We are left with an awesome picture of the majesty of God, whose word nothing can resist; yet people do resist it, and this creates the terrible position in which Jeremiah finds himself as he stands between the two sides, between God and the people. Jeremiah stands in this position unwillingly. Christ, who also occupied this position, did so willingly, even though he also wished not to have to drink the cup of the pain of reconciling God's majesty and human disobedience.

Can we learn anything about the meaning of the cross of Jesus Christ from the sufferings of Jeremiah?

Jeremiah in Egypt

Jeremiah 44

The afflictions that Jeremiah suffered lasted to the end of his life. Taken down to Egypt against his will (see 43:1–7), he warned the Jews in Egypt that they would not escape God's judgment simply by fleeing from Judah. However, the fact that his warnings about the fall of Jerusalem had proved to be correct did not dispose the Jews in Egypt to take any more notice of him than they had done whilst in Judah. With a perverted logic they attributed the fall of Jerusalem, not to the judgment of the God of Israel, but to their own failure to worship the queen of heaven. They looked back to the days of Manasseh (687–642BC) when it seemed as though the pagan religion had brought peace and prosperity (it had brought a great deal of evil upon the weak and pious people). Their misfortune, they supposed, could be reckoned to begin with Josiah's reformation and the aftermath of his tragic death.

Even if he had wanted it, Jeremiah did not have the satisfaction of seeing the people say to him, 'We didn't believe what you said about the fall of Jerusalem, but you were right. Tell us now what we must do.' Instead, the inability of the people to take him seriously lasted to the end, and provided a rebuff recorded in this chapter.

It is fitting that in the way in which the Book of Jeremiah is arranged the prophecies against the nations (chapters 46–51) should follow closely upon the words of 44:30. Jeremiah serves God, the sovereign Lord. His judgment will not be frustrated by people fleeing from one land to another. His judgment will reach as far as Egypt and the Egyptian king Hophra will be as powerless as anyone else when God acts against him. The speeches against the nations which follow spell out God's worldwide sovereignty, to bear witness to which was part of Jeremiah's prophetic calling (1:5, 10).

PROPHECIES AGAINST THE NATIONS

Battle of Carchemish

Jeremiah 46:1–24

The background of this passage is two defeats of Egypt at the hands of the Babylonians. The first (vv. 2–12) deals with the battle of Carchemish in 605BC, the second (vv. 13–24) with the Babylonian invasion of Egypt in 568BC. The battle of Carchemish was one of the most decisive battles in the history of the ancient Near East. It established Babylon as the supreme power in the area, a supremacy that was to last until the Persian triumph of 540BC. For Jeremiah, both battles showed God at work in the world, using a foreign nation to punish (first of all) Jerusalem and Judah, and (secondly) the Jews who had fled to Egypt supposing that they would be safe there from the Babylonians (see Jeremiah 44:30).

In the first passage, the extent of the Egyptian defeat is portrayed by the abrupt change from the description of the Egyptian army's preparations (v. 4) to its retreat in panic (v. 5). The fact that no battle is described serves to show that the victory is really God's, and not the victory of the Babylonians. In verse 7 the reference may be to either Egypt or Babylon. If the reference is to Egypt, then the following words (vv. 8–9) are full of irony as they describe the ambitions of Egypt to become the ruling nation of the world. The river Nile flooded annually, covering the land along its banks; so Egypt, whose defeat has already been described, thought of ruling the surrounding nations. If verse 7 refers to Babylon, then the river of the north, the Euphrates (v. 6), is in fact the river that will rise and cover the world, bringing to nothing the ambitions of Egypt. The day of the battle is described as the day of the Lord of Hosts (v. 10). Here, Jeremiah is using this idea in its more usual sense of a day of victory of God over his enemies, and not as a day of judgment over Israel (compare Amos 5:18–20). Yet God's victory over Egypt will pave the way for the punishment of Judah and Jerusalem by the agency of Babylon.

In the second passage the mention of Migdol, Memphis and Tahpanhes ties the passage to chapter 44. The name of the Egyptian king in verse 17 is meant to show his lack of fitness to rule—he does not know the decisive time to act. There follows a remarkable series of poetic images in which Egypt is in turn described as a heifer, a fleeing serpent and a forest about to be felled. At every point the inevitability of Egypt's defeat is implied.

Are we dealing here with forecasts or with interpretations of events? (If Jeremiah was still alive in 568BC, he would have been well over 70.) That prophecy has a predictive element is clear from the whole ministry of Jeremiah. It is a mistake, however, to suppose that all prophecy is prediction. To uncommitted observers, the events of 605 and 568BC would have nothing to do with God's judgment. For Jeremiah and the editors of his book, these events showed the power of the sovereign Lord.

Does it require a prophet to see God at work in the world?

The fall of Babylon

Jeremiah 51:1–58

The previous passage dealt with the fall of Egypt and the rise of Babylon; in the present passage it is the fall of Babylon that is described. Although these verses may have been added to by the editors of the book, the core goes back to Jeremiah. This is most likely in the case of verses 30–33. These envisage a cruel battle for the city of Babylon itself, whereas the city opened its gates to Cyrus in 540BC and yielded without a struggle.

Two themes that emerge from the marvellous poetry of the passage are the sovereignty of God and his care for his people. Babylon is described as a golden cup in God's hand with which he makes all the other nations drunk (v. 7). Babylon is also described as a hammer (vv. 20–23) by means of which God breaks everything that tries to resist him. Yet this mighty people that was used by God was a nation at whose heart was the worship of idols (vv. 47, 52). Such a nation cannot endure before the Creator of the world (see vv. 15–19, a passage similar to Isaiah 40:18–26). The language describing the inevitable defeat of Babylon includes striking images drawn from creation language. Thus, Babylon is described as being overwhelmed by the sea (v. 42) and heaven and earth together rejoice at the city's downfall (v. 48).

God's care for his people is expressed in verses 5, 10, 19, 24 and especially 34–37. Here, Jerusalem utters a lament in which it says it was crushed, eaten, emptied and swallowed. The city is told to ask for vengeance upon Babylon and is assured that this prayer will be heard and acted on by God.

What are we to make of the ideas expressed in this passage? It is hard, if not impossible, for us today to see God at work in the world in judgment. We would have him let us get on with our own affairs without him, only appealing to him in emergencies. But this was precisely the attitude of most of Jeremiah's contemporaries. Only he had the ability to see what God was doing, and without this insight the fall of Jerusalem would have been interpreted as the conquest of the weaker by the stronger nation. Is the fact that passages such as Jeremiah 51 are so uncongenial to us today a reflection on Jeremiah or a reflection on us?

Is God at work in the world today judging the nations through the process of war? If he is not, is there any way in which he is exercising his sovereignty, or is he a passive observer of what is going on in the world?

The vulnerable position of the Philistines *Jeremiah 47*

Although the Philistines had been subdued by David, they continued to occupy the cities of the southern part of the coastal plain, through which passed the strategic route from Egypt to the north known as the 'way of the sea'. It is possible that Necho had attacked Gaza after defeating and killing Josiah at Megiddo in 609BC. Control over the 'way of the sea' was continually disputed between Egypt, Judah and the Philistines, and no opportunity to regain control was missed.

But it is the foe from the north that really threatens the Philistines, and once more Jeremiah applied to the Babylonians the image of the Nile overflowing and covering surrounding lands. Philistia will be attacked because it stands in the path that the Babylonian army will take when it moves against Judah and Egypt. It is striking that Jeremiah does not list any offences for which the Philistines will be punished. Perhaps it was commonly accepted in Judah that Philistine religion and morality were not pleasing to God.

The main point, however, is that nothing can withstand God when he acts. Jeremiah prays for God's sword to be still and return to its scabbard (v. 6), but he answers his own prayer by affirming that what God has decided to do cannot be resisted (v. 7). The events will not be averted by ritual gashing or by vows accompanied by shaving the head (v. 5), nor will help come from the cities of Tyre and Sidon. The noise of the horses and chariots will herald an irresistible foe.

Moab's favourable position *Jeremiah 48*

Moab was the eastern neighbour of Judah. Although its northern boundaries in particular did not stay the same, it occupied roughly the opposite side of the Dead Sea from Judah. From the point of view of its position it was much more fortunate than Judah. Although a major route known as the 'king's highway' passed through it, this was not the major thoroughfare from Egypt to Syria and beyond to Assyria and Babylon. Moab was thus not in the front line in the way that Judah was. Moab was also more fertile, with a high plateau on which sheep were kept on a large scale (see 2 Kings 3:4). When famine struck Bethlehem, it was to Moab that Naomi and her family went (Ruth 1:1). Relationships between Judah and Moab were such that neither side missed the opportunity to dominate the other, although this was not possible for most of the time.

The speech against Moab draws heavily on material from elsewhere in the Old Testament. This is seen most strikingly if you compare 48:29–33 with Isaiah 16:6–10, and 48:43–44 with Isaiah 24:17–18. As we have it, Jeremiah 48 consists of a core of sayings of Jeremiah which was enlarged by the editors of the book, who drew upon other parts of the Old Testament.

Much of the material follows lines with which we are now familiar. There is the urgent appeal to the inhabitants to flee from their homes (v. 6), there are cries of wailing that follow after destruction (vv. 4–5), there is a lament over destroyed cities (v. 1). The main complaint against Moab is that the country has had it too good. It has not experienced war and exile as other countries have (v. 11) and the result is that Moab has become proud and lofty (vv. 29–30). Such pride leads to self-dependence and to the rejection of spiritual values. God, however, is on the move, and will break all forms of pride and self-dependence in order to demonstrate his sovereignty (v. 42).

The chapter ends, remarkably, with a promise that Moab will be restored (v. 47). The same is promised for Ammon (49:6). According to Genesis 19:30–38 Ammon and Moab were the incestuous children of Lot, the nephew of Abraham. There is thus a special relationship between the Israelites and Ammon and Moab, and this will not leave them outside God's mercy when, in the latter days, he establishes his kingdom visibly in the world.

Ammon and the east-Jordan tribes *Jeremiah 49:1–6*

Ammon was Moab's northern neighbour. The boundary between the two peoples fluctuated with their respective strengths and weaknesses, and this is why Heshbon is mentioned in verse 3 in connection with Ammon, while in 48:34 it is mentioned in connection with Moab. Ammon was also to the east and south of the territory that traditionally was reckoned to the tribes of Gad and Reuben and the half-tribe of Manasseh (see Numbers 32:33–42). Again, no opportunity was missed by Ammon to occupy these lands, and the background to this passage is in fact Ammon's occupation of some or all of the lands. It is also interesting to note that the murderers of Gedaliah were encouraged by the king of Ammon and that the murderers tried to return to Ammon after completing their task (Jeremiah 40:14; 41:10).

Milcom is the name of the god of Ammon (see 1 Kings 11:5) and stands in verse 1 for the Ammonite people. The prophet asks why it is that Ammon, not the tribe of Gad, now occupies the land allocated to Gad. Because of this occupation, Rabbah (Rabbat Ammon the capital, today Amman) will be destroyed.

Exile and restoration. In verse 3–4, exile is foreseen for the Ammonites. The valleys mentioned in verse 4 include the deep gorge of the river Jabbok, which was a useful natural line of defence; but all will be of no avail when God acts against Ammon.

Hatred of Edom *Jeremiah 49:7–22*

This is another passage with quotations from elsewhere in the Old Testament (compare vv. 14–16 with Obadiah 1–4). Edom lay to the south of Moab and according to Old Testament tradition was descended from Jacob's brother Esau (see Genesis 36:1). Following the destruction of Jerusalem in 587BC, Edomites occupied the southern part of Judah, an action which earned them considerable hatred, which is expressed in several passages in the Old Testament (see Psalm 137:7–9).

Edom was famed for its wisdom. Teman, mentioned in verse 7, was the home of one of Job's comforters (Job 2:11) and Job's land of Uz has itself been located in Edom.

The condemnation spoken here may be taken in two ways. The famed wisdom of Edom may be criticized because the occupation of southern Judah was not a wise action; or it may simply be that wise as the Edomites were, their wisdom was foolishness in comparison with the purposes of God.

— THE FALL OF JERUSALEM —

Jerusalem under siege and relieved *Jeremiah 34*

This chapter has something in common with chapter 37. There, the king sends for Jeremiah in order to enquire about his fate. Here, Jeremiah is sent by God to Zedekiah to speak the words of judgment. Also, the present chapter implies a lifting of the siege of Jerusalem while chapter 37 actually reports that the Babylonians temporarily withdrew when an Egyptian force approached.

We may assume that the events described here took place in about 588BC. The reference to Lachish and Azekah (v. 7) is interesting. In 1935 some 'letters' were found, written in ink on fragments of pottery. Letter 4 of these so-called 'Lachish Letters' was written in about 588 from an observation post and sent back to Lachish. The observers report that they can no longer see the fire signals of Azekah. The city has probably just fallen.

The opening words of the chapter are also significant. They speak not just of the Babylonians, but of 'all the peoples' fighting against Jerusalem. In the Zion theology of the Psalms, the peoples band together against Jerusalem, but to no avail (see Psalm 2). In the case of chapter 34, they will succeed, and the Davidic king, who in Psalm 2:9 is promised that he will break nations in pieces, is here promised defeat and exile.

The second part of the chapter deals with the famous incident of the freeing of the slaves in Jerusalem, a generous act on the part of slave-owners which was reversed at the earliest opportunity, so that the freedom of the slaves was short-lived. We do not know why the slaves were released. It may have been in response to the preaching of false prophets such as those who opposed Jeremiah (see 28:1), or it may have been a desperate attempt to earn God's favour and to ward off the Babylonians. It seems to have been accompanied by a solemn ceremony in which the freeing of the slaves was ratified by the parties walking between the two halves of a sacrificial animal (compare Genesis 15:9ff). The freeing of the slaves seems to have been successful. The siege was lifted. Immediately, slavery was reimposed.

It is amazing how inconsistent humans can be even today in their dealings with God. How often do we try to bargain with him that if we get our own way in a particular matter we will be better disciples in future! We know perfectly well, of course, that we really do not mean this, and that we simply want God to be there for our convenience.

Jeremiah's words in response to the renewal of slavery are simple in their logic. The inhabitants of Jerusalem are not the only ones who can go back on solemn agreements. God made a solemn covenant with his people. Should he take it any more seriously than the slave-owners took their agreement with the slaves?

The Rechabites *Jeremiah 35*

Chapters 34–39 are not in chronological order. The previous passage dealt with events of about 488BC, the present chapter deals with events of nine or ten years earlier, while chapter 36 is dated to 605BC. The arrangement is theological and thematic rather than chronological, and the chapters build up to a dramatic climax in spite of seeming to make time go backwards.

In chapter 35 the contrast is strongly drawn between the Rechabites, who strictly obeyed the orders of their human ancestor Jonadab (Jehonadab), and the house of Judah who disobeyed the commands of God. Jonadab is mentioned in 2 Kings 10:15–17 as having accompanied Jehu (c. 840–815BC) on the latter's journey to Samaria to wipe out the family of Ahab and the prophets of Baal. Jonadab may have ordered his family not to drink wine, sow seed, plant vineyards or build houses because he thought that this was the best way of protecting them from the fertility religion that was closely bound to the cycle of nature.

During the siege of 598–597BC, prior to its first capture by Nebuchadnezzar, the Rechabites had taken refuge in Jerusalem, and Jeremiah was commanded to take them into one of the chambers of the temple, and to order them to drink wine. We can assume that this was not a private gathering. There would have been witnesses present, and this made the event into a public sign that reinforced the word that Jeremiah was given to speak.

The chapter ends with a promise to the house of the Rechabites (vv. 18–19) and this may well account for the arrangement of the material. Jonadab will always have a successor; his house (family) will last for ever. This promise is in sharp contrast to what is said about the future of the house of David in chapter 36.

The Baruch scroll *Jeremiah 36*

We are now taken back to 605BC, the fourth year of Jehoiakim and the year of the battle of Carchemish. Jeremiah is ordered by God to dictate to Baruch the prophecies that he had spoken up to then. Baruch is to write them down, and because Jeremiah is unable to go to the temple (has his 'temple sermon' brought him a ban?) Baruch is to read the scroll in the temple when many people are gathered there. Perhaps the reason for the action was Jeremiah's conviction, following the battle of Carchemish, that the foe from the north was at last really under way, and that the earlier prophecies needed to be revived.

It is not surprising that Baruch's action should be reported to the king, and that he should order the scroll to be brought and to be read in his presence. The scene of the cutting and burning of the scroll is full of drama. Upon hearing such solemn words the king and his courtiers should have torn their cloths in fear and trembling before God. Instead, the king cut the scroll which contained God's words. The same Hebrew verb is used for 'to tear' or 'to rend' garments and 'to cut' the scroll. The king has unwittingly performed a symbolic act. His cutting of the scroll only indicates what will happen to him. His dead body will not be buried, but will be exposed to cold and to heat, as was the scroll.

In fact, the prophecy concerning Jehoiakim was not strictly fulfilled. He died three months before the city fell, leaving Jehoiachin to be taken into exile. But the more significant part of the prophecy concerned the house of David, which, unlike the house of the Rechabites would be brought to an end.

The scroll had been destroyed, but God's words to Jeremiah could not be so easily disposed of. Jeremiah dictated his words to Baruch once more, this time with additions.

The siege lifted *Jeremiah 37*

When the Babylonians lifted the siege of Jerusalem because of the approach of an Egyptian force, many must have breathed a huge sigh of relief. Exactly why the king asked Jeremiah to pray for the people we can only guess. Did he believe that the people had truly heeded God, that this was why the siege had been lifted, and that he feared a relapse on the part of the people? Or did he simply want Jeremiah to pray that the Babylonians would not come back? It is an interesting exercise to examine the motives for how and why people pray as they do, ourselves included. Jeremiah's response was not what the king wanted to hear. He spoke of the Babylonian withdrawal as a temporary one, to be followed by their return and capture of the city.

Nevertheless, Jeremiah used the lifting of the siege as an opportunity to visit his home village. As he left the city he was recognized by a guard and arrested on the suspicion of deserting to the enemy. This was a reasonable suspicion. Jeremiah had consistently forecast a Babylonian victory. What would be more natural than that he would escape to the Babylonians while he could, and reap the benefits of being a traitor? Jeremiah's protests of innocence were ignored. The truth was, however, that he was determined to suffer with the people—himself to be a victim of the judgment that he foresaw.

Jeremiah's arrest marked the beginning of an imprisonment that lasted until the city fell. He was flogged, and no doubt detained in wretched conditions until the king sent to ask if there was a word from God. The king's request was both tragic and pathetic. Surely there had been sufficient words from God already! Did he really expect that suddenly there would be a change in what the prophet was saying? Yet, like all of us in border situations, he clung to whatever straws of hope that he could find, and at least he improved Jeremiah's lot and gave him proper rations.

Was Jeremiah a traitor to his country?

Jeremiah's treason

Jeremiah 38

We can assume that while Jeremiah was detained in the 'court of the guard' he still had the opportunity to speak to those who passed in and out, and that he continued to urge people to leave Jerusalem (vv. 2–3). It is not surprising that high officials in the city found this quite intolerable. Here was a traitor, and he was being allowed to weaken the resolve of the people and solders to continue the fight. The phrase 'weakening the hands' (v. 4, i.e. undermining morale) is also found in one of the Lachish Letters, where the complaint is made.

The king was hardly in a position to quarrel with the decision that a traitor should be put to death, and he allowed Jeremiah to be taken away to be put in a muddy cistern. The words 'cistern' and 'mire' do not convey the horror of the conditions in which Jeremiah found himself. He was probably in darkness, with no food or water, perhaps up to his knees in mud, and probably unable to lie down or rest in case the mud covered and choked him. We do not know how long it was before Ebed-melech pulled him out, but Jeremiah must have given up hope of remaining alive, and he must have faced a very black period indeed.

When Zedekiah called for him for their final meeting the thought must have occurred to Jeremiah that if he displeased the king he would be put back into the cistern. Nonetheless, he refused to alter his words. If speaking God's word was to result in an unpleasant death, he still had to speak God's word.

The new element in Jeremiah's speech was the lament to be sung by the women of the royal household when they were led to captivity. It is a piece of Hebrew poetry in the lament rhythm, bewailing the false advice given to the king by his courtiers. Its reference to Zedekiah's feet sinking in the mire is interesting in view of Jeremiah's own recent experience. Although the Hebrew words for 'mire' in verse 6 and 22 are not the same, the verb translated 'sink' is, and the similarity between the two verses is striking.

In 39:15–18 Ebed-melech's action in rescuing Jeremiah, when he, too, might have been called a traitor, is rewarded with the promise that he will survive the fall of the city.

Jerusalem's capture

Jeremiah 39

The account of Jerusalem's fall, Zedekiah's capture, and his blinding after he has seen the execution of his sons and nobles needs little comment. Presumably, those nobles who opposed Jeremiah were among those to be killed. The king retained his life, as Jeremiah predicted (34:5), although we may wonder whether blindness and exile were really preferable to death.

Verses 11–14 are full of irony. The Babylonian king commands Jeremiah to be well treated, and for notice to be taken of what he says. There is a great contrast between this treatment and that accorded to Jeremiah by his own king and his own people.

Presumably, Nebuchadnezzar had spies in Jerusalem, or he learned from deserters about Jeremiah's proclamation that surrender was the only hope. On the other hand, we learn from 40:1 that Jeremiah was bound in chains and could well have been taken to Babylon.

Even though he managed, so far, to escape the fate of many, we must not count Jeremiah as a lucky person in the circumstances. It gave him no pleasure to see the vindication of his words, and we must not forget the anguish with which he foresaw the devastation of the land and its people (4:19–26).

Can we perceive, from Jeremiah's attitudes, how we might distinguish between someone who really thought that they were called to be a traitor and someone who was mistaken?

PROPHECIES OF HOPE

The redemption of land

Jeremiah 32:1–15

This chapter begins with a date which places the incidents it records in the year 587BC, perhaps not long before the fall of the city. Chronologically speaking, the passage should come between chapters 37 and 38, from the time when Jeremiah was detained in the court of the guard following his alleged attempt to desert to the enemy (37:11–15). It owes its position here to two points. First, it follows a collection of sayings about future restoration (chapters 30–31) and secondly, it is a fitting introduction to material that will have the fall of Jerusalem as its climax.

Leviticus 25:25 specifies that if an Israelite has to sell his land, his next-of-kin must buy it, because land must not be sold in perpetuity (Leviticus 25:23). Jeremiah found himself in the position of a next-of-kin during the siege of Jerusalem. We must allow that much more happened than the narrative records. How, for example, did Jeremiah come to have seventeen shekels of silver, the scales and the necessary legal documents when he was in captivity? If Jerusalem was under siege, how did Hanamel travel from Anathoth to Jerusalem? It was probably with the help of friends such as Baruch that Jeremiah obtained the necessary money and materials in order to perform a symbolic action of outstanding importance. At a time when, humanly speaking, there seemed to be no hope for Judah, Jeremiah purchased a field in order to affirm the word from God that 'Houses and fields and vineyards shall again be bought in this land' (v. 15).

The double receipt of the sale (v. 14) was the normal practice of the time. One receipt was sealed so that it could not be opened and altered, while the open receipt gave access to the contents of the sealed receipt. The depositing of the receipts in an earthenware vessel symbolized a long period during which there would seem to be no hope; but Jeremiah's certainty that God was in control of events and that he would restore the people to the land could not have been more forcefully demonstrated.

God speaks tenderly *Jeremiah 30:4–22*

It is unlikely that all the words in this passage come from Jeremiah himself. Verses 10–11, although not exactly paralleled in Isaiah 40–55 have so many similarities with the language of those chapters (see Isaiah 41:10–13) that it is likely that they come from the compilers of Isaiah 40–55. It does not matter if some of these words come from someone other than Jeremiah. Chapter 32:1–15 has already made it clear that Jeremiah hoped for a restoration of the people to the land, and the compilers of his book were not being false to him by including in it material about restoration from other biblical traditions.

What is important about these words is that God speaks in the first person. Many passages that we have read presented God as though he was a heartless tyrant. It is Jeremiah who has to plead for the people, or who feels the anguish of the effects of the coming judgment upon the people. Is God not moved by what is going to happen? Does he enjoy punishing his people? Chapter 30 gives us a glimpse of what has been called the divine 'pathos'—the suffering and anguish which God has as he sees the afflictions of his people. He knows better than anyone the physical pain of the untreatable wound (v. 12) and of the emotional pain of rejection by friends and lovers (v. 14). He comforts his people by assuring them that Jerusalem and its palace will be rebuilt (v. 18), that their captivity will end (v. 8) and that the bond which makes him their God and them his people will be renewed (v. 22).

Promises to the northern kingdom *Jeremiah 31:2–14*

This poem of hope and restoration is addressed to the northern kingdom Israel, whose independent existence as a nation was ended by the Assyrians in 721BC (see 2 Kings 17:1–6). Some of the language is similar to that in Isaiah 40–55, for example the references to the coastlands and to the shepherd keeping his flock (v. 10; compare Isaiah 41:1 and 40:11). We probably have a poem, the core of which goes back to Jeremiah, but which was enriched from other parts of biblical tradition by the editors. It is difficult to know where to date the poem within Jeremiah's ministry. Some commentators compare the poem with the call to Israel to repent in Jeremiah 3:11–25, and they date it to the early period of his preaching, 627–622BC.

The poem alludes to the events of the wilderness wanderings, a period already mentioned in 2:2–3 as one of sincere love on the part of Israel for God. In chapter 31 the references to the wilderness are less idealistic. Those who 'survived the sword' in verse 2 may be those who escaped the killings that followed the making of the golden calf (Exodus 32:25–29). The reference to timbrels and dancing may hint at the tradition that after the overthrow of Pharaoh at the Red Sea, Miriam and the women rejoiced with timbrels and dancing (Exodus 15:20). The references back to the Exodus and wilderness traditions recall something fundamental to the Old Testament, that God loved Israel not because Israel was worthy but because God's love made Israel into something to be loved (Deuteronomy 7:7–8). Thus we have the beautiful words of verse 3, 'I have loved you with an everlasting love'.

In verses 5–6 a restoration of the northern kingdom is envisaged, but a northern kingdom that will look to Jerusalem (Zion) as its capital, not Samaria. The words of verses 7–14, whether or not they come from Jeremiah himself, present one of the most beautiful pictures of restoration in material terms anywhere in the Bible. God's power in bringing this about is stressed by the references to expectant mothers and to blind and lame people making the long journey back to Israel. In a land where water is short, to live as in a watered garden is indeed a blessing. But Jeremiah's hope of restoration of the northern tribes was not fulfilled.

Rachel weeping for her children *Jeremiah 31:15–22*

In this passage the promises to the northern kingdom are continued. The opening words, 'Rachel is weeping for her children' will be familiar to many readers from the story of the killing of the children in Bethlehem by Herod (Matthew 2:18). In fact, there are two traditions in the Old Testament about the location of Rachel's grave. The best known, in Genesis 35:19, places it near Bethlehem, which is the reason why Jeremiah 31:15 is quoted in the Gospel narrative, and why the traditional site of Rachel's grave is on the road from Jerusalem to Bethlehem. The less well-known tradition is in 1 Samuel 10:2, and locates the grave in the land of Benjamin. As a Benjaminite himself Jeremiah probably knew this second identification, and thus begins his poem with a striking picture of the wife of Jacob crying for her exiled children many centuries after her natural death. God cannot resist these cries for help and he comforts the crying mother: your children shall come back to your own country.

In verses 18–20 Ephraim speaks, admitting that he was headstrong, but now confessing that he knows better, and that he is ashamed of what he did in his youth. In reply, God speaks as a tender father. The bond of love that ties God to his firstborn will not be severed. God yearns for his son's return, and will have mercy.

The poem concludes with a call to the people to come back. God speaks as though he has already created the conditions necessary for their return. All that they have to do is to retrace their steps from the land of their exile.

Verse 22 has been interpreted in many ways. In the Hebrew it means 'a woman surrounds a man', and thus 'protects' is a reasonable translation. We can guess that the text means that when God establishes his kingdom there will be no more war or danger. A woman will be ample protection for a man against his enemies, because he will have none.

The new covenant *Jeremiah 31:31–34*

In the previous passages the restoration of Israel was pictured in material terms—the repossession of the land, the planting of vineyards, the joyful gathering together of young and old, sick and healthy. The famous verses of the present passage strike a deeper, spiritual note, without which all the descriptions of restoration in material terms would leave us with an unanswered question: if they come back, will they be any better than they were before they were exiled?

Whether or not the words about the new covenant come from Jeremiah is disputed by the experts. There is no reason why they cannot go back to him. He saw as clearly as anyone in the Old Testament how weak and deceitful human nature could be. The likelihood of Israelites doing or being good was the same as the likelihood of Ethiopians changing the colour of their skin or leopards getting rid of their spots (13:23). Nobody would appreciate more than Jeremiah the need for radical change in human nature. But whether or not the words go back to Jeremiah, they touch on one of the most important themes in the Old Testament, that of human rebellion in the face of divine grace. The theme is found in Genesis 3, where Adam and his wife eat the forbidden fruit in spite of having everything else that they need. It is found in Genesis 12 when Abraham leaves the land that has been promised to him at the first hint of hardship, in the form of famine. It is found in the story of the golden calf when the people worship an idol that they have made at the very moment when Moses is receiving the Law from God. It is found in the unwillingness of the people to enter the Promised Land (Numbers 14:1–4). Deuteronomy 1:27 sums up this attitude in the words 'you murmured in your tents, and said "Because the Lord hated us he has brought us forth out of the land of Egypt . . ." '.

Granted that within the experience of Israel there was a persistent desire not to obey God's Law, what was to be done? The Law itself was not at fault. The weakness of the covenant came from the fatal combination of God's Law and grace on the one side, and Israel's desire to be rid of God on the other. What was needed was not a new Law, but a new Israel and a new humanity.

It is easy for Christians to think that Jeremiah's words about the new covenant have been fulfilled in the Church. Did not Jesus ratify a new covenant by the shedding of his blood, and did he not command his followers to celebrate the new covenant when they met to break the bread in his name? Yet Christians must hesitate before they apply Jeremiah 31:31–34 to themselves or the Church. Of which Christians can it be said that the Law of God is written on their hearts? Where is the situation in which no missions are required because all the people know God 'from the least of them to the greatest'?

The truth is that the Book of Jeremiah and our present verses touch on the deepest problem of Jewish and Christian faith. How can God win us to perfect obedience to his Law and to pure love for himself? If he does it by force then the obedience and love are worth nothing. If God tries other ways he is vulnerable to our rejecting him. For much of the Book of Jeremiah, the prophet speaks on behalf of the sovereign Lord who, even if he will not compel obedience, will not ignore disobedience and leave it unpunished. But this awesome picture of God has to be set alongside the tender promises that we have seen in chapter 30.

The Book of Jeremiah does not answer the dilemma that it touches upon, and as a result it points beyond itself. The new covenant is not yet fulfilled in the Church, but for Christian faith there is a fulfilment in Jesus Christ, of whom alone it can be said that God's Law was written in his heart and that his life was a life of perfect love and obedience.

The sufferings of Jeremiah were not cruel punishments imposed upon him by a heartless God. For Christian faith, God himself took up the cross that lies at the heart of the process of bringing men and women to the point where they all know and love him, from the least to the greatest.

Is there the risk that Christians think that they have a 'spiritual' rather than a 'legal' covenant with the result that their faith lacks any moral content, apart from generally being 'good' and 'decent'?

EZEKIEL

The strangeness of the book and of the prophet

Of all the prophetic books, Ezekiel is perhaps the most difficult for the ordinary reader to get to grips with. It presents us with a character who sees curious visions and who acts in a most extraordinary way. So peculiar is the prophet that some earlier commentators regarded him as a suitable case for psychoanalysis and tried to apply its methods to him. This approach did little to illuminate the meaning of the book and in its more extreme forms it misled readers concerning the nature of prophets in general. It implies that they were in some abnormal state of mind when they spoke their prophecies. Some, and especially Ezekiel, were regarded as 'ecstatic' prophets who, under the influence of external forces, lost control of themselves. Ezekiel, therefore, had periods when he couldn't speak or move or was otherwise 'beside himself'. This concentration on the personality of the prophet often obscured the important message he had to convey.

The importance of the message

Nowadays the visions tend to be understood as based on things actually familiar to Ezekiel which he described in colourful language and the curious actions are seen as non-verbal expressions of the message he has received from God. So we are more concerned with his message than with theories about his personality.

Priest and prophet

There are, however, certain things we can say about Ezekiel which will help us to understand his message better. We are told (1:3) that he was a priest. Without ceasing to be a priest he was also called to be a prophet. His priestly role could not be fully exercised because he was in exile in Babylon (see below) and therefore far from the Jerusalem temple which was the only place where sacrifice could legitimately be offered. But a priest was also responsible for teaching the Law and making judgments on the basis of it. This side of his priestly work he could still fulfil among his fellow-exiles. The consequence of this combination of roles is that his speeches bear the marks of both priestly and prophetic influence. The former is clearly and especially shown in passages such as 3:16–21, 18:1–20 and 33:1–20 which are concerned with the issues of responsibility; but we ought to keep it in mind throughout for it can help us to get a clearer understanding of what he is saying.

Divine inspiration

Although Ezekiel may clothe his message in words which are his own and are derived from his experience as priest and prophet, there is no doubt that he regarded the message itself as coming from God. The opening vision and the many references to the influence of the 'spirit of God' make this clear. As a priest he needed God's inspiration to interpret and apply the Law to the circumstances of his day; as a prophet he needed divine guidance to interpret the events which were happening around him for they were beyond human understanding alone. Certainly those in exile with him could not make head or tale of what was happening and when they tried they were often, in Ezekiel's view, mistaken. God's will for the present and purpose for the future must be revealed to the people through his prophet. Consequently, though we may recognize the conventions of priestly and prophetic speech, we have to be open to the word of God which finds expression in them.

Ezekiel in Babylon

This word from God is applied to a particular situation though it is also capable of application to different ones. Throughout the first half of the seventh century BC, Judah had been dominated by Assyria and King Manasseh was left with little room to move independently. He had been forced, humanly speaking, to comply with the demands of the king of Assyria and if these conflicted with Judah's beliefs and practices, so be it. He had little option but to be obedient. Consequently religious practice had become debased and for this later historians and theologians blamed Manasseh (see 2 Kings 21). When Assyrian power began to weaken, the possibility for reform opened up and King Josiah, who had come to the throne as a child in c. 640BC, instituted a whole series of reforms when he was old enough to take personal responsibility in 621. These were meant to restore the purity of Judaean belief in and worship of the Lord (2 Kings 23). Josiah was killed in battle in 609 by the Egyptians who were passing through Judah to help the Assyrians against the emergent Babylonians. Soon, however, under his successor, Jehoiakim, the reforms were forgotten and resistance to Babylon became the order of the day. The prophet Jeremiah advised submission but was not heeded and in 587 the Babylonians under Nebuchadnezzar attacked Jerusalem and carried off Jehoiachin, who had recently succeeded his father, along with many officials from the royal court and the temple. They were deported to a site outside the city of Babylon. We have so far assumed that Ezekiel remained in Jerusalem until 587 and that the first 24 chapters of the book contain threats which he spoke directly to the people there. Certainly he does appear to have addressed Jerusalem and he was very much aware of all that was happening there. However, his familiarity with affairs in Judah can be explained by reference to the correspondence conducted between those in Jerusalem and those in Babylon (see also Jeremiah 29). The question is not settled beyond doubt but the editor of the book clearly believed him to have been in Babylon and that is the view taken here. It is generally held that he was taken to Babylon in the first deportation of 597BC.

New hopes

The first years of his ministry were therefore marked by warnings and threats that the punishment was not yet complete. In this he was proved right, for in 587BC Jerusalem was captured again when the walls and the temple were destroyed and further exiles joined those already in Babylon. It was at this point that Ezekiel, recognizing that the threat of judgment was now fulfilled, began to look forward with renewed hope to the future which included a return to the homeland and a rebuilding of the temple. These hopes are expressed in chapters 34–48.

Later use of the prophet's words

The fact that a number of oracles are rather precisely dated between 595 and 572BC suggests that Ezekiel may not only have spoken God's word to the exiles but may also have written down what he said, or at least made notes of it. In any case, it was left to others to preserve and collect what he had to say. Moreover, since this was recognized as being the word of God, it was seen to have relevance not only to Ezekiel's contemporaries but also to later generations. The result is that we have in our present book of Ezekiel both his words to the exiles in Babylon and the reflections of others who sought to apply them to their own later circumstances.

The editing of the book

Whoever 'edited' the book, putting it into its present form, included both types of material. These 'disciples' of Ezekiel were probably for the most part at work in the latter part of the exile and were concerned to put more flesh on Ezekiel's often rather vague hopes for the future. It is important not to dismiss these later interpretations as unimportant. They are a part of our present Scripture and they have to be taken every bit as seriously as the words of Ezekiel himself. There may be marked differences in outlook, and the tension between the two is often instructive in demonstrating differences of outlook in Judah and throwing light upon differences of outlook today.

The process of interpretation

In fact, there may well have been more than these two levels of material, that from Ezekiel and from followers later in the exile. The process of reinterpretation of prophetic oracles went on for a considerable time and here and there we find evidence of people from a much later age still using Ezekiel's words to inform their thinking and to address their situation. We modern interpreters, therefore, stand in a tradition which goes back to the time of the prophet himself as we seek to apply his words to ourselves and our contemporary affairs.

Occasionally I shall depart from the order in which the prophecies now stand in the Bible and in any case I shall not be able to deal with them all; but I hope the selection will help to grasp the message of the book.

By and large the English version followed is the Revised Standard Version, though this should not cause any problems for those who wish to use a different version.

Further reading

J. Blenkinsopp, *Ezekiel*, (Interpretation), John Knox Press, Louisville, 1990

B. Vawter and L.J. Hoppe, *A New Heart: A Commentary on the Book of Ezekiel*, Eerdmans, Grand Rapids and Handsel, Edinburgh, 1991

CALL AND RESPONSE

The setting

Ezekiel 1:1–28

The compiler of the book, as the custom was, sets the scene by giving us some historical information. He tells us that Ezekiel had his vision 'in the thirtieth year'. A further comment in verse 2 makes clear that this was 592BC, and so he could have meant the 'thirtieth year' after the great reforms of King Josiah in 621BC. But he could equally well be referring to the prophet's age. Ezekiel would have been twenty-five when he was taken into exile from his home in Jerusalem in 597BC, and according to Numbers 8:24 twenty-five was the age at which a priest began his priestly work. So the would-be priest who would have officiated in the Jerusalem temple now became a prophet in Babylon.

The vision. We could spend a long time thinking about the details of this strange vision which brought about such a change in Ezekiel. No doubt some features of it are derived from what he had seen in the temple; others may be drawn from contemporary mythology. It is important, though, simply to read this through without worrying about the details and to let it make the impression on us that the vision itself did on Ezekiel. It certainly represented God seated on his throne, something indescribable in ordinary language. God is seen in his *holiness*, and this is not just one quality among others in the nature of God; it is his divine nature itself. The 'glory' of which the prophet speaks is what men and women can see of that holiness. However much the prophets believed that God was present with them, they never lost this sense of his divine majesty.

The response

Ezekiel 1:28—2:7

Confronted by such a vision it is hardly surprising that Ezekiel was overcome by it. It was dangerous to get too near to such holiness—as Uzzah discovered when he touched the holy ark (2 Samuel 6:7). The very words used in the second half of verse 28 distance Ezekiel from God and he can only fall on his face in awe, for the belief was strong that no man could see God and live (Exodus 33:20). Isaiah had earlier survived his vision (Isaiah 6) and Ezekiel survived his. By addressing him as a 'son of man', an expression often used in Ezekiel, God emphasizes the prophet's humanity over against his own divinity. Yet even a human being in all his weakness may stand up when God calls.

The commission. Then he can receive his commission. Ezekiel's is difficult. He is to threaten his own people who, instead of being the chosen people of God, as they were meant to be, had rebelled against God. According to Jewish law any son who rebelled against his father was punished by death. According to ancient custom any people which rebelled against its king or overlord could expect the severest punishment. The exact nature of Israel's punishment is not yet revealed to Ezekiel. For the moment the only thing he is told to say is 'Thus says the Lord.' Any messenger, sent on an errand, began his message with 'Thus says so-and-so,' but the phrase had come to be used especially by prophets who were seen as God's messengers to his people. When Ezekiel used this phrase it would indicate to his hearers that though he was a priest he was now speaking as a prophet.

To do so required enormous courage. Some previous prophets with a message of criticism had lost their lives (Jeremiah 26:10–23). Ezekiel therefore needed reassurance from God.

Eating the scroll

Ezekiel 2:8—3:15

There is no need to take this passage about the eating of the scroll literally! The metaphor of digesting what a book says is familiar to us, but it is expressed here with extra vividness. The message on the scroll, still not specifically revealed to us, is one of lamentation, mourning and woe. Is it not rather strange, then, that Ezekiel found it as sweet as honey? There is nothing elsewhere in the book to suggest that it gave him any special pleasure to condemn and threaten his own people. It may be that Ezekiel had not yet fully grasped that the message in the scroll was to be directed against Israel. Sometimes the prophets were called to threaten other nations and they often did so with relish. Indeed, later in this book there is a collection of prophecies against other nations. It is not unlikely that Ezekiel thought the message was meant for them—indeed, the original Hebrew text in 2:3 has the plural 'nations' where some of the early versions and most of the English translations have the singular 'nation'.

The unpalatable truth. Whether or not this is so, the words which are now recorded in 3:4–11 make it unmistakably clear to Ezekiel that the rebellious people is Israel, and it is they who will have to lament. Foreign nations might have the good sense to listen to a prophet, but the very people who ought to be most responsive to the word of God have become the most obstinate. The exiles in Babylon believe that their present suffering will come to an end. They have been there five years and will soon be on their way home. Ezekiel's unpleasant message is that there is still more trouble to come.

So, with the assurance of his vision to support him and impelled by the God to whom he has submitted himself, he must now present himself to the exiles. There, like the friends who visited the suffering Job (Job 2:13), he sits quietly sharing the hardship of his people and unable to say anything to them 'for seven days' (a conventional phrase for a week or so). Only then is he able to fulfil his commission and pass on the message which God has given him.

A prophet's responsibility *Ezekiel 3:16–21*

At this point the person who put together the Book of Ezekiel included a further passage before recording the beginning of the prophet's work. It is similar to another passage in chapter 33 which opens the second part of the book, the part in which Ezekiel promises that now Jerusalem has fallen the Jews will be allowed to return to Judah. The passage fits the context rather better there than it does here but the editor has placed it here as well because he felt it was important to say something about a prophet's responsibility to speak out even when his message was as unpopular as Ezekiel's.

There could be no backing out of this responsibility now. While the passage makes clear the weight of responsibility for proclaiming the word of God, it equally makes clear the limits of it. It is easy to take too much responsibility. The initial picture is of a sentry on watch, looking out for any danger on the horizon and reporting it at once—or failing to do so. The picture is soon left behind, though, and its meaning applied directly to the prophet. He has this enormous responsibility—to warn people of their sin. To that extent their 'blood', that is their 'life', is in his hands. He is answerable to God for their safety, and, if he fails to give warning, God will take his life. So it is a matter of life and death for him.

The limits of it. Great as it is, there his responsibility ceases. Provided he has given warning, he has discharged it and the outcome is then in the hands of others. First, it is in the hands of God who has passed a death sentence on the people. 'You shall surely die' is a formal death sentence in court. Secondly, it is in their own hands. Whether they heed his warning and change their ways, so averting the death sentence, or whether they ignore it and persist in their ways, so suffering death as the penalty, the prophet himself is innocent.

Who is to blame? *Ezekiel 18:1–20*

Since the question of responsibility has an important place in the Book of Ezekiel, let us look at another passage which takes the matter up in a different way. Here in chapter 18 Ezekiel begins by quoting the proverb about sour grapes which Jeremiah had also quoted (31:29–30). Both prophets agree that it should not be used to excuse present behaviour and attitudes.

Ezekiel then continues with some examples of 'case law'. Here a certain 'case' is supposed, and the appropriate judgment given. In the course of this he makes clear what kinds of behaviour are right and what are wrong. Then he deals with three generations. A man who does what is right is pronounced innocent; if his son does what is wrong he is pronounced guilty; if his son in turn does what is right he too is innocent.

The generation gap. It is often said that this and other passages in Ezekiel stress the responsibility of the individual whereas earlier the emphasis has been on the whole community. This, however, is not strictly true. The emphasis in both the proverb and the case law which follows is on the responsibility of each generation for its own sin. Then, as now, it was all too easy to blame past generations for the misfortunes they were experiencing. It was widely believed that righteousness generally ensured prosperity and wickedness brought adversity, and so it remained a puzzle why such a good king as Josiah had been killed in battle in 609BC at the age of about 30 whereas Manasseh before him had done every wrong thing in the book and yet had reigned for a whole forty years. There was a tendency for people to say they were now reaping the harvest of Manasseh's sins. Such shifting of responsibility Jeremiah and Ezekiel would not allow, for Judah had gone back on Josiah's reforms and fallen again into evil ways.

However true it may be that a previous generation's sin has an effect on succeeding ones, this must never be used as an excuse for failing to recognize and repent of current wrongs.

Bound and dumb *Ezekiel 3:22–27*

There is one more strange event before we are allowed to hear the message Ezekiel has to proclaim. The prophet has another encounter with the God whom he saw in his vision, and it has an odd outcome. Not only must he threaten his own people, not only must he accept the heavy responsibility of his office, he must now suffer two appalling restrictions on his activity. He is to be bound and confined to his house and he is to be struck dumb. But surely it is inconceivable that anyone called to be a messenger of God should be prevented from going on his errand and from passing on the message?

A number of explanations have been suggested. First, it has been thought that the dumbness really came later in his career, when his wife died. This was at the same time as Jerusalem was captured. We are told that he was promised relief from it when news arrived about the fall of Jerusalem (24:15–27) and this promise was fulfilled (chapter 33). Secondly, some think it began at his call but applied only to ordinary conversation; he was still free to proclaim God's will as necessary. It is not impossible, however, that Ezekiel did suffer these restrictions from the outset. On the one hand, people do seem to have to visit him at his house to receive his message; on the other, the strange actions described in the following chapters, and the fact that certain of his prophecies are dated (8:1) and were therefore possibly written rather than spoken, may suggest some restraint upon his activities. Unable to speak, he had to find other ways of making known God's message to the people.

The editor's intention. Whichever of these suggestions is correct we must in any case ask why the editor put the story here and what he intended by it. It may be, having already placed a passage similar to chapter 33 at this point, he inadvertently included with it this account of Ezekiel's dumbness which was closely related to that chapter. More likely, however, it is meant to explain the curious prophetic actions which follow.

Sometimes, in these days when we use Christian names freely and speak very familiarly with each other, we are tempted to treat God in the same way. The coming of Jesus in human form and our use of his name, along with his invitation to call God 'Father', have all contributed to this. The sense of wonder, mystery and awe has diminished, and God has almost become 'one of us'. It is healthy, therefore, to read the Old Testament, and especially a passage like the description of Ezekiel's vision, to remind ourselves that he is God and we are human beings. This is what we mean when we call him 'holy' and speak of his 'glory'. We are not saying what he is like, *we are saying what he* is. *That is worth thinking about.*

All the same, this holy God is not distant from us. He is approachable, and he approaches us. He calls men and women to be his servants and even his friends. He uses human people with all their weakness and sin to fulfil his purpose. The fact that God became man in Jesus and yet remained God is the supreme example of this.

To speak for God is never easy, especially when it involves being critical of people and institutions we love and respect. There is an inner suffering which we have to accept. To help us to do this we need to keep alive our vision of God. Yet we cannot and must not shelve that responsibility. We do so at our peril.

Ezekiel will not allow us to think that we are totally responsible for the world and what happens in it. People are free to make their own response to God's message. Jesus, too, invited people to follow but never compelled them. Provided we have been faithful we need not feel guilty when the message is rejected. Being faithful, however, involves using every means at our disposal to proclaim the message, not complaining about the abilities which have been denied to us, but discovering and using those we do possess.

— OBEDIENCE IN PREACHING —

Prophetic actions

Ezekiel 4:1—5:6

Ezekiel begins his new career as a prophet not by speaking his prophecy but by *acting* it, as Isaiah (chapter 20) and Jeremiah (chapters 19 and 27) had done before him. Such actions were not intended merely as visual aids. Both the acted and the spoken prophecy were expected to bring their own fulfilment nearer because they passed on the word which God had already spoken (Isaiah 55:10–11). The actions, then, were not magical acts seeking to compel God; rather they were expressions of God's will. When the prophet acted out his message from God the act was an integral part of the process by which God's purpose would be fulfilled. The Book of Ezekiel as it now stands tells us that the prophet had been struck dumb; so Ezekiel used prophetic actions which are just as effective and powerful as prophetic words.

Jerusalem under siege. The passage records three such actions. The details are not easy to understand but the general message is clear. In the first action, Ezekiel plays the part (as it were) of God and acts out the siege of the city, allowing no relief. In the second, he represents Israel and Judah under siege. The length of time he is said to have remained lying down is probably meant to correspond with the number of years Israel was said to have spent in captivity in Egypt (Exodus 12:40). His diet was to be of mixed grain, which was forbidden in Deuteronomy (22:9), and the method of preparation made it unclean. All this is meant to show the severity of the siege which Jerusalem was still to undergo. In the third action, what he does with the hair he has shaved off represents the siege, the defeat and the exile of the people of Judah. Any who are spared will gain only temporary relief.

The exiles to whom his message is addressed hoped and believed that Judah's punishment was over and that they would soon be on their way home again. Ezekiel assures them that since the lesson of loyalty to God has still not been learned ,there is yet more punishment to come.

Another vision

Ezekiel 8

A year or so after his call Ezekiel had another vision in which the God he had seen earlier now carried him bodily to the temple in Jerusalem. The description of what he 'saw' there is so vivid that some people have thought Ezekiel was actually present. But this need not be so. We know from Jeremiah 29 that letters passed between Jerusalem and Babylon, and no doubt messengers had brought him the information on which his vision was based.

First, he saw what he calls the 'image of jealousy' (v. 3), probably an image of Astarte, the Near Eastern goddess also known as the 'queen of heaven'. To worship any deity alongside the Lord was a breach of the first commandment. To allow her actually to displace him was even worse.

Secondly, he saw pictures of animals on the wall of an adjoining room (v. 10). It was the Egyptians who represented their gods by animals, and, since Jerusalem was under Babylonian control, it had to be done in secret (through a 'hole in the wall'). The family of Shaphan were pro-Egyptian and later compelled Jeremiah to flee there (Jeremiah 43:5–7). Because it seemed as though their God had been defeated, they turned secretly to Egyptian gods.

Thirdly, there was the worship of Tammuz (v. 14), the Babylonian god who, by dying and rising each year, was thought to guarantee renewal and fertility to the land after the hot, dry season. Loyal Israelites and prophets had fought against this type of religion for over 500 years.

Fourthly, in the inner court he saw sun worship (v. 16), probably worship of Marduk, the chief Babylonian god. To face him they had to turn their backs to the holy of holies where stood the ark, the throne of God. They 'put the branch to their nose', a gesture of the utmost disrespect. We would say 'they cocked a snook'.

All this was happening in the place where God had promised to meet his people. Such open idolatry provoked him to punish them further.

God's departure from Jerusalem *Ezekiel 10*

The vision which began with the sight of idolatry in chapter 8 continues in chapters 9–11 with God's 'glory' (his presence) departing first from the ark (9:3 and 10:4), then to the east gate of the temple (10:18–19), and then to a mountain on the east side of the city (11:22–25). Left without his protection they will be destroyed. The idolatry has resulted in God leaving the very place where he had promised to meet his people. Probably the implication also is that he has now made himself available to them in Babylon.

Chapter 10 is very complex. Its description of the vision is similar to that in chapter 1 and yet it is also significantly different. Many scholars think that later editors grafted a version of the throne vision on to Ezekiel's original vision of the happenings in Jerusalem. Be that as it may, the chapter heightens the sense of shock associated with the destruction of the capital.

Earthly and heavenly thrones. First the 'living creatures' of chapter 1 have become 'cherubim'. There were two cherubim, one at each end of the ark, God's earthly throne (Exodus 25:18–22), but the cherubim mentioned here are now the bearers of God's heavenly throne. The ark presumably perished in the destruction of the temple and the city, but the writer was insisting that, though the earthly throne of God may be destroyed, the heavenly one cannot be. His rule extends beyond Judah.

The holy fire. Second, the 'fire' or 'coals' which were under or between the cherubim on the ark were another symbol of the presence of the holy God. That very same fire was to be scattered over the city to destroy it (v. 2). It was a striking picture of God's holiness turning to destroy his holy city.

The flight of the Judaean king *Ezekiel 12:1–20*

This passage describes two more prophetic actions performed by Ezekiel to proclaim his message. The differences between these and those described in chapter 4 suggest that these come from a slightly later period in the prophet's life and ministry.

In the first, Ezekiel plays the part of someone leaving his home by stealth. Those watching may well have thought that he was predicting the flight from Babylon back to their homeland when their exile was over. Therefore they ask for clarification. Ezekiel makes it clear that this is not the meaning. Instead it is a symbol of the flight of the king of Judah (here called 'prince') from Jerusalem. This 'prince' is Zedekiah who had been put on the throne by the Babylonian King Nebuchadnezzar to replace Jehoiachin after the first attack in 597BC. The Book of Jeremiah tells us that he was unable to make up his mind whether to submit to Babylonian rule or to rebel with the support of Egypt. Ezekiel does not mention this but simply predicts his departure from Jerusalem and exile in Babylon. In 2 Kings 25:6f we are told that he was blinded before being taken to Babylon in 587BC. The apparent reference to this in verse 12 of this chapter is probably a comment by a later editor after it had happened.

The shock of further disaster. The second action (v. 18) indicates the shock and distress which the Judaeans will experience when the second Babylonian attack comes. The RSV suggests that 'people of the land' refers to those living in Judah (v. 19); but the Hebrew actually says he spoke '*to* the people of the land'. Normally they are the free landowners in Judah but Ezekiel may be referring to the exiles around him with extreme irony. They are now neither free nor landowners owing to their refusal to listen to God or his prophets.

'I am the Lord'. At the end of each of these episodes is a phrase which Ezekiel uses often. The events he predicts will remind people that the God who speaks through him is the Lord (Yahweh, the personal name for Israel's God) who has a claim on their total loyalty.

True and false prophets *Ezekiel 13*

At the very end of chapter 12 the people had been saying that the things the prophets said never came true, or, if they did, their fulfilment was so far ahead that it made no difference to them. So here Ezekiel turns to the question of how you can tell a true prophet from a false one.

For a start they both make claims to divine inspiration, using exactly the same language. There seems to be no objective test by which you can tell the difference. All Ezekiel can do is reaffirm the truth of his own message as he sees it and claim that those who say anything different have not been sent by God.

How can you tell? Both Deuteronomy (18:15–22) and Jeremiah (chapters 27 and 28) had been concerned with the same problem. One of Jeremiah's tests was whether a prophet preached 'peace'. By this he means they say, 'All's well; don't worry.' The best response to such prophecies was to wait and see whether they came true, but since true prophets up to then had always threatened disaster, it was best not to take too much notice of these prophets of 'peace'. Ezekiel makes a similar point in verses 10–16. The wall daubed with whitewash is a weakly built wall suitable as a partition wall but plastered over to make it look like a durable outside wall. It will not stand up to the weather. Prophecies of peace will also crumble and fall because they have no basis in the will of God.

Magic and witchcraft. Then Ezekiel turns to the women who prophesy, but these turn out to be people who engage in magic and witchcraft which were long condemned and forbidden in Israel. These things are no substitute for the will of God. What is more, they do it just for the money.

A glimmer of hope. Such false prophecies will come to nought and the people who prophesy them will be outlawed from Israel. In saying this perhaps Ezekiel is beginning to see some hope for 'Israel' beyond the impending destruction of Jerusalem and the temple.

Against foreign nations *Ezekiel 28:1–19*

Before turning to that part of the Book of Ezekiel which offers the exiles a hope of restoration to Judah, it is worth looking at just one of the prophecies against foreign nations which form a central part of the book. There are several against Egypt and three against Tyre. This one, addressed to the king of Tyre, is especially interesting because it resembles the story of the fall of man in Genesis 3. It consists of a threat (vv. 1–10) and a lament (vv. 11–19).

Equal with God. The threat is issued on account of the king's pride in regarding himself as a god because his wisdom is equal to that of a god. It is almost certain that the Phoenician kings were honoured and worshipped as divine. Such a view was intolerable in Israel because the Lord alone was God and the king was a man. The proud king of Tyre must die, and that will prove him to be a man.

The garden of God. The lament speaks of the exalted position which the king had. His home was in the garden of Eden on the mountain of God. He wore clothing studded with precious stones and was guarded by a cherub. His success in trading led to pride in his own achievements, and so the cherub which guarded him will now evict him from the garden and he will return to ashes. The similarities with Geneses 3 are striking. There Adam and Eve were offered wisdom which would make them gods. Not content with the high status God had given them in creation they hankered after divinity. They too were driven out of the garden and became subject to death, returning to the dust from which Adam was made. Ezekiel can therefore use this story of the perfect man in the garden in an entirely new way.

Tyre doomed. Tyre was a great commercial centre and on several occasions had been allied with Israel (1 Kings 5; 1 Kings 16; Jeremiah 27:3). It was almost impregnable; but Ezekiel threatens its destruction and that of its proud king.

When Christians try to perform their prophetic tasks of commenting on what is going on around them they run into several difficulties.

- *They will almost certainly arouse opposition, especially if they comment on affairs which are not strictly 'religious'. The Old Testament prophets made no distinction between religious and social. For them life was all of a piece and they were concerned with it all.*
- *Christian people with different opinions often claim that they are saying what God wants them to say and it is hard to distinguish the true from the false. In these circumstances we have to be true to what we believe while making sure we do nothing to stifle God's word to us by being set in our own ideas. We do have the additional advantage of being able to look to the life of Jesus for guidance as well.*

- Christians often ask what are the modern 'idols' equivalent to those condemned by Ezekiel. The answer is that an idol is anything which displaces God from the centre of our personal or social life. So it is not only something 'out there'; it is also something within ourselves which needs to be put right. Jesus said 'Seek first the kingdom of God.'
- An even greater temptation for modern men and women is to put themselves where God ought to be and to believe that they do not need God. There is no doubt about the skill and intelligence of twentieth-century people. The mistake we sometimes make is that we think we have gained these things solely by our own effort instead of recognizing them, as the Bible does, as gifts from God in the first place, needing to be developed and used by human beings. We must never imagine that we are God. Jesus did not think equality with God a thing to be grasped at. To be the perfect man he humbled himself (Philippians 2:5–11). According to Ezekiel human pride can only be met with the humbling experience of the judgment of God.

MESSAGES OF HOPE

The death of Ezekiel's wife

Ezekiel 24:15–27

Towards the end of 589BC the Babylonians besieged Jerusalem (24:1), as Ezekiel had threatened in chapter 4. As the fall of the city drew nearer, possibly in 587BC, the prophet was told to proclaim that it was now imminent. This proclamation was through a sign which affected the very centre of Ezekiel's personal life. God told him that he was going to take away his wife by death. The phrase 'at a stroke' (RSV) does not describe the illness but simply means that God will strike her down suddenly. Prophets like Hosea had seen their personal lives used by God in this way; but here we have perhaps the most poignant example of a prophet's personal involvement in his message. This tragic event paves the way for another prophetic action. Ezekiel must not perform any of the normal mourning rites. Imagine the people's astonishment and bewilderment. Naturally, they demand an explanation. It is this. The temple which was just as precious to the Jews in Babylon as Ezekiel's wife was to him would also be struck down. They must not look back in mourning, but forward in hope. The inner pain of both events here and the account of their fulfilment in 33:21–22 pave the way for the prophecies of hope and promise which occur in the following chapters.

Word of prophet or word of God. In verses 21–24 Ezekiel speaks again as God's messenger and the 'I' in the passage generally refers to God, but in verse 22 it refers rather to the prophet himself. Various explanations have been offered, but it may simply indicate how closely the prophet, as messenger, was identified with God who had sent him.

The promise of the end of Ezekiel's dumbness in verses 25–27 is also fulfilled in 33:21–22 and we dealt with the questions concerning this when we read 3:25–27.

The bad shepherds of Israel *Ezekiel 34:1–31*

Whenever in the Old Testament references are found to shepherds and sheep it is most important to stop and ask whether they are meant literally or metaphorically. Here, as is often the case, the shepherds are the rulers of Israel and the sheep are the people. When Micaiah foretold the death of Ahab in battle (1 Kings 22:17) he said the Israelites would be scattered 'as sheep without a shepherd'. Ezekiel's complaint about the succession of Judaean kings is that they have been looking after their own interests instead of their people's and this ran contrary to the Israelite ideal of kingship. Just as a shepherd was responsible to his master for the safety of his sheep so were the rulers responsible to God because really the people were God's sheep (Psalm 95:7).

So, in verses 11–16, the prophet described God as the good shepherd, the divine king who will see to it that his people have all they need (Psalm 23).

But it is not simply the rulers who are to blame. The sheep, the people themselves, have jostled one another out of the way to gain their own advantage. So God, the shepherd-king, will judge them too.

The new under-shepherd. In verse 23, God promises them a new human shepherd-king, a new David. Whereas previous kings had failed to carry out God's rule on earth, this one would succeed. He was not to be a son of David, but rather a new David whom God would provide to make a fresh start. He would be all that the first David was, and more. Ezekiel avoids calling him king and uses the term 'prince' instead, just in case there should be any misunderstanding as to who the real king is—God himself.

The reign of this new David would be marked by peace and prosperity (vv. 25–31). A similar promise of a new David, son of Jesse, had already been made in Isaiah 11:1–9. There too he would rule with justice and his reign would see the restoration of peaceful relationships within nature itself.

God's reputation at stake *Ezekiel 36:22–32*

The prophet here starts by telling people why God is going to restore them to their own land. It is not out of pity, nor because they have changed in any way. His motive is to 'vindicate the holiness of my great name' (v. 23, RSV). Because of their disobedience and idolatry God found it necessary to drive them into exile, but then the other nations assumed that he was unable to keep them safe and so his reputation as a great and powerful God who cared for his people had been badly tarnished. He is determined to prove his 'holiness', his divinity, to the other nations by restoring his people to the land from which he had driven them.

God's renewal of his people. Three things will be needed. First, God will cleanse them from their sin and idolatry (and here we may see the interests of Ezekiel the priest). Secondly, he will give them a new heart, and by 'heart' the Old Testament usually means 'mind' or 'will'. Thus he will free them from self-will and give them a new resolve to do his will. Thirdly, he will give them a new spirit, that is, his divine power which will enable them to fulfil their resolve.

A new covenant. Throughout the passage the emphasis is wholly upon God's new activity, the change he will bring about in his people's way of life when he restores them to Judah. Jeremiah has a somewhat similar passage in 31:31–34, where he speaks of a new covenant to replace the old one in which human hearts (wills) will be so attuned to God's that they will do what he requires of them.

The new future to which Ezekiel looks forward will involve not only the rebuilding of the cities but the renewing of the fertility of the land to a level comparable with that set out in the story of Paradise in Genesis 2.

The new creation *Ezekiel 37:1–14*

This must be one of the best-known passages in the Book of Ezekiel. The event it describes happened soon after the fall of Jerusalem in 587BC because the Jews are clearly despondent and in need of the encouragement which Ezekiel's account of his vision is intended to give them.

The 'hand' of the Lord is a symbolic way of speaking about God's power which is now given to Ezekiel to enable him to see the vision. So, too, is the 'spirit' of the Lord.

The interpretation of the vision which is given in verses 11–14 suggests at first sight that it is a vision of the resurrection of Israel, but it is very unlikely that any of the Jews of this period held any belief in personal resurrection which could have provided the basis for it. Indeed if we look closely at verses 1–10 it is more concerned with the new creation than with personal resurrection *per se*. The dead bones are reminiscent of the dust from which man, Adam, is said to have been made in Genesis 2. There also the body was moulded by God into its human shape and there too the entry of the breath of God into the body made it into a living being. Israel, then, is to be re-created. This same view is to be found in the other prophet writing during the exile (Isaiah 43:14–15). God will make a fresh start with Israel.

Freedom from prison. The Isaiah passage may also give us a better clue to the meaning of verses 11–14. It shows that the exile was seen as an imprisonment but that God would break down the bars. Now the grave was also a place of imprisonment in Old Testament thought, and so Ezekiel could use that also as a metaphor for the exile from which the new-created, living Israel would be set free. Later, when a belief in personal resurrection had arisen among certain Jews, the passage was understood to be a prediction of the resurrection of Israel and this probably influenced the final wording of the passage.

The two sticks *Ezekiel 37:15–28*

The striking thing about this prophetic action is that it represents God as re-uniting Israel and Judah. 'Joseph' represents the old northern kingdom of Israel (or Ephraim) and 'Judah' the southern kingdom which had just been destroyed. There had been a united Israel only for a very short time, perhaps seventy years or so, during the reigns of David and Solomon. On Solomon's death in 922BC the northern kingdom had broken away under its own king and remained a separate state until 722BC when it was finally absorbed into the Assyrian kingdom and its people scattered far and wide through the Assyrian provinces. So, in the days of Ezekiel, there was no identifiable 'Israel', even in captivity. These were the 'lost tribes'. How then does Ezekiel come to predict this virtually impossible reunion? Already, in books like Deuteronomy, people were looking to that period of the unity of the people of God as the golden age of the past, and so it came to be used as a model for the golden age of the future. It is, of course, an ideal which was never realized.

It was further enhanced by the promise of the new David. If the old David had ruled over a united Israel, so also should the new David.

A theological hope. This hope therefore arises more from theology than from the realities of the historical situation. It is nonetheless a very real hope in the Old Testament, found not only in Ezekiel but also in the book of Hosea in its present form (1:11) and in the book of Jeremiah (31:31).

Although the prophecy of the return of the Judaeans to their homeland was fulfilled, those of the return of the northern Israelites were not. Nor was the prediction of the new David.

The literary problem *Ezekiel 39:1–8*

The preceding reading ended with God's promise to establish a sanctuary in Israel again; and later in chapters 40–48 there are plans for such a sanctuary. Chapters 38 and 39 therefore interrupt the argument of the book. Not only so, but they are in themselves the most difficult part of the book. For this reason, the first eight verses of chapter 39 have been chosen as an example because they seem to make the point intended by the chapters in the simplest form. It is highly unlikely that any of the material in 38:1–39:24 comes from Ezekiel himself, though some of the phrases used show the writers to be familiar with his prophecies. Perhaps 39:1–8 were written first and on these, layer upon layer of further materials has been superimposed, so that now no real design is recognizable. Much in the chapters is quite similar to the apocalyptic writings in the books of Daniel and Revelation.

If we really keep our eyes open in the modern world, it is not easy to go on believing that God is all-powerful. But then, it never has been easy. It wasn't easy for Ezekiel and when Jerusalem was destroyed many of his contemporaries jumped to the conclusion that God was defeated. It took courage to put the blame on them for their thoughtlessness, carelessness and sin. Often, though not always, these are still the cause of much of the suffering and hardship which we see around us and which cause people to doubt the power and love of God. We should hesitate to say that God inflicts personal tragedy upon people in order to convince them of his power, but the fact remains that in such times innumerable people have discovered the depths of God's love and the heights of his power.

They discover, too, that out of the ashes of disaster God can raise new life. It is not only Ezekiel who points to God's re-creating power. Paul, writing to the Corinthians, assured them that 'if any one is in Christ he is a new creation' (2 Corinthians 5:17). When we are at the end of our tether, whether through our own fault or other people's, God is able to remake our lives.

Ezekiel's hopes for the future were not all fulfilled. Many of the Jews returned to Judah, but there was no united kingdom which included those northern people who had once been part of Israel, and there was no new David. However, the hope continued to be held down to the time of Jesus. The Jews of his day could not see him as the Davidic king; the Romans could and so he was crucified. His followers came to believe that he was precisely the one whom Ezekiel and others had hoped for. In and through him God had created for himself a new people. Jesus is the good shepherd (John 10), the new king offering his people love and care, but demanding from them their trust and obedience.

Gog and Magog. Throughout these chapters Israel is settled peacefully back in her own land, only to be attacked again by wild hordes from the north, given the names of Gog and Magog. Gog is not found elsewhere; Magog is mentioned in the table of nations in Genesis 10:2 along with Tubal and Meshech. There is no point, however, in trying to identify them. It may well be that a later disciple of Ezekiel realized that the return of Judah had taken place but that other nations had failed to recognize that the Lord had done it. Therefore this part of Ezekiel's prophecy was still awaiting fulfilment. So in these few verses the restored Israel is to be attacked again by a fearsome enemy, brought upon them by God who will then turn and destroy the enemy so that 'people may know that I am the Lord'.

All this illustrates how people in a later period used and re-assessed the prophet's words in the light of their own situation, incorporating into the book their own interpretations alongside the words of the prophet.

— RESTORATION IN JERUSALEM —

The new temple in the new Jerusalem *Ezekiel 40:1–16*

This last section of the Book of Ezekiel appears to be the least interesting and rewarding of the whole book. All the more reason, then, why we should try to discover what it has to say. Certain parts of it derive from Ezekiel himself, but much more of it has been added later by people of another generation with different interests.

Chapters 40–42 contain a vision of a new temple in Jerusalem. The first sixteen verses give a sample of the chapters as a whole.

The vision was given to Ezekiel in the spring of 574BC, some thirteen years after the death of his wife and the fall of Jerusalem. The 'high' mountain is undoubtedly Zion. There were higher mountains around, but it could be described as the highest place because God lived there (Isaiah 2:2–4; Micah 4:1–4). The idea of gods living on high mountains was common in the ancient world. The 'structure like a city' was the walled temple on the crest of the hill. The man 'like bronze' was clearly an angelic figure. He and Ezekiel set out to measure the temple they saw, which was entirely symmetrical. Too little information is given about it for it to have been meant as a blueprint for the future temple which was to be built there. For Ezekiel it simply meant that God would be enthroned again in a perfect, ideal dwelling place. Later, other people were more concerned with the plan of the structure and so filled out his description with details about the various rooms and the preparation of sacrificial victims.

God the builder. Almost certainly Ezekiel saw God as the builder of this ideal temple. Everything to do with the return from exile was due to God himself. He was the king who would provide himself with a perfect home in Jerusalem.

The Lord's return *Ezekiel 43:1–12*

These verses describe the return of the Lord to his new temple. The details of the vision of God are not spelled out but it is surely the same vision as Ezekiel saw at the outset of his work and it has the same effect. In it God's glory returns from the east, that is from Babylon, the direction in which he had departed in chapter 11:22–25. Again it is the 'glory' of the Lord which the prophet sees. As before, his coming is preceded by a great noise. Ezekiel again falls on his face and is then raised to his feet. This time he is transported into the temple which is filled with God's glory.

The permanent presence. As in chapter 1 the prophet is addressed as 'son of man', but this time he hears the words of promise that God would now remain in Zion for ever. The 'place of my throne' and 'the place of the soles of my feet' recall expressions which are found in Isaiah 60:13, Lamentations 2:1 and Psalm 99:5. Perhaps before the destruction of the temple they had referred to the ark, the symbol of God's presence with his people. Although after the exile the ark is no longer available, yet his presence is assured. Never again will God be constrained to leave his temple because of the idolatry of his people (compare chapter 8).

A later writer wished to specify more clearly what defilement meant in his day, and so added words about corpses and the proximity of the royal cemetery to the temple. In the words 'neither they . . . between me and them' in verses 7 and 8 we can discern later priestly concern for the ritual holiness of the site.

Laws of the sanctuary. Finally, Ezekiel is told again to describe the temple he has seen. From verse 10 onwards, however, interest shifts from the presence of God to laws regulating the use of the temple. These verses form a link between Ezekiel's own vision and the later collection of laws concerning the sanctuary in the succeeding verses.

From vision to Law *Ezekiel 44*

Although chapter 44 begins in the same way as chapters 40 and 43 with the prophet being led by his heavenly guide, the concerns of this and the remaining chapters are very different. It is worth pausing here to recall that chapters 34–43 all deal with different aspects of the new future which God will bring about. He will create for himself a new people with a new resolve and a new ability to do his will. He will unite them along with the dispersed northern tribes under a new David whom he will provide. He will lead them back to Judah and will himself return to Zion to live for ever in a temple he has provided for himself. From this tremendous vision of the future, the book now turns to detailed legislation about priesthood, sacrifices, property and possession of the land. It is almost impossible that Ezekiel himself should have become bogged down in this legal morass. Far more likely, later writers, finding that the ideals of Ezekiel had not materialized and that the old dangers of defilement of the temple and its worship were still there, found it necessary to revert to detailed legislation. They were probably priests whose fathers and grandfathers had collected Ezekiel's prophecies during the exile and brought them back to Jerusalem some time after 538BC when the Jews began to return.

The present chapter begins with a regulation about the closing of the east door probably to keep out defiling intruders. Even the coming prince would have to use the side door!

Levites and Zadokites. By now the 'Levites' and the 'Levitical priests, the sons of Zadok' are distinguished from each other. The former will be demoted to take on the work done by foreign slaves who are now excluded because they are uncircumcised. The reason given is that they had once sacrificed at altars outside Jerusalem. The latter are descended from Zadok, the priest appointed by David alongside Abiathar and made sole priest by Solomon when Abiathar was banished. They are now given rules about dress, behaviour, duties and benefits.

The real concern is for purity of faith and proper regulation of its ministry.

One of the problems facing Christian people is whether we can be content with a broad framework of belief or whether we must at once begin to fill in the details.

First, we believe that we are saved by God's grace alone and so, as Paul puts it, we no longer need the 'schoolmaster' of the Law. Yet when we try to live the life of grace we find we need a law, for without it we too easily fall into irresponsibility. We need the Sermon on the Mount as well as the story of the cross. We need the ethical demands of Romans 12–13 as well as the offer of free salvation apart from the Law in Romans 5–7. Ezekiel's belief in a new-created Israel, with the ability to do God's will arising purely out of their close relationship with him, proved insufficient for his followers, who needed a controlled set of laws to regulate the relationship.

Secondly, on a different level, hopes for the future rarely give us the detailed information we want. What will the second coming be like? When will it happen? Is it due any moment? Even Jesus claimed not to know. What will heaven be like? Shall I see my loved ones there? They are unanswerable questions. The framework of hope is provided but we should like more information. Ezekiel believed in a new act of God by which Israel would be recreated and restored to their own land under a new king with a new will to obedience, assured that 'the Lord was there' in his own temple. His followers needed to try to fill in the detail.

Freedom and self-discipline, broad outlines of hope and detailed information, free worship of the spirit and ordered liturgy—the tension between these is felt in these closing chapters of Ezekiel. Perhaps this tension is always a part of our Christian life and experience.

The holy portion *Ezekiel 45:1–8*

In chapter 48 we shall find that the Promised Land is to be divided up between the tribes but there is a central section of it which belongs to the Lord. The present short passage anticipates this, perhaps because towards the end of chapter 44 it had been said that the priests had no inheritance and now it was necessary to qualify that statement.

The picture that emerges is of a piece of land 25,000 cubits square, that is, about 8¼ miles square. This is divided into three strips running in an east–west direction. The northern strip of 10,000 cubits is for the Levites to possess and build cities. The next strip to the south is again 10,000 cubits and is for the priests. In the centre of this is a square of 500 cubits for the Temple. They are not said to possess this but to have the use of it. South again is a further strip of 5,000 cubits which is meant for the city itself. The coming 'prince' will have land adjoining this plot on the east and on the west. Such an account takes no notice at all of the geographical and topographical features in and around Jerusalem and is clearly an idealized picture, purely notional.

Such a picture must have been imagined before Jerusalem and the temple were rebuilt and while the people were still in exile. In anticipation of their return, Ezekiel's disciples are putting some detail on to his vision about the temple which God will provide for himself on the hill of Jerusalem.

The temple at the centre. Behind the passage stands the view that at the heart of the newly occupied land there must be the holy place, the place which belongs to God, and close to that must also be proper provision for those who will minister there.

Priest and prince — *Ezekiel 45:10—46:24*

This rather long section is a collection of laws from various periods mainly about worship and sacrifice. Very probably the basic material, to which various layers have been added, concerned the responsibilities of the 'prince' in this matter. It will be remembered that Ezekiel had avoided using the title 'king' in case of misunderstanding. Now his disciples felt it necessary to spell out the responsibilities of the prince. In Judah the king had always had a place alongside the priest in the worship offered by his people. David made a sanctuary for the ark near his own home. He chose Zadok as priest alongside Abiathar and himself shared some of the priestly functions (2 Samuel 6). Solomon built his palace next door to the temple and was crowned by Zadok (1 Kings 1). After a short break in the Davidic line, when Athaliah, the queen mother and a daughter of the northern king Ahab, seized the throne, it was the priests who restored a son of David to the throne. What, then, was to be the relationship between the new David and the Zadokite priesthood?

The prince's tasks. Just as Samuel was said to have written down the 'rights and duties of kingship' for Israel's first king (1 Samuel 10:25), so the functions of the new prince must be laid down. In 45:7 he is allocated land adjoining the holy district. In 45:16–17 he is to act as mediator: the people will make their payments to him and he will then pay for the sacrificial offerings out of them. In 45:21ff this is his main responsibility at the Feast of Passover and Unleavened Bread, as at the Feast of Tabernacles or Booths. In 46:10 he is to lead the people out of the temple.

There never was any separation between religious and social life in the Old Testament but there was always the danger that the king, who had a rightful place in worship, would usurp the authority of the priest (1 Samuel 15). Precautions are here being taken to get things right.

The river in the city *Ezekiel 47:1–12*

Chapter 47 opens with the continuation of the vision which began in chapter 40 and which we left behind in chapter 44 onwards. Here we may well have some of Ezekiel's own words again. The same angelic guide pilots him to the door of the temple from which he sees water pouring out. The further east they go, the deeper it becomes, until it becomes a river with trees on each bank. It flows southwards towards the desert land in the south of Palestine and into the Dead Sea where the water becomes fresh enough for people to fish in it! Ezekiel's new Israel is made prosperous, fertile and happy by God alone.

The river of life. Jerusalem never had a river. The spring Gihon, from which water was channelled into the city through Hezekiah's tunnel, was the source of its water supply, and this was certainly not a river. But Psalm 46:4 had spoken of a river which gladdened the city of God and the story of paradise in Genesis 2 tells of four rivers flowing from the garden to water the whole earth. Ezekiel is again using the language of myth, just as he did when he spoke of Zion as the highest mountain. The same idea is found again, of course, in Revelation 22:1.

The new creation. This mythical language is now used simply as a figure of speech by which the prophet can express his belief about the new future which God will bring about. It is this-worldly in the sense that it takes place on the present earth, but it represents a complete transformation. The act of the new creation extends beyond Israel to the whole world. The new king, the new covenant, the new people, the new relationship between divine and human king and between the divine king and human people opens out into a new creation. Isaiah 11:1–9 had already pointed the way, as had Hosea 2:16–23. It could be taken up again by Paul in Romans 8:19–25 and in Revelation 22 where again the leaves of the tree are for the healing of the nations.

From this high point chapter 48 descends again to the drab detail about the division of the land, but the whole book ends in great confidence with Jerusalem being given the new name—'The Lord is there'.

DANIEL

The modern reader coming to the book of Daniel for the first time may well feel like a member of the audience watching an historical play acted in period costumes and spoken in the language of a bygone age. The language of the book, its bizarre imagery involving curious animals and heavenly beings, and its strange form of dreams and visions which have hidden meanings needing to be correctly interpreted, all combine to make it seem remote. Yet the book was written for its first readers with a burning and immediate sense of purpose, and its message proved to have lasting and haunting significance, as its frequent use in the New Testament, and its fascination for many generations since, especially in times of suffering and crisis, have shown.

The twelve chapters of Daniel fall very clearly into two parts. Chapters 1–6 tell stories about Daniel and his friends who are portrayed as being among the Jews in exile in Babylon following the fall of Jerusalem in 586BC. These stories show how God supported and prospered them even in this alien environment because they remained loyal to him. Such stories were, understandably, very popular during the many years Jews were under foreign domination with many of them living in the 'Diaspora' far from their homeland. Whatever their original setting and date, they would clearly have had continuing relevance over the years. The second part of the book, chapters 7–12, records visions of Daniel himself concerning coming events and the interpretation of them given to him by an angel.

Although the stories and visions are set in the time of the Babylonian exile (sixth century BC), most scholars agree that the book in its final form was written in the second century, between 167 and 163BC.

In spite of the devastating effect the Babylonians had on the Jews, their empire was not long lived. In 539BC Babylon fell to the combined forces of the Medes and Persians under Cyrus and for long afterwards Judah was part of the Persian empire. In 333BC the Persians in their turn fell to the fast-growing power of Greece under Alexander the Great, who came to control all the Near East including the area we know as Palestine. After Alexander's death this empire was divided between his rival generals. For about one hundred years Judah was ruled by Ptolemy and his successors from Egypt, but soon after 200BC it came under the successors of Seleucus, rulers of the area of Syria.

At the time of the book of Daniel, the current ruler was Antiochus IV, 'Epiphanes' as he was known because he claimed to be a manifestation (Greek: *epiphanes*) of Zeus on earth. Faced with the growing menace from Rome, Antiochus sought to gain cohesion throughout his disparate empire by uniting all his subjects in a common worship of himself. Most of his subject peoples could take one more religious cult on board without problem, but for faithful Jews, called to exclusive worship of the one God, this presented an unavoidable conflict of loyalties. When Antiochus had a statue of Zeus erected in the Holy of Holies in the Jerusalem temple ('the abomination that makes desolate', Daniel 11:31, see Mark 13:14), it was the final straw for many Jews devoted to the Torah (the *hasidim*, 'devoted ones') who resisted and, as a result, faced Greek attempts to stamp Judaism out. Copies of Torah were burned publicly, Jews were forced to eat pork and parents were forbidden to circumcise their children. This led to the armed resistance and guerrilla warfare of the Maccabaeans. The *hasidim* did not approve of armed resistance and only reluctantly joined them when many of their number were massacred. The writer of the Book of Daniel is clearly of their number as his rather lukewarm allusion to the Maccabaeans shows (11:34), but the revolt secured religious freedom by 163BC when the temple was cleansed and 'pure' Jewish worship was resumed. The book knows of the temple's profanation in 167BC but still looks forward to its cleansing in 163 and so it must have been written within those years.

Daniel was a hero known from earlier times. He is referred to in Ezekiel 14:14, 20 and in the literature of Israel's neighbours as a legendary figure of virtue. Why does the writer give Daniel's name to this book? Perhaps, as we shall see, it was because he believed that the hopes held out to the people in the earlier crisis of the Babylonian exile by prophets like Jeremiah, Ezekiel and the author of Isaiah chapters

40–55 still applied. He expounds them in this later crisis assuring his readers that they too will know the same delivering mercy and power of God as did their forefathers in that earlier time of crisis. There are many differences between the book of Daniel and other prophetic books in the Old Testament and these have led to its description as 'apocalyptic' in distinction to 'prophecy'. The word suggests the 'unveiling' of hidden mysteries and secrets and thus obviously fits the the book in many ways. However, it is a vague term and scholars have used it variously either to describe a particular kind of outlook on the future, or a certain type of literature or 'literary genre' with distinguishing characteristics. Earlier prophets had visions and some needed an angelic interpreter to explain them (such as Zechariah, see Zechariah chapters 1–8). They also looked to a future action of God just as Daniel does. Yet we are somehow in a different worldview in this book with its picture of the bitter struggle on earth as a projection of a struggle between heavenly powers (e.g. 10:13, 20), and its picture of human history as the working out in detail of a divinely predetermined plan revealed long ago to a sage, to be 'unveiled' only now at the climax of the whole process.

While it has its roots in prophecy, and shares with the Wisdom literature (e.g. the Book of Job) a concern to explain the terrible evil and suffering in God's world, such literature does have a slightly different view of how God acts in history, even if this is a difference in emphasis rather than of kind. The prophets believed God was acting in this world's history here and now, working out his purpose. But the Book of Daniel is written at a time of such suffering and such rampant evil that it is hard to discern that process even with the eye of faith. The only possible explanation can be that God has given this stage of world history over to the powers of evil. However, all this has been known to him and is part of his plan from the beginning as revealed to the faithful man of God in the past. He also has a fixed time, however, when he will break into this process from above and beyond, bring down the powers of evil and establish his everlasting kingdom in which his suffering, faithful servants will reign and know peace and justice. That is the theme of the Book of Daniel.

The book is thus written to encourage God's people to remain loyal and to assure them of God's power to keep them through their ordeal and of the certainty of the final victory of God's kingdom.

Further reading

P.R. Davies, *Daniel*, Old Testament Guides, JSOT Press, Sheffield, 1985

D.A. Russell, *Daniel: An Active Volcano*, Saint Andrew Press, Edinburgh, 1989, also Westminster/John Knox Press, Louisville, Kentucky.

D.S. Russell, *Divine Disclosure: An Introduction to Jewish Apocalyptic*, SCM Press, London, 1992

For those ready to embark on a fuller commentary:

N. Porteous, *Daniel*, second revised edition, Old Testament Library Series, SCM Press, London, 1979, also Westminster Press, Philadelphia

THE STORIES: DANIEL 1–6

Food laws and religion

Daniel 1:1–16

Many stories like this one of Daniel and his friends in the Babylonian court circulated among the Jews. To a people who had known what it was to be under foreign rule the faithfulness and power of God were cherished themes. The stories were aimed at exhorting and instructing the community to show a similar faithfulness.

One thing which tells us that the Book of Daniel was written later than the time in which it was set is that the author is hazy about the actual history of the Babylonian and Persian periods. There never was a siege of Jerusalem by Nebuchadnezzar in 605BC (v. 1), but one might gain the impression there was by reading certain earlier Scriptures (see 2 Kings 24:1–2 and 2 Chronicles 36:5–8).

The story is about obedience to the Jewish 'kosher' food laws, to be kept even in a Gentile society. These still matter very much today to dedicated Jews but they would have had a special 'edge' in the persecution under Antiochus IV. In his attempt to bring the Jews to heel he forced some of them to eat swine's flesh, an abhorrence under their law (Leviticus 11:7). For them to obey God was a life-and-death issue, and this story of Daniel and his friends would have encouraged them.

For many people today such laws seem totally incomprehensible. Yet what we eat does have a bearing on our obedience to God. Is the 'wealthy West', or the 'nourished North', to go on hogging an unfair share of the world's food resources? And can we really square our extravagance with proper husbandry of the earth and care for the undernourished? Perhaps if we dared lower our pampered standard of living we should, like Daniel and his friends, find that God gives more than we sacrifice.

The limits of human wisdom *Daniel 2:1–16*

Interestingly, the language of the book changes in verse 4 from Hebrew to Aramaic until the end of chapter 7.

All the courts of the ancient Near East had their 'wise men' who acted as counsellors to the king and court, advising them on matters of national and foreign policy. We know such men also played a part in the Israelite court before the exile. Jeremiah speaks of prophets, priests and 'wise men' together as advisers of state (Jeremiah 18:18). It was believed that the highest human wisdom was that which God 'gave' as a special gift. Solomon was remembered in tradition as one who asked for, and received, such a divine gift (1 Kings 3:5–14).

The limit of human wisdom is a familiar theme of some of the 'wisdom' literature of the Old Testament:

> *Trust in the Lord with all your heart and do not rely on your own insight.*
>
> *Proverbs 3:5*

So there is an especial irony in the understandable cry of despair from the Babylonian wise men (v. 10) when the king asks not only to be told what his dream meant, but what his dream was! Jewish readers would have seen the implications of that and so, apparently, do the Babylonian sages: 'The thing the king asks is difficult and none can show it to the king except the gods' (v. 10). The sequel will show that *the* God is present and able to give 'wisdom'.

'Cleverness' and 'wisdom'. This 'Wisdom' language may seem strange to us. Yet we all know that some very clever and knowledgeable people can yet act remarkably foolishly. To see how to live well, and not to miss the values that matter beneath the purely expedient, needs an insight which comes from beyond ourselves.

God gives wisdom *Daniel 2:17–35*

The first part of our reading makes explicit what we saw to be implicit earlier in this chapter. It is not that Daniel is shown to be cleverer than the Babylonians. But he trusts the God who alone can give true wisdom (v. 30).

This is the theme of the Wisdom 'hymn' in verses 20–23 and in his words to the king. There is a 'God in heaven who reveals mysteries' (v. 28).

Nebuchadnezzar's 'image'. The dream was a vision of an image made of materials of descending value, gold, silver, bronze, iron, degenerating even further into an alloy of iron and clay. Whatever the original significance of the vision, it has now been used to 'prefigure' the course of world history in a succession of four world empires stretching from the sixth to the second centuries BC. The gold represented the Babylonian empire, the silver the Median. The writer thought, mistakenly, that Babylon fell to the Medes (see 5:30). In fact it fell to the Persians, but some earlier Scriptures might have led one to suppose that the Medes were successors to the Babylonians (e.g. Jeremiah 51:11). The bronze thus represents the Persian and the iron the Greek empires. The mixed iron and clay portray the divided rule of the Ptolemies and Seleucids.

All human kingdoms fall. The whole picture is an ironic comment on the illusions of grandeur in human empires. Each becomes worse than the one before and all are doomed and transient. The writer would have agreed with the words, 'All empires carry the seeds of their own destruction.'

The kingdom of God remains. This statue was brought down by a stone 'cut out by no human hand' (v. 34) which then grew to become a mountain which filled the whole earth (v. 35). This represents the kingdom of God, perhaps suggested by the 'Mount Zion' tradition which was seen as the dwelling of God (e.g. Psalm 132:13f) and which prophets had predicted would become the 'highest of all mountains' to which all the nations of the earth would come.

God acting in history

Daniel 2:36–49

Here Daniel gives Nebuchadnezzar the interpretation of his dream. The themes of God's power (the authority, even of heathen kings, is given them by God, v. 37) and 'wisdom' (Nebuchadnezzar owns that there is no God like him, v. 47) and his ability to cause his people to prosper even in unpromising circumstances (vv. 46, 48–49) are all sounded here again.

But we should not miss another theme. The picture of history presented in this dream is of a steadily deteriorating succession of world powers. History gets worse and worse. God is in control—in fact he is foretelling it all before it happens—but he apparently allows evil powers to flourish. Then, at the end, he breaks into history from beyond. The stone 'cut out by no human hand' crashes into the present world system. A new era begins in which God reigns (vv. 44–45).

The prophets stressed that God acts within this world's present history. If Assyria marches, God is sending them (e.g. Isaiah 10:5–6). If Israel goes into exile, God has sent them there as judgment (e.g. Amos 5:25–27).

We shall see that the writer of this book believes God is at work in the present time of distress. He helps his people to face their ordeal and even uses their sufferings for his purposes. On the other hand, the prophets did believe that God was working towards a decisive 'end' when he would establish righteousness in the earth. Yet, perhaps, the kind of view we find in Daniel is more characteristic of periods of great suffering and turmoil. This kind of literature is often referred to as 'apocalyptic'. The name means that God is 'unveiling' to someone what he will do at the climax of this world's history.

God's present and future action. Perhaps the people of God need both lenses for a proper view of our world. One of these perspectives alone can breed escapism, the other alone can breed despair.

The Book of Daniel reminds us that the judgment of this world is always now. If we do not see Christ and our neighbour today, we shall almost certainly miss them tomorrow.

No man can serve two masters

Daniel 3:1–18

This story would have produced an immediate response from the Jews of the second century BC who were suffering persecution under Antiochus IV. For Nebuchadnezzar to demand worship of himself, represented by the image, was to present faithful Jews with an 'either-or' situation which those of other nations would not have known. For, unlike the gods of other nations, the God of Israel demanded exclusive worship (Exodus 20:3).

When Antiochus set up 'the abomination which makes desolate' in the temple (see 11:31, 1 Maccabees 1:54 and 2 Maccabees 6:2), he faced the Jews of his day with a similar choice. Many, like Daniel's friends, chose suffering and death rather than compromise, and it is the purpose of this story to urge them to remain obedient.

The theology of these stories is 'crisis theology'. The people of God are in a life-and-death situation. The issues are unmistakable. It is clear who are the friends and who the enemies of God. It may be costly and painful to do what is right, but it is not hard to discover what is right.

For us there appears to be no crisis. The edges are blurred. It is not easy to know how to act in our moral dilemmas. Indifference is sometimes a deadlier weapon against faith than the sword.

God is able to keep his people. There is a fine irony in the question of Nebuchadnezzar to the friends (v. 15): 'Who is the god that will deliver you out of my hands?' There would be no doubt about the answer for this writer. The God of Israel is more powerful than any human king. The answer of the friends is a little puzzling, for it seems to express uncertainty about this. Probably they are saying, 'We do not doubt that he can deliver us. But even if (for whatever reason) he does not, we shall remain faithful.'

In the second century BC many Jews did die under torture and in battle. The writer calls for trust in God which is not just dependent on outward circumstances or on the good fortune God may be expected to give. Later, another will call for a discipleship which involves taking up a cross (Mark 8:34). Beware of those who prophesy, falsely, that true discipleship can be measured by the prosperity and security God sends.

Christ has brought life and light, life which challenges our half-existence and light which throws up the shadows of our shabby compromises. His coming, his life, his love, his grace, his cross judge us and our world. The values of this world claim us by stealth, not by heroic slaughter. Moral insight, faith, holiness, fall by slow erosion rather than in the heat of battle. Wrong triumphs not so much by the deliberate actions of wicked men, but by the inaction of many good people.

The 'fires' of suffering *Daniel 3:19–30*

This remarkable story gains in pace and suspense with the description of Nebuchadnezzar's anger and punishment. It echoes a number of biblical themes. 'Why do the nations rage and the people plot in vain?' asks the Psalmist (Psalm 2:1). He went on to assure the king as representative of God's people that God would subdue their enemies. Nebuchadnezzar's 'rage' would be no more effective than theirs.

Again, the slavery of Israel in Egypt had been pictured as a 'furnace' from which God rescued them (e.g. Deuteronomy 4:20). This probably inspired some of the prophets to liken the exile in Babylon to a furnace in which God tested and refined them:

> *Behold, I have refined you, but not like silver; I have tried you in the furnace of affliction.*
>
> *Isaiah 48:10*

The writer of the Book of Daniel is assuring his readers that God will deliver them from their 'furnace of affliction' just as he had done before in their history.

The appearance in the fire of 'one like a human being' (v. 25) brings home another great truth. Not only will God deliver his people but he enters into their suffering with them. They are never alone.

This story is an exposition in narrative form of that great theological certainty. But yet another biblical theme is hinted at here. Through the faithful suffering of these servants of God even a heathen king comes to see and hear what he had never known before. He confesses, 'the God of Israel is able to deliver' (v. 29, compare v. 15). Second Isaiah had promised that through the suffering of God's faithful servant, 'Kings shall shut their mouths . . . for that which has not been told them they shall see . . .' (Isaiah 52:15). Suffering borne for God has many times proved to be not pointless but a powerful proclamation of his love and grace.

Human pride must bow to God *Daniel 4:1–27*

The placing of this story is significant. It occurs immediately after that of Nebuchadnezzar's 'image' which all people were called upon to worship. While he acknowledged the power of Israel's God to deliver the Israelites whom he had punished for disobedience, he had shown no signs of contrition for putting up the image in the first place. He must learn what the story of Adam taught. All human pride which wants to be equal with God is doomed to frustration. Human honour and dignity are safe only when God is given first place.

The appearance of a 'tree' in the story again makes use of a familiar Old Testament picture. Ezekiel had told a parable about a great tree which symbolized the mighty power of Tyre, so great that it brought other nations under its rule, likened to birds of the air making their nest in its branches (Ezekiel 31:1–9). However, this also was directed to be cut down, as later interpretation of the picture shows (Ezekiel 31:10–18). The same idea is found in Psalm 37:35f. Familiar with these pictures, readers languishing under the rule of Antiochus in the second century BC are reminded of the fate God has dealt out to earlier pretenders to divine power.

Judgment on Nebuchadnezzar. The 'watcher' (v. 13) is a term describing one of the angels through whom God exercises his 'watch' over the affairs of men and women, and carries out his purposes, either for judgment or deliverance (compare 8:15f; 9:21). The great Nebuchadnezzar is to be reduced to the level of an animal for seven 'times' (probably = 'years', v. 16). It was especially suitable for our writer's purpose of showing that all great kingdoms are more 'bestial' than 'human' (compare Daniel 7:3–8).

The real point of the story is found in verse 25. God is the real sovereign in the earth, King of kings and Lord of lords. Only in submission to him and trust in him can the full potential of human personality be realized. To submit to him is to become fully human and truly free.

Intellectual and real belief

Daniel 4:28–37

There was a topical allusion in this story which would not have been lost on second-century Jewish readers. Antiochus, under whose persecution so many were suffering, had called himself Antiochus 'Epiphanes' which means one in whom God is 'manifest' or has 'shown himself'. However, this had given rise to a rather cruel nickname. He was known popularly as Antiochus 'Epimanes'—the 'Madman'. Nebuchadnezzar, so the story ran, was forced by his 'madness' to bow down before the true God and acknowledge him. So, the story assures the faithful, would the dreaded and apparently all-powerful Antiochus be judged.

It is strange that Nebuchadnezzar, who had apparently digested the lesson of the power of God (v. 17), is yet found strutting round his palace confident that he was lord and master of all he surveyed (vv. 29–30). It is often said that the 'self-made' man ends up worshipping his creator! And there is a strange contradiction between 'notional' belief, that which we know intellectually, and 'real' belief, that which we have made our own and by which we live.

It is the same with all of us. So often, even hard and difficult experiences in our lives can be a high road by which God comes to us in a more real way and at a greater depth than we have known before.

Belshazzar's feast

Daniel 5:1–12

This well-known story of Belshazzar's feast has been linked with chapter 4 by the writer in a number of ways. Belshazzar is referred to as Nebuchadnezzar's 'son'. Although it is the 'queen mother' who refers to him as such (v. 11)—his wives were present at the feast already (v. 3)—and she might be thought to have known who his father was, Belshazzar was in fact son of Nabonidus and was not even descended from Nebuchadnezzar. Nor was Belshazzar ever king, although he may have acted as 'regent' sometimes during his father's absences from Babylon. Again, the queen mother reminds Belshazzar of the part played by Daniel in the story related in chapter 4 (vv. 11–12).

Pride before a fall. In some ways the sin of Belshazzar echoes that of his father. He shows overweening pride in the way he flaunts the vessels sacred to one whom he regarded as a defeated god (vv. 2–4). The particular manifestation of that sin is seen here as sacrilege, even bordering on blasphemy. Later, the restoration of these very temple vessels to Jerusalem will show that the God of Israel is sovereign (Ezra 6:5; compare 7:19).

Jewish readers would be reminded of the sacrilege committed by Antiochus IV, who had the Jerusalem temple plundered. Yet they would be encouraged by the reminder that an earlier monarch who had similarly defied God had been brought down in judgment.

The writing on the wall. The 'writing on the wall' which suddenly appears (v. 5) is written by a 'finger'. This would recall to Jews that God's 'finger' had written the ten commandments, which called for exclusive worship of God alone (Exodus 31:18; see Deuteronomy 9:10). But their tradition also recalled how Egyptian magicians and wise men had ascribed the confusion brought about by the plagues to that same 'finger' acting in judgment against their disobedience: 'And the magicians said to Pharaoh, "This is the finger of God" ' (Exodus 8:19).

The readers are assured that the God who delivered their fathers from the power of Egypt and brought the exiles home from Babylon is still active on their behalf.

Ignoring past lessons *Daniel 5:13–31*

Daniel does not waste much time in diplomacy! Brusquely rejecting the king's offer of lavish rewards (v. 17), the messenger of God speaks without fear or favour not because of what he gets out of it but as he is constrained by God. Belshazzar knew what happened to his father but he has not acted accordingly (vv. 22–23). Again, arrogance and contempt for the sacred will bring inevitable judgment.

The message written by the finger is nearly as difficult for us as it was for Belshazzar. It is possible that it represents three different measures of weight and that with withering irony, Belshazzar is depicted as the 'lightweight' among them, inferior both to Nebuchadnezzar who had preceded him and the Medo-Persians who were to follow him as they captured and seized his empire. Verse 25 takes the three words as verbs, but this is a kind of popular 'sermonizing' exposition. What is clear is that the words warn of imminent judgment and their warning is tragically and immediately fulfilled (v. 30). 'Darius the Mede' is unknown to history. Babylon fell to Cyrus, the Persian. The second-century writer has probably confused him with the Darius of the time of Haggai and Zechariah.

The writing on the wall today. To us a story in which a hand appears and writes on a wall seems unreal and strange. Perhaps we should think again. When a nation confines many school-leavers to the scrap-heap of unemployment, the writing on the wall appears in rising crime and drug abuse. When a society pens its poor and immigrant population into derelict slums in city centres, the writing on the wall appears with riots and looting. When one third of the world's population is left to hunger and poverty, the writing on the wall appears with a threat to world trade and the world's banking system. When a society ignores God and the 'spiritual' dimension of life, the writing on the wall appears with a breakdown in moral values. It is to be hoped that our generation is better at reading the writing on the wall than Belshazzar was.

God's laws and human laws *Daniel 6:1–13*

A good deal in this chapter, which is a close parallel to chapter 3 with its story of Daniel's three friends in the furnace, shows that the writer is much more concerned with the second century than the sixth. The king is supposed to be the Median Darius who, as we have seen, is unknown to history. Greek authors suggest that a re-organization of the empire was in fact carried out by the Persian, Darius I. The command to pray to no god but to the king himself is improbable and uncharacteristic of Darius who was a highly religious man, while there is no evidence to show that the laws of the Medes and Persians were regarded as being particularly irreversible.

On the other hand, Antiochus did present faithful Jews in the second century with an 'either-or' situation. Just as Darius is shown as being bound by 'the laws of the Medes and Persians' (vv. 8, 12, 15), so Daniel is bound by the laws of the living God. It was this clash of loyalties which tore the Jews under Antiochus in two ways.

The envy of little men always snaps at the heels of great men, and that is what happens here (vv. 4–5). To this, no doubt, is added the hostility that those who are faithful to God arouse in those without faith. Envy of either kind can always rationalize and justify itself, and these courtiers could disguise their personal enmity as concern for the internal security of the kingdom. It would not be the last time that personal scores would be settled under the label of 'official secrets in the interests of national security'.

Prayer prepares. Daniel prayed three times a day (v. 10). The Psalmist of Psalm 55 talks of praying 'at morning, noon and evening' (vv. 16–17) and he speaks of this at the exact moment the Psalm switches from lament to a spirit of certainty of deliverance. As with Daniel, there can be no doubt that it is the regular practice of worship, corporate and private, that prepares us to withstand the sudden moment of crisis.

An irritant ('salt') in the life of the body politic, witnessing to the truth of God's purposes for all and his just claim as 'Lord of lords' and 'King of kings'—is not this a Christian's calling?

God's deliverance

Daniel 6:14–28

The story of Daniel's deliverance from the 'lions' pit' illustrates the truth of a number of passages in the Old Testament Scriptures. Several of the Psalms testify to being delivered by God from 'the pit', a synonym for 'Sheol', the abode of the dead (e.g. 40:2; 57:6). They confess their belief that God is able to deliver those who trust him from death and this is expressed metaphorically in Psalm 57:

> *I lie in the midst of lions that greedily devour the sons of men.*
>
> *Psalm 57:4*

In the Psalm the 'lions' represent those who 'set a net for my steps' and who 'dig a pit in my way' (v. 6).

Perhaps we catch here an echo of a 'salvation' theme in the Old Testament, for Joseph was delivered by God from a 'pit' in which he had been placed by his hostile brothers (Genesis 37:24) and so was Jeremiah (Jeremiah 38:6). So Jews who now faced the same kind of suffering, from hostile enemies, and even from their own 'brethren' who had apostasized, were assured that the God of the fathers, the God who had not abandoned the Psalmists of old, was with them still. He would not leave them alone in their own 'pit of lions'.

THE VISIONS: DANIEL 7–12

Daniel's visions

Daniel 7:1–18

The book changes dramatically in chapter 7. Instead of stories about Daniel and his friends in which Daniel often interprets the dream of a foreign king with the aid of the wisdom God gave to him, we now begin a series of four visions seen by Daniel himself which he describes in first-person speech and which he needs an angel to interpret for him.

As in chapter 2, so here history is seen as a succession of four great empires of increasing severity and cruelty. Human world powers are seen as 'bestial' and are symbolized by the four beasts which rise up out of the 'deep' (v. 2). It is like the creation story in Genesis 1 where all was dark, a watery chaotic ocean, until God by his word reduced it to order and gave light to it. So the picture in this chapter of God's 'final' act of salvation is of a 're-creation' or of a 'new creation'.

God is king. Another Old Testament theme in this chapter is that of the universal 'kingship of God', celebrated in a number of Psalms, such as Psalm 93. Though his kingship is sometimes threatened by the forces of chaos ('the floods', v. 3), God overcomes them (vv. 1–2, 4), and so establishes his kingdom founded on his just decrees and characterized by his holiness (v. 5).

God's final victory. The last of the beasts which rise up against God in chapter 7 sprouts 'the little horn' (v. 8), which represented Antiochus Epiphanes, with his arrogant words and defiance against

God and his threats against temple and people. Yet God, on his throne, conquers him, and the 'bestial' human kingdoms are succeeded by the kingdom of God, the kingdom with a 'human' face (vv. 13–14). In times of deep distress and darkness, the assurance that ultimately God will defeat every form of evil, and his writ of peace and justice runs everywhere, is the one beacon by which his people have often kept hope and faith alive.

The 'son of man' receives the kingdom *Daniel 7:19–28*

In this second part of the chapter we, like Daniel, hear the 'explanation' of the vision which must be seen as early commentary on its meaning. For us much interest centres on 'one like a son of man' who was described in verse 13. The Hebrew idiom 'son of man' can mean simply 'a man' and it is used in this way in the Book of Ezekiel (e.g. 2:1). In this vision the one like a son of man comes to God on his throne (v. 13) and *receives* 'dominion, glory and kingdom', a world-wide and everlasting rule. In verse 21 this figure has become 'the saints of the Most High' who 'received the kingdom' (v. 22). Whether the saints of the Most High are heavenly, angelic beings or the faithful people of Israel is not spelled out. What is clear is that 'one like a son of man' is seen as a representative figure who receives and exercises rule from God. Clearly what happens in heaven has its effects on earth. Through him the people of God will know deliverance from their oppressors and enjoy the eternal rule of God. His kingdom is described as 'human' in contrast to the evil oppressive empires which have darkened the pages of history.

Two ages, two worlds. As we have seen, it is a mark of the literature sometimes described as 'apocalyptic' that it sees history very much in two contrasting stages. This present time in the historical world is evil and may be expected only to get worse. But something new and different will break in from beyond space and time when the kingdom of God comes. Since Christ's coming, Christians see the first signs of this kingdom already present here and now. But the hope that all its partial victories will ultimately be completed, its dimly glimpsed hopes realized, is surely one we must never lose.

Current affairs *Daniel 8:1–14*

Daniel's second vision, in which the language reverts to Hebrew for the rest of the book, introduces a surrealist picture of a ram and a goat in conflict. To us this seems more and more 'other-worldly', more removed from any kind of reality on this earth as we know it. In fact, from this point on, the visions begin to sharpen their focus on the history of the time of the writer and his readers.

The ram with two horns represents the Medo-Persian empire which spread to the west (vv. 3–4). But there it was confronted with a 'he-goat' (a symbol of power and leadership, see Ezekiel 34:17), which represents Alexander the Great who defeated the Persians at Issus in 333BC. Thereafter he rapidly extended his power to the east as far as India, and south as far as Egypt (vv. 5–8). However, Alexander died young and his vast empire was eventually divided between his generals. One of them, Ptolemy, ruled from Egypt, controlling Palestine; another, Seleucus, ruled in Syria (v. 8). Eventually the Seleucids, the successors of Seleucus, gained control of the Jews and their land (v. 9). Later, Antiochus IV came to power, and his arrogant defiance of God by his desecration of the temple and his persecution of faithful Jews are described in verses 10–14.

The God who fights for us. The term 'Prince of the host', for God (v. 11) reminds us of the power of Israel's God who fought their battles. The phrase would have reminded Jews that they were not alone in 'their darkest hour'. Arrogance and power, however great, stand no chance before God and an angelic interpreter assures Daniel that Antiochus' time is strictly limited (v. 14).

The cry 'How long?' is a familiar feature of the prayer of the sufferer in the Old Testament. Today's reading assures us that God does hear our cry and responds.

Daniel and Ezekiel *Daniel 8:15–27*

The setting, the content and the manner of Daniel's vision are strongly reminiscent of Ezekiel's 'call vision' in Babylon (Ezekiel 1). That, also, was by a river in Babylon. There, too, the prophet saw one who had 'the appearance of a man'. Ezekiel, like Daniel, fell on his face in fear. God spoke reassuringly to Ezekiel, telling him to get up and hear what he had to say in order that 'he might make it known' (Ezekiel 2:3; compare Daniel 8:26; 12:4). Just as God had shown his power to the Jewish exiles in Babylon, so now the same promise will be fulfilled in the experience of their successors who, although in Judah, are really 'in exile' in their own land, cut off from the true worship of the temple (vv. 11–14).

Divine and human power. The promise that Antiochus, for all his power and for all the terrible consequences of his persecution (vv. 24–25) will be broken 'by no human hand' reminds us of the great stone 'cut out by no human hand' which brought down the statue in Nebuchadnezzar's dream (2:34–35). This author does not think that human effort and military power effect much. He damns with faint praise the followers of Judas Maccabaeus who hoisted the standard of rebellion against Antiochus.

In fact, it was a combination of human action, bravery, persistence and determination, *and* the action of God which brought deliverance to the Jews. We have to do all we can, for God uses us and the powers he has given us. Yet our efforts are effective only in so far as God owns them and acts through them.

The repeated emphasis on how 'overwhelmed' Daniel was by the visions (e.g. v. 27; see 10:2–3) perhaps suggests that it is always costly to be chosen to bear witness to truth God has shown us.

The 'sabbath rest' of the land *Daniel 9*

Daniel's third vision arises from his reading of Jeremiah. It is interesting that by the time of the writer of the Book of Daniel some, at least, of the words of the great prophets are known as 'the books' (v. 2). Their words are obviously becoming well known in written form and are on their way to being regarded as authoritative. Later books, like Daniel itself, assume increasingly the form of 'exegesis' (interpretation) of these writings, in the conviction that God still speaks through them to those in the changed situation of a later time.

After a prayer which is ascribed to Daniel (vv. 3–19), Gabriel appears to him in a vision to explain that when Jeremiah predicted a seventy-year exile in Babylon (Jeremiah 25:12; 29:10), he really meant 'seventy weeks of years' (v. 24). This, however, is not just a convenient 'get-out' to explain why the end of the exile in Babylon did not bring in the promised rule of God. It also is scriptural 'exegesis'. In 2 Chronicles 36:20–21, the writer also quotes Jeremiah's 'seventy year' prophecy. He explains that the reason for the exile was that the holy land had been contaminated by the people's sins and so God had to leave it to lie fallow for its 'sabbath rest'. That is what is in the writer's mind in Daniel. He sees the whole period from the fall of Jerusalem to his own day in the second century as a 'continuing exile'. That is the burden of the prayer in verses 3–19. It has been a 'seventy weeks of years', not because it lasted a literal 490 years, but because it has been a 'fallow' period, a time of judgment, to let the land recover from the people's sin.

Gabriel makes this clear in verse 24. This period has, for their sin, to atone for iniquity and end the impurity. Now, however, God is about to act to save his people. His 'righteous' kingdom will be victorious, the words of Jeremiah will be fulfilled, and a holy temple and holy people will again know God's presence with them as they worship him (vv. 24–25).

Darkness before the dawn of God's 'day'. The details of the 'weeks' of this history are obscure to us as probably they were to the writer. The crisis, however, is coming. They are in the last 'week' in which Antiochus has joined forces with apostate Jews (the 'many') and desecrated the temple. They have known persecution for three and a half years (167–164BC). In fact, in 164BC, the Jews reclaimed and rededicated their temple. To that extent the prophecy was 'fulfilled'.

Birth-pangs of God's new age *Daniel 12*

The last chapter of the book brings the climax. The final vision, which has been described at length and in detail in chapters 10–11, narrated the course of history during the various military campaigns of Antiochus IV. It describes in particular the suffering, and even death, of many of the 'wise', that is, those who have remained faithful to God and his laws (11:33–35). Yet it assures the readers of Antiochus's death (11:44–45, a prophecy which was not fulfilled in the manner described here) and that this will mark the 'beginning of the end', the birth-pangs of God's new age. The secrets revealed to Daniel are to be preserved as a sure promise for those who are 'wise' enough to see God's hand in these terrible events which were driving so many to fear and panic (v. 4).

Resurrection from the dead. Two questions occupy the writer in this chapter. One is that the victory of God's kingdom will come too late for those who have suffered martyrdom. We have to remember that most of the Old Testament was written without any hope of a real life after death. Here, however, the promise of 'resurrection' for the faithful who have died breaks surface. They will be raised to share in the triumph (just as the wicked who appear to have escaped judgment by death will be raised to suffer punishment, v. 2).

'Vicarious' suffering. Yet it is not only that they will have been victorious. God will have used their suffering vicariously to influence the careless, apostate 'many' (v. 3). Indeed, there is a quotation from Isaiah 53:11 here, likening their sufferings to those of the 'suffering Servant' who, by his suffering, would make 'the many to be accounted righteous' (v. 3).

The 'time of the end'. The other question for later readers of this book was, 'When will all this happen?' (v. 6). All Daniel is told is that the witness is sealed 'until the time of the end' (v. 9). The 'wise' will understand and keep the faith (v. 10). That has not stopped some later editors from adding different guesses in the last two verses! One is reminded of the impatience of the disciples who wanted to know from Jesus exactly when 'he would return the kingdom to Israel' (Acts 1:6). Jesus's answer was that they were to be faithful to the mission on which he was sending them out, confident that God had fixed 'the times and seasons' by his own authority. That is the real faith of the writer of the Book of Daniel and it is this which makes his book a word of hope for the people of God who live and serve long after the days of Antiochus. His kingdom was swept away. God's kingdom remains and, at the last, will triumph.

The witness of a book such as Daniel is that we do not have to wait until the 'End', whenever and whatever that will be, to know God's presence. Here and now the king is with us in our living, our suffering and our witness to the reality of the kingdom. Indeed, he uses the service and suffering of his people in his work of bringing others to the light of knowledge of him and experience of his power and love. The sufferings of 'the Servant of God' are never futile. They are the paving stones along which the divine love reaches into his world and extends his guiding hand to those who, as yet, have not seen the significance of 'the times and seasons' in which he is now at work.

Books of the Bible like Daniel, with their talk of 'times' and 'seasons', with visions interpreted by angels and predictions of 'the end' pose real problems for Christians today. As with all biblical 'prophecy', is it not true to say that the great promises the visionaries attached to events of their own lifetime have long since been overtaken, and discredited, by history?

Perhaps we have to read these books at two levels. In fact, the immediate hopes of the writer of the Book of Daniel were fulfilled. The temple was reclaimed for freedom of worship, rededicated, and again became a centre for the faith of a growingly worldwide Judaism. Judaism also was to become the womb of Christianity. Yet the book also witnesses to a hope that, beyond all the partial victories of the kingdom and the limited effectiveness of our service, we live in the light of the hope of an ultimate victory of God as king over all which mars his creation. Only such a hope can sustain the community of faith in all its work, its conflict and its suffering. How it will happen, and what form it will take, are 'sealed books' to us. History shows that God often acted in a way different from that envisaged by the prophets, but he acted just as surely as they foresaw he would. God's glory always bursts the framework of the agendas we set for him.

THE BOOK OF THE TWELVE

Grouped together at the end of the Old Testament are the twelve shorter prophetic books, or 'minor' prophets as they are sometimes called. It is important, however, to remember that this description refers to their length, not to their significance, for certainly Amos, Hosea and Micah belonged to the great age of classical prophecy in the eighth century BC, and indeed all twelve have a challenging message to give. By the third, or possibly the second, century BC the twelve prophets had come to be regarded as one book written on a single scroll. It seems likely that the arrangement of the books was determined for the most part by what was regarded as their chronological order, ranging from the eighth century, to which the story of Jonah (though not the writing of the book) also belongs, through the seventh and early sixth centuries with Nahum, Habakkuk and Zephaniah, to the last three prophets, Haggai, Zechariah and Malachi, which all belong to the post-exilic period. It is difficult to fit Joel and Obadiah into this scheme and it may be that they owe their place alongside Amos to certain similarities of content (compare Amos 1:2 with Joel 3:16, and Amos 9:12 with Obadiah 19–21). To read the Book of the Twelve as a whole is to see in perspective the judgmental words spoken against hostile nations, particularly in Obadiah and Nahum, for included here, too, is the message of Jonah that God's forgiveness is not limited to Israel.

HOSEA

Hosea is well known to many Christians as a prophet whose message to his people was embodied in his own life. Through his troubled marriage, he expressed in action the love of God which he proclaimed. Less familiar is the strong note of divine judgment which he shared with the other prophets, especially his near contemporary, Amos. But none of the great prophets in ancient Israel spoke purely of God's blessing on his people, and Hosea is no exception. If God is to save Israel, it can only be after ruthless punishment, carried out through an enemy army and resulting in devastation of the country and much loss of life.

Yet Hosea is distinctive in believing that God is never satisfied with justice alone. Hosea's God is not an impartial observer, watching Israel get what it deserves from a position of detachment. Hosea's God is torn between his love for his chosen people and his own justice, which demands that they should be punished. At times it seems almost as though God cannot make up his own mind about what is to be done (see 11:8–9).

Later theology has tended to stress that God does not have to 'make up his mind' after deliberation, but always knows exactly what he is going to do. But Hosea conceives God in more human terms. We could say that he shows us the human face of God, which Christians see still more clearly expressed in the life, death and resurrection of Jesus.

Hosea lived in the northern kingdom of Israel, which had its capital at Samaria, in the second half of the eighth century BC. We know almost nothing about his life, except for the account of his marriage in chapters 1–3 of his book, and even here the details are far from clear.

He prophesied at a time of turmoil for the kingdom. Internally the country was unstable; there was political intrigue and assassination as king followed king in quick succession (see 2 Kings 15:8–31). Hosea himself points to a political leadership that had long since lost interest in the good of the nation, and was interested only in self-indulgence (7:1–7). He also saw the national life as religiously decadent and corrupt, with many practices borrowed from the old Canaanite religion. Externally there was a growing threat of annihilation by the major world power of the day. In 745BC the Assyrians, an ancient nation based in what is now Iraq, began to expand westwards and to build an empire by conquering the small states in Syria and Palestine. Neither of the Hebrew kingdoms, Israel and Judah, stood much chance of withstanding the Assyrians. Israel tried to resist the Assyrian advance in 735 by forming a coalition with Syria.

Samaria eventually fell to the Assyrians in 721BC after a long siege (see 2 Kings 16:1–9 and 17:1–6). Hosea may have lived to see all the leaders of Israel deported and the countryside pillaged.

More than any other prophetic book in the Old Testament, the book of Hosea suffered from miscopying by scribes in ancient times, and sometimes the meaning is very difficult to grasp. This commentary follows the New English Bible (NEB), and you will sometimes notice wide differences from other versions. In places it is not clear where individual sayings of the prophet begin and end. Nevertheless a clear and distinctive message still emerges from a careful reading of the book.

Hosea is the only prophet from northern Israel whose words have come down to us (Amos prophesied in the north, but was a Judaean). Perhaps this is why he felt such personal agony at the thought of the nation's impending destruction, whereas Amos could contemplate it with greater detachment.

A century later Jeremiah, in Judah, would speak in similar terms of the fall of Jerusalem and Judah to the Babylonians; like Hosea, he experienced the national disaster as a personal tragedy. Nowhere is the sense stronger that the prophet is bound up with the fate of the people he speaks to, even when his appointed task is to tell them of God's judgment, than in Hosea and Jeremiah. With Hosea there begins the tradition that prophets weep over the sinful nation as well as denouncing it (compare Luke 19:41–44). They then begin to think of God himself as having the same compassion for sinners, even if justice demands that he punish them. 'The kindness and the severity of God' (Romans 11:22) have been a central theme in both Jewish and Christian theology ever since.

Further reading

H. McKeating, *Amos, Hosea, Micah*, Cambridge Bible Commentary, 1971

For more detailed study

G.I. Davies, *Hosea*, New Century Bible Commentary, 1992

Hosea's unfaithful wife

Hosea 1:1—2:1

Often, in the Old Testament, prophets are told to perform actions which symbolize some aspect of God's relation with his people, a kind of acted parable: see, for example, Jeremiah 27:1–15. But few cases are as startling as God's command to Hosea to 'take a wanton for your wife'. This was to symbolize the faithless character of Israel, the people whom God has chosen and to whom he is therefore 'married'. Hosea did not need to invent the picture of God's relationship with his people as a marriage. In his day the Israelites practised a form of their ancestral religion which had been heavily influenced by the Canaanites, the original inhabitants of Palestine; and in Canaanite religion Baal, the chief god, was said to be 'married' to the land. The marriage was celebrated by festivals involving what we should call sexual orgies. Gomer, Hosea's wife, may have been a 'sacred prostitute' employed for these rites. Considering how Hosea detested this perversion of Israel's religion, his willingness to obey God's command is even more remarkable. He was able to find a positive use for the idea of a 'marriage' between God and his people in spite of the danger of being misunderstood by those who practised a religion of fertility.

The unfaithfulness of God's people. Hosea gives his children symbolic names, pointing to the divine judgment that will fall on an unfaithful people. 'Jezreel' reminds the people of the oppressive rule of Ahab and Jezebel (1 Kings 21), but also of the equally sinful vengeance wreaked on their dynasty by Jehu (2 Kings 9:30—10:11). The other two names are direct threats that Israel will receive no pity, and will cease to be God's people. By having a family with names like these, the prophet was a standing reproach to his people, constantly reminding them that they had made themselves hateful to God and could expect nothing but destruction.

A promise of salvation. Yet already Hosea seems to look beyond disaster to a great deliverance, in which Israel will be God's people once more, and will even be reunited with their neighbours to the south, the kingdom of Judah, as in the days of David and Solomon two hundred years before. Hosea insists on both the severity *and* the faithfulness of God, who is not frustrated by his people's unfaithfulness but will in the end find a way to restore them.

Israel: divorced and remarried — *Hosea 2:2–17*

Chapter 2 begins in the law-court, as God presents the case for the prosecution against his faithless wife, Israel, and announces his intention of divorcing her if she does not repent. Marriage in Israel was hardly an equal partnership: husbands could divorce their wives at will, whereas wives could not divorce their husbands under any circumstances whatever. But in proposing to 'divorce' Israel, God does not claim the right to sever his connection with his people arbitrarily. On the contrary, he spends a long time explaining why his action is fully justified. Israel, he says, has been disloyal, going after her 'lovers'—that is, the many other gods the people have been worshipping. Hosea sees this disloyalty as ruining their relationship with their God in the same way as promiscuous adultery will ruin a human marriage. What is more, Israel is positively deluded, accepting the claim of the gods of Canaan to be the source of the land's fruitfulness when in reality it is Yahweh, the God who had rescued his people from slavery in Egypt, who *also* provided the good things with which the Promised Land abounded.

But God's punishment is not meant to annihilate his people: he is being cruel to be kind. By interfering with the land's fertility his purpose is to bring Israel to recognize that it is he who has the power over nature which they wrongly ascribe to Baal. Once they come to their senses, he can receive them again as his own people (vv. 14–17). Thus God's judgment is not his last word: it is part of a larger plan, in which his people's relationship with him will ultimately be even better than it was in the beginning, at the time of the exodus from Egypt. It will be founded, not on blissful ignorance of the temptations of life in the Promised Land, but on a mature and open-eyed loyalty to a God whose nature and power are fully appreciated.

The universal God. In the ancient world it was usual to believe in many gods, who shared out among themselves the tasks involved in governing the world. To claim, as Hosea does, that the God who had directed Israel's history was one and the same as the God who made the land fertile was a radical step. Hosea speaks as though his audience ought to have realized that all good things came from the one God of Israel, and so should have avoided getting embroiled in the fertility rites of Baal. But he may have been more original than he thought he was. People were probably quite puzzled by the idea that 'it was I who gave corn, new wine, and oil' (v. 8). Christians tend to take the idea that there is only one God for granted. But Israel arrived at it by a long and often thorny route. In this chapter of Hosea we can catch a glimpse of one vital stage along that route. Hosea's experience of his own marriage seems to have been crucial in this. He sees God's outrage at being rejected as being like his own anger at his wife's infidelity, and God's love as like his own inability to abandon the person he had once loved.

Heaven on earth *Hosea 2:18–23*

In this short passage the promises of 2:2–17 are extended to embrace the transformation of the whole world. Israel is still at the centre of God's concern: this remains true throughout the Old Testament. But in order to bless Israel to the extent that will do justice to his love for her, God has to transform the entire world, indeed the entire universe, making peace among the nations, peace between human beings and animals, peace between heaven and earth. Hosea's vision is like that in Isaiah 11:1–9, where even the natural enmity between carnivorous animals and their prey yields to the new order which God will one day bring in. God and Israel, surrounded by a recreated world, will speak to each other like reunited lovers, saying, 'You are mine.'

Prophecy and politics. To the political leaders of Israel in the eighth century, Hosea's threats *and* promises must have seemed equally remote and unconnected with the daily reality they knew.

They did not see the nation as hopelessly sinful, but as a God-fearing state whose God was not giving it the support it needed against powerful enemies. One the other hand, their hopes for the future were also less extravagant than Hosea's. For the prophet, God's relationship with his people is a game played for higher stakes than political 'realists' recognized.

A time of discipline *Hosea 3:1–5*

It is not easy to say whether this chapter tells of a further marriage, at some later date, or a re-marriage after divorce, or is an alternative version of the events described in chapter 1. Probably the simplest answer is that here we have the prophet's own account of his marriage ('The Lord said to *me*') whereas in chapter 1 someone else is telling the story. The parallel between Hosea's experience with his wife and God's with Israel is drawn very clearly: Hosea is to love her just as God loves the Israelites—even though she has slept with another man just as Israel has resorted to other gods. But, as in 2:6–13, the relationship cannot be restored to what it was until Israel comes to its senses. This is symbolized in the marriage by a period of waiting, in which Hosea and his wife are to have no sexual relations. In the same way, Israel is to pass through a time in which God no longer communicates with the nation, since all the national institutions, both political and religious, will cease to exist (v. 4). This clearly implies that the country is to lose its independence and pass through a period in which it has no control over its own national life. But this time of discipline is the prelude to a renewed relationship with God in a kingdom restored to prosperity.

Hosea found in his own experiences and emotional life a model for the way God felt and acted in relation to his people. What can we learn of God's purposes and intentions from our own life-story up to the present?

'No knowledge of God in the land' *Hosea 4:1–11*

In the next six chapters Hosea surveys the sick state of Israelite society in his day. His presentation is not systematic, and many of the same themes keep recurring. First we have a general summary of what is wrong: there is 'no good faith or mutual trust'. In the anarchic condition to which Israel had sunk by the mid-eighth century none of the traditional ethical standards of Israelite life was maintained, and the sense of brotherhood which underlies all the laws in the Old Testament had broken down. In what looks like a reference to the ten commandments (v. 2), Hosea points out that the most basic moral standards are being broken.

For the prophets, a failure to live by God's standards can be described as a failure to 'know God' (v. 1). They would have had no time for the idea that people could know God through prayer or in mystical experience without living the kind of life God requires. To know God is to serve God, and God is served when people behave to others in accordance with God's Law. 'A man may say, "I am in the light"; but if he hates his brother, he is still in the dark' (1 John 2:9). Knowledge of God is tested by its fruitfulness in leading to a life that accords with God's own standards.

The responsibility of the priests. How were people to know what kind of life God required? According to Hosea, responsibility for instructing people in God's Law rested with the priests, who were the main religious teachers in his day. Like all the prophets, Hosea is hardest on those who influence the lives of others, and it is for the priests that he saves his sharpest words. Instead of keeping the people loyal to God and just towards each other, the priests take the lead in putting all their energies into the worship of Baal—with all the sexual licence that involves, as the next section makes clear.

'A people without understanding' *Hosea 4:12–19*

One of the strangest aspects of the teaching of the prophets is that they often told their hearers not to offer sacrifice to God, not to visit temples and shrines, and not to spend time or money on the practice of 'religion' in the ordinary sense. This seemed to their contemporaries not just mistaken, but perverse—as if church leaders were to appear on television to try to persuade people not to come to church, read the Bible, or pray. 'Do not come to Gilgal,' says Hosea—Gilgal was the home of a major sanctuary. Amos, a few years before, had said the same: 'Go not to Gilgal' (Amos 5:5).

There are two reasons for this strange attitude. The first is that, in the prophet's eyes, 'religion' divorced from morality was a hollow mockery, which deluded people into thinking that when they had gone to the sanctuary and sacrificed, they had done all that God required. Better that they should not go, and be made to realize that God's real demands were for right dealing between people. It did him no honour to offer expensive sacrifices bought with money stolen from the poor!

But the second reason was that what went on at the sanctuaries was in any case a complete travesty of 'religion'. An Israelite festival was not a 'service', it was a feast, an opportunity for eating and drinking. That was inappropriate enough in itself, when times were so bad for the poor. But, worse still, now that the national religion had come to be so heavily influenced by fertility cults, the feast soon deteriorated into an orgy. If that is what passes for religion, then the only option is to scrap the whole thing, and start again. Since the people and their leaders showed no inclination to do this, God himself would have to step in: 'The wind shall sweep them away, wrapped in its wings' (v. 19).

For the prophets, knowledge of God and the practice of religion have much more to do with how people behave towards each other than with the external (or even the internal aspects) of worship and religious ceremony. Yet they cannot be accused of 'reducing' religion to the 'social gospel'—they are clear that God always come first and have a vivid awareness of his transcendence. How can the life of the churches reflect this double truth in our own day?

Military disaster *Hosea 5:1–13*

From about 745BC, when the strong and successful king Tiglath-Pileser III came to the throne, Assyria began to look west and to threaten the pocket-states of Syria and Palestine. Continual petty disagreements, usually sparked off by disputes about territorial rights, prevented these states from presenting a unified response to Assyrian threats. Temporary coalitions would be made and broken; and from time to time one small country would invite the Assyrian king to deal with its neighbour's claim to territory, thus foolishly allowing him to extend his sphere of influence. Both Hosea and Isaiah thought that Israel and Judah should have avoided any entanglement with foreign powers, and they condemned both the unstable little anti-Assyrian coalitions and the appeals to Assyria to intervene. But the northern kingdom of Israel, where Hosea lived, suffered worse from blunders in foreign policy than Judah. The disastrous attempt to force Judah to join an anti-Assyrian campaign in 735BC resulted in an appeal to Assyria by King Ahaz of Judah, and from then on Israel was never to be free of Assyrian interference in its affairs until Samaria fell in 721BC.

This is the background to Hosea 5:8–13. After repeating many of his previous charges against the false religion of priests and people, Hosea turns here to questions of international relations. He seems equally incensed at the conduct of both kingdoms, believing that the Assyrian army would soon prove the downfall of the whole of 'God's people'. We know of Israel's attempt to invade Judah and Judah's appeal to Assyria (see 2 Kings 16:5–9 and Isaiah 7:1–9), but in this oracle Hosea seems also to refer to a similar attempt by Judah against Israel (whom Hosea calls 'Ephraim'), and an appeal to Assyria by the northern kingdom. This suggests that the events of these years were even more complicated than the record in 2 Kings makes them sound.

'A festering sore'. Through all the complications of the two kingdoms' inept foreign policy, Hosea sees one root cause of disaster: the abandonment of Yahweh, Israel's God. Verses 12 and 13 graphically portray the nation as terminally ill, with festering sores and ulcers (see Isaiah 1:5–6; Jeremiah 8:21–22). In one of the most extraordinary pictures of God in the Bible, he sees God himself as the illness from which the people suffer: 'I am a canker to the house of Judah.' In modern terms, we might put this by saying that the nation has become so alien from God to whom it is related that its system rejects God as a foreign body. No medical care can heal this incompatibility—certainly not the kind of treatment that will be dispensed by the Assyrians.

'On the third day he will restore us' *Hosea 5:14—6:11*

This passage contains a verse that was important to early Christians: 'after two days he will revive us, on the third day he will restore us, that in his presence we may live' (6:2). They saw it as foreshadowing the resurrection of Jesus on the third day, and it is possibly this verse the creeds have in mind when they affirm that 'on the third day he rose again *according to the Scriptures*'. We shall see that in its original context the verse had a very different meaning.

'Loyalty is my desire, not sacrifice'. Jesus is recorded in the Gospels as having quoted Hosea 6:6 in disputes about whether it is more important to keep the provisions of the Jewish Law strictly, or to help others to live and flourish (see Matthew 9:13; 12:7), 'I desire mercy not sacrifice'. 'Mercy' (or 'loyalty', as the NEB translates it) means faithfulness to God's will, loyalty to him, and a commitment to behaving towards others as God himself behaves towards those he loves. Hence it serves as a kind of shorthand term for just those qualities of living that, according to Hosea, were being replaced by the empty, outward show of religion in Israel in his day.

'A harvest of reckoning'. If we now replace these famous verses in their context, we find that they contribute to one of Hosea's sternest denunciations of his people in God's name. The passage begins (5:14) with another surprising and disturbing picture of God, which shows how wrong is the popular idea of Hosea as a gentle spokesman for an indulgent and kindly God: 'I will be fierce as a panther to Ephraim, fierce as a lion to Judah—I will maul the prey and go, carry it beyond hope of rescue.' Like a beast of prey, Israel's God retires to his den with the carcass of the nation he has killed, and waits there for what is left of his people to venture near enough to beg for mercy. Hosea 6:1–3 should be put in inverted commas, as the words with which the Israelites will try to encourage each other as they nervously approach the mount of Yahweh's lair. The words they speak are true enough in themselves, for God's justice *does* 'dawn like morning light'; it *is* 'sure as the sunrise'. But, says God, that is far from good news for people such as they are. Their loyalty to him is no more than lip-service, transient as the early morning dew, for which the certainty that the sun will rise is merely the certainty of swift extinction (6:4). The fact that God is utterly reliable in his justice is thoroughly bad news for a country where people are murdered and the 'covenant' (the special bond between Israel and its God) repeatedly violated. All the sacrifice in the world will not remedy this (6:6), and nor will fine-sounding words of penitence.

There is indeed comfort in Hosea, but not in this passage. All his efforts here go into shocking his hearers out of their easy complacency, their assumption that God is a machine for dispensing sweetness and light. God is not Israel's pet; he cannot be domesticated. He is indeed reliable, but that does not make him predictable. There is nothing cosy about Hosea's kind of God.

In the central section of Hosea (chapters 4–9) there is scarcely any gleam of light. Later we shall find hopes of eventual restoration, as we found them in the first three chapters. But there is never any suggestion that national disaster can be avoided, only that God may decide to do some new thing *beyond disaster. People think of the prophets as preachers of repentance: but Hosea scarcely ever calls on his hearers to repent. The time for repentance has come and gone, and divine judgment is now inevitable.*

A nation in decline *Hosea 7:1–16*

This chapter is among the most obscure passages in the book, and in many verses it is almost impossible to say what the Hebrew means. Nevertheless, the overall theme is clear: the anarchy and confusion into which the kingdom of Israel has fallen in its declining years.

The previous chapter might leave the reader feeling that God has not even *tried* to bring his people back to himself preferring instead simply to abandon them to their fate. Hosea now begins to describe the state of mind into which Israel's leaders have fallen, and thus to show how hopeless is the task facing both God and his prophet. Leading members of the community think nothing of committing robbery with violence (v. 1), and their religion is nothing but the celebration of rites involving a mixture of drunken sexual orgies (vv. 4–5) and self-mutilation (v. 14). 'King after king falls from power' (v. 7) because of the political instability of the country (see 2 Kings 15:8–31). Meanwhile international relations are in the hands of people with neither sense nor judgment, so that alliances are made and broken with Assyria, which was obviously serving only its own interests in getting involved in Palestinian affairs, and with Egypt, by now a spent force for several hundred years but always ready to meddle in Palestine in a quest for its own long-lost empire (vv. 8–11).

'A half-baked cake'. Such a country is so half-baked (v. 8) that it could not recognize its God if it met him: 'I long to deliver them, but they tell lies about me' (v. 13). In yet another startling image, Hosea presents God as a fowler, who with little effort will capture Israel as it flaps aimlessly around (v. 12). Their claim to be loyal to God is patently insincere (v. 14): 'their talk is all lies' (v. 16). It is not that God is unwilling to help them, but simply that they would not recognize help if they saw it.

'Israel has forgotten his maker' *Hosea 8:1–14*

Chapter 8 provides further variation on themes that are now familiar. As at the beginning of chapter 6, Hosea notes the people's perfect unawareness that anything is wrong in their relationship with God: 'We know thee, God of Israel', they say (v. 2). Israel seems to Hosea to be governed by people who always insist that they know best, and can provide the solutions to the country's problems: new kings and a fresh administration (vv. 4, 10); extra altars and special sacrifices (vv. 11–13); and skillfully constructed images of God (vv. 5–6).

God had been worshipped in the image of a bull (or 'calf' as the Old Testament calls it, probably contemptuously) since Jeroboam I had established shrines at Bethel and Dan as northern rivals to Jerusalem in the tenth century BC (1 Kings 12:25–33); and the story of the 'golden calf' (Exodus 32) may reflect an even older use of bull images. Most people probably thought of the bull as an image of Israel's own God, Yahweh (or maybe even as a mount for him to ride). But its associations with the fertility cults of Canaanite religion made it, in Hosea's eyes, worse than useless. Like all the prophets, he believes that *no* image can do justice to God, and that in practice (whatever the theory may have been) those who used images in worship were concerned more with the human skill and money expended on them than with the God they symbolized. People may have thought they were honouring God; in reality the were merely celebrating their own achievements. And in God's eyes Israel has no achievements: the nation is 'a worthless nothing' (v. 8), for which nothing but exile is in store (v. 13).

The end of prophecy *Hosea 9:1–9*

One of the ideas in the Old Testament that is hardest for the Christian is that of the 'hardening of the heart', where God is sometimes said to be the *cause* of people's inability to respond to him in obedience. We meet this idea in the stories about Moses and Pharaoh in Egypt (see Exodus 7:3, 22; 10:1), and also in Hosea's contemporary, Isaiah (see Isaiah 6:9–10). This sounds as though God has decided in advance that certain people are to suffer, and that he (dishonestly) ensures that they will 'deserve' their suffering by making them unable to obey him. Such an idea would certainly be repudiated by most Christians and by most Jews.

In fact the Old Testament is more subtle than this suggests, and does justice to a feature of human personality that we can recognize as a terrible reality. It is possible to persist so long in a wrong way of life that one's perception of good and evil becomes blunted, and in a certain sense it is actually impossible to change one's ways. The Old Testament holds that, once this stage is reached the blunting of moral vision which prevents repentance (and hence makes forgiveness impossible to receive) is itself God's punishment on persistent sinfulness. It is not that God ceases to seek the sinner, but that there comes a point when even he has to admit defeat.

It may seem difficult to love a God who declares that there are some sins he simply will not forgive, and Christians will feel that they have seen more of God's endlessly forgiving love than was revealed to Hosea. Nevertheless, it would not really be better to have a God who smiled indulgently at absolutely any kind of human conduct. A God who cannot help but forgive, whatever we do, is not a God worth worshipping; nor is a God who has favourites.

Point of no return. For Hosea, this point has now been reached by Israel, for whom nothing remains but hopeless exile. In the event it was not to Egypt (v. 6) but to Assyria that the inhabitants of the northern kingdom were taken; but in a symbolic sense it was indeed 'Egypt', for the people lost the land of promise and were no better off than they had been before Moses freed them from their bondage in Egypt. Other 'prophets' than Hosea had apparently been proclaiming what they presented as a word from God (v. 8), but (like the priests of chapters 4 and 5) they had spoken nothing but lies. And now the point of no return had been reached, at which Israel's heart had been 'hardened': from now on, true prophecy would cease altogether. 'The prophet shall be made a fool, and the inspired seer a madman by your great guilt' (v. 7). The people have lost the ability to discern between good and bad advice, and their punishment will be to continue for ever in this bemused condition. 'Their prison is only in their own minds, yet they are in that prison; and so afraid of being taken in that they cannot be taken out' (C.S. Lewis, *The Last Battle*).

'Their root is withered, and they yield no fruit' *Hosea 9:10–17*

If anything, the gloom of the prophet about his people deepens still further in the second part of the chapter. The present is black, the future blacker; but surely there was once a time when Israel had a fruitful relationship with its God? No, Hosea replies. God adopted the Israelites as his own when they were a nomadic people, and expected that they would repay his loving kindness in giving them the Promised Land; but even before they entered it, they began to rebel. 'Baal-peor' is the God worshipped at Beth-peor, one of the last places at which the Israelites stopped east of the river Jordan before crossing into the land of promise; Numbers 25 tells the bloody story of what happened there.

The gift of the land was a gift that Israel spoiled the very moment it was given. God had by now had several centuries in which to regret having made it, and little that had happened in that time had given him cause to think that anything could be salvaged of its original intention. Tainted from the beginning, Israel had now sunk into such total ruin that nothing remained but to make an end.

Whether meant literally or metaphorically, the image that comes first to Hosea's mind is *sterility*: 'no childbirth, no fruitful womb, no conceiving' (9:11)—a fitting punishment, it must have seemed to him, for a long history of both literal and metaphorical 'unfaithfulness' to a God who had been the 'husband' of his people (compare 2:16). No doubt there was also for him a sense of poetic justice in the idea that barrenness should be the result of so much misused sexuality. The total extinction of the race seems to be what Hosea has in mind here: a prediction which mercifully failed to come true, but a good measure of his own complete disillusionment with the people to whom he belonged.

The gravest problem in Hosea's message lies more in his assumption that there can be national *sin, which God can justly punish through national disaster. Can Christians really see the hand of God at work in the destruction of small nations by their more powerful neighbours, as Hosea saw it in the imminent fall of Israel to the Assyrians? What of all those who suffer undeservedly in such events? If it is unjust of oppressive rulers to crush the poor and helpless, is it any more just of God to punish them in a way which leaves their victims every bit as dead as if he had let things take their natural course? Questions like these are not easily set aside, once we step outside the assumptions within which the prophet worked and try to apply their message to our own world.*

The human face of God *Hosea 10:1–8*

The last chapter ended with a threat of sterility, the end of all the fruitfulness which the rituals of fertility were supposed to ensure. This oracle uses the imagery of fertility in another, equally hostile way. Like richly fertile soil, Israel provides the perfect condition for the growth of weeds. The more fruitful life in the Promised Land had become, the more the people had built altars and 'sacred pillars' (standing stones, as we should call them) in honour, not of Yahweh, the God who had given them the land, but of Baal, the native god of the Canaanites to whom the land had belonged. Thus, according to Hosea, they had turned the God-given fruitfulness of the land into a cause for sin; and the more God blessed them, the more sinful they became.

'Fertility', both literal and metaphorical, has been Israel's downfall: so it is fitting that it should also be the nation's punishment. When the people have gone into exile, the land will go on bearing fruit, though Baal is no longer being worshipped there, and the bull images have been taken to Assyria. The fruit it bears will be 'thorns and thistles' (10:8), and it will gradually cover up the altars that caused so much trouble. There is a grim irony here, as if the land itself is taking revenge on its former inhabitants. The oracle ends with words which Jesus (Luke 23:30) quoted as he was being led to execution: 'They will say to the mountains, "Cover us".'

There is a clear sense here, as in the previous few chapters, that God has failed to achieve the purpose he had in choosing and blessing Israel.

Hosea conveys, as no other prophet except perhaps Jeremiah, the immense *frustration* which Israel's God felt at his people's perversity in taking everything he had given them and turning it to evil. 'They are crazy now, they are mad.' If he blesses them, they attribute the blessings to other gods, make his fruitful land the subject of endless lawsuits (v. 4), and willingly submit to humiliating treaties with foreign powers to deprive themselves of the freedom their prosperity could give them. If, on the other hand, he tries to show them his power by causing national disaster, then, instead of repenting or reforming, they simply lament over the fact that they have been deprived of their 'idols' (v. 5). God is at his wits' end: what can be done with people so stupid?

Both Christians and Jews have inherited a sense of caution about ascribing emotions—especially feelings like frustration, irritation, or despair—to God. There are indeed grave difficulties in believing that the God who made the world can be frustrated by his own creation, or can meet with problems that he cannot deal with or has not foreseen. But the prophets did not yet feel this theoretical difficulty. Thinking of God in such human terms had not yet set limits to people's religious ideas. The prophets felt free to present God as suffering all the pain and anger that a human person would feel if confronted with infuriating and deliberate perversity. For them, God's ability to feel such emotions was part of his 'aliveness'. It is dumb idols that feel no emotion (compare Psalm 115), the living God has more, not fewer, feelings than a human being. This is, in the end, good news, because the God who can be truly angry can also truly love, and Hosea's last word is that he indeed does so.

Reading the prophets shows us how one might think of God as a warm, living person and yet not lose sight of his power and infinity. The Christian idea of the incarnation stresses especially that God regards a human personality as the most fitting vehicle through which to reveal what he is eternally like.

For Mercy has a human heart
Pity, a human face;
And Love, the human form divine,
And Peace, the human dress.

William Blake

'It is time to seek the Lord' *Hosea 10:9–15*

In an oracle that continues to use pictures drawn from agriculture, we find here one of Hosea's very few calls to repentance: 'Sow for yourselves in justice, and you will reap what loyalty deserves; break up your fallow (land), for it is time to seek the Lord, seeking him until he comes and gives you your just measure of rain' (v. 12). Did the prophet really think there was still hope of safety, if the people abandoned their obsession with the fertility of the land and the rituals that were supposed to ensure it, and turned instead to the real 'fruitfulness' that God desired—fruitfulness in 'justice' and 'loyalty' (compare 6:6)? Perhaps; but the sequel seems to show that he did not think they were at all likely to take his advice. So far no one had sown justice: 'You have ploughed wickedness into your soil, and the crop is mischief' (v. 13).

Like his contemporaries Amos and Isaiah, Hosea called for justice in the knowledge that his hearers had already decided against it even before he opened his mouth. They had been rebellious since earliest times—the 'day of Gibeah' is the occasion referred to in the horrible story in Judges 19 (see also Hosea 9:9). The long history of disobedience would end once the Assyrians arrived. No one in the days of Hosea was in any doubt about the Assyrians' record for brutality in war. They had the reputation the Vikings have in northern Europe, and the prophet has only to recall one incident, unknown to us but evidently notorious to them (v. 14).

'Out of Egypt I have called my son' *Hosea 11:1–11*

The prophecy which Matthew's Gospel quotes as an allusion to the 'flight into Egypt' (Matthew 2:15) refers, in its original context, to the exodus, God's deliverance of Israel from Egypt through Moses. It stands at the beginning of an oracle in which at last we see the other aspect of God's human face: his love and concern for his people, which cannot be set aside even by their most infuriating rebellions.

Even here, Hosea holds out no hope that the military disaster he fears will be averted. God's continual care for Israel from the days of the exodus down to the present does not at all imply that he will not punish them. On the contrary, Hosea describes God's love in the most human and intimate terms (like the love of a parent to a child or of an owner to a pet, vv. 3–4) chiefly in order to heighten the sense of outrage produced by an awareness of Israel's repeated acts of ingratitude: 'the more I called, the more they went from me' (v. 2). As a punishment, the exodus will be reversed (v. 5). But *beyond* judgment, the prophet clearly foresees restoration. For the first time in the prophets we encounter the idea of a 'new exodus' (v. 11; see Isaiah 43:16–21; 51:9–11; Ezekiel 36:22–32). The 'pigeon' that fluttered aimlessly from one foreign power to another (7:11) will now become a *homing* pigeon, returning to its own land from exile, never to leave it again (v. 11).

'How can I give you up, Ephraim?' Just as it is inconceivable that God should not punish Israel, so it is unthinkable that he should destroy them for good. Despite Israel's rejection of its special obligations, it remains precious to God, not to be destroyed without trace as were 'Admah' and 'Zeboyim'—probably alternative names for Sodom and Gomorrah (see Deuteronomy 29:23).

'I am God, and not man'. It is characteristic of the Old Testament that this warm compassion, which leads God to think better of his plan for Israel's total destruction, is what marks him out as 'God, not man'. God is greater than man, in this perspective, not because he is more powerful and implacable, but because he is endlessly merciful. His patience is tried to the utmost, and if he were human it would snap, as it seems virtually to have done in chapter 10. Because he is God, he has reserves of love left even in the most extreme case.

The Old Testament does not reach an understanding of God by visualizing a human being and then removing all the features that make such a being human—anger and compassion, hatred and love. Instead it insists that all these characteristics exist in God in a heightened form; and if it has to insist on one as more ultimate than the others, it is God's love and mercy that remain. Both Jews and Christians have emphasized the 'changelessness' of God, but sometimes this has been at the expense of what we have called his 'aliveness'. For the Old Testament, God's changelessness means that he never ceases to be responsive in mercy to the need of his people, however undeserving they may be: 'I am the Lord, I do not change; therefore you, O sons of Jacob, are not consumed' (Malachi 3:6, RSV).

'Practise loyalty and justice, and wait upon God' *Hosea 11:12—13:3*

Most of the major themes of Hosea appear in this section, including both the harsh message of coming judgment (e.g. in 12:2 and 12:14) and the promise of undeserved mercy (e.g. in 12:9). But it is impossible to find any sequence of thought, and it seems likely that the section is simply an anthology of various oracles, perhaps from different times in Hosea's prophetic career.

The lesson of history. In one of the very few reterences to a story in Genesis to be found in the prophets, Hosea recalls Jacob's struggle with his twin, Esau (Genesis 25:26) and his wrestling-bout with the angel at Penuel (Genesis 32:22–32)—apparently regarding both as examples of the sin that goes back to the very first existence of 'Israel' (the new name given to Jacob by the angel). Yet Jacob is also an example of the unfailing mercy of God (12:4), who listens with favour to those who repent as he did to Jacob at Bethel (Genesis 28:10–22). The same implication is perhaps behind the reference to Moses ('a prophet', 12:13), who manifested God's care for his people by preserving them from destruction at the hands of Pharaoh.

'O death, where is your sting?' *Hosea 13:4–16*

When St Paul quoted Hosea 13:14 in 1 Corinthians 15:54–55, he took it as a rhetorical question: 'Where is your terror now, O death? It is destroyed.' But it is virtually certain that the prophet meant us to imagine death and Sheol (the underworld) as executioners, whom God calls on to carry out their appointed task and to fulfil the vow he makes in the second part of the verse: 'I will put compassion out of my sight.' If we thought that we had reached safety in 11:8–11, we were mistaken, and this oracle takes us back to Hosea's most violent threats of disaster, as in 5:14. There are few more savage predictions in the prophets than 13:7–8, where God changes his shape from panther to leopard to she-bear to lioness, and rips open the living body of his people. Nor is this merely vivid imagery. Hosea 13:16 reflects only too accurately the atrocities Israel could expect at the hands of the Assyrians, who to the prophet will be God's *own instrument* of punishment (compare Amos 1:13, RSV; 2 Kings 8:12; 15:16).

There is really no way of telling whether this terrifying oracle represents a foreboding which Hosea later modified, or whether, even after he was convinced that God would eventually restore Israel, he still saw the dreadful destruction predicted here as a necessary prelude to the restoration. But we have already seen plenty to convince us that Hosea was far from hopeful about the immediate future, and on the whole it seems likely that he really did expect the carnage spoken of in these verses. Though it can have been small comfort to him, he was proved right: Samaria was sacked, no doubt with every ounce of the brutality of which Assyrian kings regularly boasted in their official propaganda. The 'store of costly treasures' (13:15) seized from Samaria has been rediscovered by archaeologists excavating the Assyrian city of Nimrud, on the Tigris; it included many expensive ivory ornaments (see Amos 3:15; 6:4), some of them now to be seen in the British Museum's Assyrian galleries.

'I will be as dew to Israel' *Hosea 14:1–9*

Hosea's last word about God's plans for Israel—if this last chapter is really the last word—returns to the theme of God's enduring love. It looks forward to a time when Israel will not only be freed from the threat of destruction, but will in fact do nothing that would merit punishment: neither foolish political intrigues nor the worship of gods they have 'made with their own hands' (v. 3). This vision of a restoration that actually eliminates the tendency to sin, and hence makes it impossible that the need for punishment should ever recur, is a familiar theme in later prophets: see Jeremiah 31:31–34 and Ezekiel 36:26–27. It is possible that this chapter has been added to Hosea's words, to form a 'happy ending', by an editor of the book who had come under the influence of such ideas, perhaps during or soon after the exile of the sixth century (two hundred years after Hosea's own time). Even if this is so, however, it develops a theme which we have seen to be firmly grounded in the prophet's message: the theme of restoration beyond judgment, and of God's inability finally to cast off his own people.

The images for restoration are completely appropriate to the context, for fertility is once again the theme. This time it is not the fertility wrongly attributed to the gods of Canaan, nor the parody of fertility represented by the weeds growing up to cover the places where Israel had abandoned its God, but the fertility that God himself causes and blesses: the fruitfulness of a garden or an orchard, filled with fruit trees and fragrant flowers (vv. 5–6). The language is reminiscent of Isaiah 55:6–13, where again the restored plants and trees symbolize the healthy relationship between God and the people, now returning to their own land, and the assurance that God's promise comes to fruition as surely as seeds germinate in the soil.

A word to the wise. The book ends with a verse (14:9) which is surely the reflection of an early reader, added as a kind of 'blurb' to encourage others to profit from Hosea's words. It suggests a 'moral': God's commands are a clear and reliable guide to how one should live ('the Lord's ways are straight'), and he will reward those who keep them but punish those who do not. On one level, this certainly is implied or assumed by Hosea. But by now it should be clear that there is something a little 'tame' about such a way of looking at this explosive book, whose promises and threats are alike more dramatic than this rather bland footnote might lead one to expect. It shows, however, that in ancient times readers were already doing what we still do today: reflecting on the ancient prophet's words, and trying to make them fruitful in a situation different from that in which they were uttered, yet alike in being in the hands of the one God who seeks his people's good.

JOEL

Joel is one of the prophetic books, but what a strange prophecy it is! Almost nothing is known about Joel, when he lived or what his background and circumstances were. He quotes other prophets yet differs from them strikingly. Some scholars suggest that the book in its present form has more than one author. To know this is more help than hindrance because it helps to read the chapters as part of a lament, that is as a liturgy which is timeless.

Joel is written in the form of a national lament like some of the Psalms. Laments are cries to God for deliverance from calamities usually judged to be undeserved. They are not just moans. The cries of woe are made in the faith that God will hear and will save. In this case, he does. The book tells us how disasters can lead to redemption and restoration via the cries, protests and appeals of a stricken people. It moves from bad news to good news and in this it is like most of the other prophets—indeed like most of the Bible. It is a journey from darkness to light—from cross through a cry of dereliction, to resurrection.

Written after Amos and Micah (some time between the late sixth and early fourth centuries BC), it is placed before them as a kind of preface. The particular disasters referred to are varied and the imagery used to describe them extremely rich. Based, no doubt, on specific historical experiences, it is not limited to any one of them. Like the rest of Scripture, it is rooted in the particular but speaks to all times and beyond time. Conscious that it has been speaking hopefully for over 2,000 years, we shall try to hear what it says to our time.

In our society today we are not encouraged to lament. We admire the stiff upper lip! But Scripture gives a high profile to lament. It may be that journalism, television, rock music or feminist literature which, at first, distress or even appal, are hidden laments and in our chaotic and suffering age should be received as such.

The notes are based on the Revised Standard Version.

Further reading

G.S. Ogden and R.R. Deutsch, *Joel and Malachi*, International Theological Commentary, 1987

For more detailed study:

H.W. Wolff, *Joel and Amos*, Hermeneia, Fortress Press, 1977

A word for all seasons *Joel 1:1–4*

The whole book is 'the word of the Lord' and not only the parts directly attributed to him. This solves a lot of problems for the reader because it provides the book with unity and authority even if it was written at different times by different people, as it may well have been. We are told the name of Joel's father (a most unusual name) and nothing more. This almost mocking silence both challenges our 'scholarship' and warns us that the book of Joel is not cocooned in a distant time warp but is a word for all sorts and conditions of people, and for all seasons.

The word is first to the elders, as custodians of the tradition and the tribal memory. But the word must not stop there. The senior citizens have responsibility for instructing succeeding generations. This is a momentous word; a word about God and nations, about good and bad, about past, present and future. It is a family matter that extends to the whole family of nations because it is concerned with the family of God.

This religious education which begins in the home is not just a Bible story and a prayer detached from real life and designed for the innocent young and the credulous aged. It starts with the worst possible worldly bad news that affects everyone. There has been an economic disaster of unimaginable proportions. This total economic collapse is described with images far more powerful than feverish stock exchanges and soaring inflation; the locusts have passed over. The extent of the devastation is heightened by four different words being used for locusts. The words may refer to different species but, more likely, they describe the locust at various stages of its development. Either way the result is a picture of complete and continuous destruction. Later the picture of disaster and horror will be magnified by the use of other images, of wild animals, of warfare, of drought and fire. This poses two questions. The first asks whether we are dealing with a series of distinct disasters, or what might be better described as a sea of troubles. I shall opt for the latter and think of Disaster with a capital D: the Disaster which always threatens. The second question is concerned with the confusion resulting from 'all these mixed metaphors'. Try to do what one writer suggests the Old Testament writers did. They used images but didn't visualize them. They were verbal and each one could be 'sucked dry' without remainder, leaving the mental field completely free for the next.

You must lament *Joel 1:5–14*

There are five divisions in this section (vv. 5–7, 8–10, 11–12, 13, 14), and each one begins with an imperative. In the first four divisions the commands are followed by the reasons why the nation should be told to 'awake', 'lament', 'be confounded' and 'gird on sackcloth and lament'. The final verse (v. 14) is all imperative: they must 'Sanctify a fast . . . Gather the elders . . . Cry to the Lord.' With great urgency and with good cause, Judah is called upon to lament and they must do it publicly and ritually. But isn't there something missing? Isn't the prophet doing less than his duty? Where is the blame and the scathing indictment? Even the drinkers are not criticized for drinking; only warned that the drink will run out. Wasn't Joel 'against sin'? Didn't he want contrition and repentance? Maybe he had read Isaiah 40:2 and believed that Judah was already forgiven. Or do we assume that he would have replied that a lament is a lament and not a mission meeting? Perhaps there is truth in both suggestions, but deeper truth lies in two other directions.

God is a saving and rescuing God. This is his nature, and Scripture records that he saves and rescues in many varied ways. There is, however, what appears to be a classical pattern of rescue, and within the pattern God responds savingly to the victim's cry for help, asking for nothing more, only a cry. From Israel's woeful cries in bondage which resulted in the exodus, to the despairing cry, 'Why hast thou forsaken me' which leads to the resurrection, the Bible abounds in examples of this pattern. The lament almost seems to be a necessary and constituent part of salvation. It does not save us but as free creatures God will not force salvation upon us. We must cooperate even if it is only to howl in pain.

Such a pattern in no way belittles the need for remorse, confession and repentance. The 'lament' pattern is not the whole story but it is a most significant and necessary part of the great whole. And it is a wonderfully reassuring part, because sometimes all we can do is shout 'Help!' The drowning man needs first to be pulled out of the water. Time enough later to ask whether he had slipped or been pushed.

More often than we care to admit, as communities we are completely at a loss and don't know where to turn. As individuals or families we sometimes reach the end of our tether and are *in extremis*. At such times 'out of the depths we cry', for the simple reason that there is nothing else we can do. Joel encourages us to do precisely this. The Lord is waiting to hear and to save.

The public lament *Joel 1:15–18*

The call to lament has been answered and both rulers and people are assembled. First they lament their present condition which is described in some detail in verses 16–18. Then they relate the present suffering of 'today' to an even greater disaster of which 'today' is only the herald: the judgment of the 'day of the Lord'. This is near at hand and is seen as destruction unmistakably caused by God.

What is the day of the Lord? Amos had told Israel that it was darkness and not light (Amos 5:20). The Book of Joel (2:18–32) tells Judah that for them it is comfort and not the destruction they obviously expected (in 1:15). So what is it? Can't these prophets make anything straightforward? The day of the Lord is when God acts decisively, openly and victoriously, when justice triumphs and the good and the bad, the faithful and the unfaithful all get their just deserts. So, for some it is light and comfort, for others it is darkness and destruction. For the oppressor it wounds and kills, for the oppressed it severs the bonds of enslavement.

Harder to accept than a God of surprises and apparent contradictions is the belief that the good God can be the cause of disaster and destruction. Can a loving Father harm his children? Can a concerned Creator destroy what he had made? The answer is 'yes', when the children corrupt or reject the love which the family relies on and exists for, and when the creatures repudiate the purposes that give creation its meaning. The two-edged word of God which we find in Scripture never allows us easy answers but it does give us some help. It assumes that if trouble comes from God then at least it isn't coming from other gods who have defeated the true God. God is still in charge. Then, of course, much of the trouble is our fault, the result of human sin and rebellion, not God's unconcern. And the God who wounds is the best one to heal the wound. Someone in one of Hitler's prisons said, 'No one who has not known God as enemy can ever know him as friend.' A hard saying, but one to which millions inside the Bible and outside can say 'Amen'.

The Day of the Lord

In much of human experience it seems that things are not as they should be. Ruthless people seem free to create havoc and the very forces of Nature conspire against our happiness. If only there would come a time when the goodness and the beauty and the love which we have known fleetingly would rise up victorious, a time when God would mightily make all things well!

The people of the Old Testament longed for such a turn of events, which they called yom Yahweh, 'the day of the Lord'. Several of the prophetic books depict it vividly, and it will have been in mind also in most of their announcements of a great change to come. It was especially at the chief pilgrimage festival of New Year and Tabernacles that the 'day of the Lord' was spoken of. Perhaps this was because great 'days' of salvation in the origins of the people were then being recalled. Or perhaps it was because on the high day of the festival the Lord was proclaimed as having now come into the midst, showing anew his sovereign power, deciding fates, putting things to rights—this climax in the annual round of worship was then like a foretaste of the full 'day of the Lord'.

At all events, it is in the midst of a great festival, about 750BC, that the earliest known episode concerning the day of the Lord takes place (Amos 5:18–24). The worshippers are massed in rows in the temple courts. Sacrifices are offered up. Psalms of prayer and praise are sent up to God with the sound of harps. And in the prayer is a longing for the day of the Lord, when God will say again, 'Let there be light!'

But our heart easily takes a false road, wanting the pleasures of salvation without having first been cleansed and redirected in the ways of God. So Amos denounces the people in that assembly, for they have not repented of their ruthless and corrupt ways. For them the day will be thick darkness—retribution rather than salvation.

In the following century, about 630BC, the pilgrimage assembly heard another presentation of the day of the Lord. The words of the prophet Zephaniah are preserved in three well-constructed chapters, something like a drama, an awesome vision of the day's different aspects. Rushing in rapidly with all the terrors of war, fire and smoke, the day will consume all the corrupt world (Zephaniah 1). The Lord will conquer all that oppose him—but here a positive purpose is glimpsed, and hope is offered to the truly humble (2:1—3:8). And the day of the Lord will achieve a perfect world, the humble remnant growing into a new people beloved of God their king (3:9–20).

Other prophets give a similar message (see Isaiah 2:12–23; Joel 1:15; 2:1, 11, 31; 3:14; Malachi 4). The early Christians were also alerted to a decisive day (Romans 2:5–16; 1 Corinthians 3:13; 2 Corinthians 1:14; 1 Thessalonians 5:4). Our world is still urgently confronted by the day of the Lord—the definite certainty that God will sweep away all that has usurped his rule, and he will become all in all. Even now there are 'multitudes, multitudes in the valley of decision' (Joel 3:14).

J.H. Eaton

In what way does Joel prepare us for the cross?

Is Joel 'Scripture' for you in the same way that John's Gospel is? When was God last your 'enemy'? In what ways did you learn more of his love from his enmity?

The private lament *Joel 1:19–20*

The public lament is all in the plural. There now follows a lament in the singular which takes up some of the themes from the public ritual, but introduces the image of fire to supplement the earlier descriptions. In this are words about unity and cohesion which can be addressed to our fractured and divided culture.

The public worship leads to the personal worship. The public needs the private and the private is fed by the public. There are similar themes in verses 19–20, but a new image. The public and private are continuous but different. They complement and complete each other. They are not two, but one.

Both in the public and private there is concern for the animals. The economic disaster and consequent famine are just as much a tragedy for the beasts as for the people. Land, wine, grain, oil, cattle and people are all bound together in the burden of life. They are not many, but one. And they are not only one in the more obvious physical and material senses, there is even the wonderful suggestion that the harmony extends to the moral and beyond the moral to the spiritual. The moral element is there in the sympathy shown for the animals and in the way human perplexities and dismay are attributed to them. The spiritual oneness is present in verse 20 where the wild beasts are included in the lament. Joel gives us a wonderful vision of the unity of all creation. Each part has its given role but each role is essential to the greater whole. But what is the greater whole? It is something different from our ecological ideals, our environmental objectives; the true oneness envisioned here only exists because all creation is united in turning to the Creator in lament and worship. Creation is only one because it is one with the true God.

And who is the 'I' in this private lament? Presumably it is the prophet Joel. Joel has heard God's word. Faithfully he has delivered the message to the nation, convened the assembly and joined in public prayer. Now he is just a layman, one of the people crying with the rest. Does he give us a pattern for ministry—both lay and ordained? His calling distinguishes him from others but does not separate him. He is one with God, one with his vocation, but at the same time one with the nation in its suffering and lamenting, and one lonely individual before God with his private grief.

The prophet as watchman *Joel 2:1–11*

Private grief set aside, Joel returns to the prophet's role as watchman: a one-man intelligence service with infallible intelligence direct from the supreme HQ. Terrifying danger is at hand, the alarm must be sounded and the nation warned to prepare. The imminent threat is described in minute if contradictory detail. It is darkness, cloud and gloom. It is fire, cavalry, chariotry, infantry. It is earthquake and thunder. But what is 'it'? Is it locusts, foreign troops or natural disaster? If locusts, are they the same ones as in chapter 1? If foreign troops, whose are they and what is the date of the invasion? All these are good questions but not important, because 'it' is God and 'it' is the day of the Lord.

We modern Christians don't like Joel chapter 2. We rejoice in verses 28–29 of course, but we choose to ignore or marginalize the rest, often with pious rationalization. It has the flavour of an old-style revival meeting! We don't like it at all. For us 'God is love' (as he is—but the Bible only says it once), Jesus is gentle (as he is—on rare occasions), and we have no place for threat, intimidation or fear. Such things are outmoded and out of place, inappropriate in a civilized society.

Joel, like most of our forefathers, thought differently and thought correctly. He saw a place for warning, alarm, dread and fear in religion, as we do everywhere else but in church. We expect our national intelligence services to give us due warning of danger, to know what threatens and to sound the alarm so that the nation can prepare to meet it when it comes. When we are choosing a new car, one of the deciding factors is safety because we fear an accident. We have all been warned, we are very alarmed (at least I am) and we take precautions to avoid the dread threat. What we readily accept in 'real life' but shun in our religious life, is present everywhere for Joel, because for him life is one whole and his faith the most 'real' part of it. He knew very well that it was a terrible thing to fall into the hands of the living God (Hebrews 10:31), but he also knew that it was a good deal more terrible to fall out of God's hands. Do we fear the fear of God because we no longer fear the loss of God? If God is really God, and our faith is really what we say it is, then the loss of God is the worst possible thing that can happen to us, and the threats and fears, though perhaps a second or third best, have their place. A most valuable place.

Turn again Judah *Joel 2:12–17*

The writers of history in the Old Testament speak to their own day out of the past; prophets speak to their day by pointing to the future. In verses 1–11 Joel has described what can soon happen, now the 'sermon' turns to the present with a plea for Judah to return. As Joel doesn't stress Judah's 'sin', 'return' doesn't include all that is meant by repentance. Indeed, it is God who might 'repent' or 'relent'. 'Return' stresses two things. First, they belong to God; they are being called home. To be with God is their natural habitat.

Second, in order to return they must turn. They are going in the wrong direction. What is involved in this about-face?

For Judah it must be a wholehearted change, with all the pain of bereavement and mourning as they break with the past, but the mourning is not to be external; it must be heart-rending. It must be done by the whole community, men and women, young and old, high and low, lay and ordained. This is total mobilization for prayer. The demand is not just addressed to the 'religious'. For Joel the word has no meaning. In the Bible, all are 'religious'; but not all worship at the same shrine. Most pray to idols. Joel's God is not just a churchgoer's God. He is God of all people, all creatures and all activity. All Judah must turn to this all-embracing God. Judah's return also means much for God, and throughout the passage there are hints (fully justified by later events) that when Judah turns, God turns. Divine strategy is unchanging but divine tactics are new every morning in response to human need. A repenting Judah finds a relenting God. He turns from anger and the need to punish to the delight of showing mercy and love. Judah hasn't earned such treatment, it flows from God's grace and is done out of faithfulness to his own nature as a God of love who rejoices in rescue. Judah is bidden to return in the hope that they will find a turning God: a Father of all who, when they were still far off, would meet them and bring them home. Judah is almost promised that 'the clouds they so much dread are big with mercy and will break in blessing on their head'.

- *Is the meaning of Joel modified (deepened, heightened, extended, reduced, expanded or contradicted) for you when set in the context of the whole of the Bible?*
- *List as many times as you can recall when the clouds you had so much dreaded broke, with mercy on your head.*

Now God turns *Joel 2:18–20*

Judah has lamented and turned to God. Now God responds, and he responds at the point of that final taunt in verse 17: 'Where is their God?' Why just here? Two clues to an answer lie in the pronoun 'their'. First, Judah was God's special possession. (Hosea had said that

God and his people were married.) They were identified with God. They were his responsibility. In their suffering God suffered. The second clue is that 'their' God was invisible. You didn't have to look for the gods of the nations—they were very visible. Idols could be seen and touched. The whereabouts of deity was a question peculiar to the God of Judah. He was known only through his deeds and not through the human senses of sight and touch. A defeated and distressed Judah implied a powerless and diminished God. Perhaps a non-existent God.

The powerful pronouns continue in verses 18–19. God is jealous for his land, and has pity on his people. The inseparability of God and his people is stressed time and again. He abides in them and they abide in him. In consequence, he 'saves' them. He restores their shattered economy, he feeds them, he removes their reproach and overturns their enemies. The invisible God triumphs over the ravaging forces of both nature and the nations. All things shall be well. All manner of things shall be well.

Can we today respond to this change of 'fortune' with 'Amen' and 'Praise the Lord'? I hope we can—but first we must look at some questions. What about God's jealousy? What about the special relationship with one tribe? And wasn't God saving his own face as well as Judah's?

First, the jealousy is partly 'zeal' or 'enthusiastic protection as promised' or 'covenant-keeping'. But also it really is jealousy, the kind of jealousy that is not out of place at all. To be jealous of something not your own, like your neighbour's wife or his Jaguar, is a deadly sin like envy. To be jealous over something or someone bound to you by mutual love and promise like your wife or husband is absolutely right and proper. God's jealousy over Judah was consummate affection. It was active faithfulness and a source of peace and comfort to Judah. The same 'jealousy' is now the inheritance of all who call upon the Father in the name of the Son.

The outcome for Judah *Joel 2:21–27*

For many Christians, 'salvation' means going to heaven when you die. That is part of the meaning, but salvation is also much more. It is earthly as well as heavenly. For Joel it is loss of fear, it is gladness and rejoicing, an unthreatened and green environment, plentiful harvest, clement weather, adequate food, assured security and the one, true, only rescuing God, always at hand to rescue when needed. Salvation includes the worldly and the unworldly, the physical and the spiritual, the personal and the social. The Lord of all promises the renewal of all he has created.

All? Really all? Now we are back with our questions. Why the blatant favouritism shown to the tribe of Judah? 'How odd of God to choose the Jews!' Odd, but not crazy. Look at the account of God's choosing in Exodus 19:5–6. The special relationship between God and his people was because 'all the earth is mine'. Israel was called to priesthood and holiness on behalf of all creation. They were chosen as representatives of mankind and also as agents of God. They were called to be the first missionaries, sent as God's servants. And let us never forget their history as suffering servants, the forerunners of the Israelite in whom there was no guile; the gloriously supreme 'oddity', the chosen High Priest who was also the sacrifice but who now intercedes for us and who is superbly jealous for all in distress who lament and turn to him in prayer.

There is still the problem of God 'saving his face' and being concerned for his reputation. A problem for us but not for Joel or for the Bible in general. Read verse 27. The Lord is God 'and there is none else'. Joel, unlike ourselves, didn't think of a variety of competing religions. He had no philosophy that gave him concepts of truth and justice. He had no independent ethics with a supermarket of 'values', no free-floating human rights, no ideological utopias. Only God 'and none else', and you either worshipped him or you committed your life to some falsity of your own making. A stark choice: God or yourself. This meant that God's 'face' or 'reputation' was everything that was good and true. It was righteousness and love, it was justice and severity, faithfulness and nobility, beauty, honour, virtue, hope. It was light and guidance in this world and the companion when you walked through the valley of the shadow of death. It was not (and is not) a theological problem. It is the be all and end all of what life is all about.

The day of the Lord: good news *Joel 2:28–32*

God's word in the mouth of the prophet is still God's word. It is given to do God's work, not the prophet's. Isaiah 55:10–11 tells us that God sends the word, that it does not return empty, but accomplishes what God purposes. Joel's words are greater than he knew. He himself built upon Ezekiel 39:25–29 and on much else that had gone before. In turn

Acts 2:16–18, Romans 10:13 and much else that followed, build upon Joel. Joel's 'day of the Lord' is but one link in the great chain of understanding that joins us to the Word which became flesh and dwelt among us. These few verses need all Scripture for their explanation.

They speak of God's Spirit and therefore of his creative power (Genesis 1:2). They speak of prophecy, of dreams, of visions, of portents. They are therefore speaking of communication. God had never stopped communicating, but for some time it had been in the language of disaster and calamity. The great reversal brings a new language which begins to interpret the disasters and calamities and to tell of deliverance, escape and survival. The coming Spirit is not only creator and communicator. He is also the energizer, and the enabler who prepares men and women for God's service (Exodus 35:31; Judges 3:10). And look who he prepares. He comes to all flesh, and in case that is not clear enough the meaning is spelt out: it means that sons and daughters shall prophesy, old men shall dream (not only pipe dreams), and young men become visionaries. What a lay movement is envisaged (it even includes downstairs: the manservants and maidservants) and what a mission! The work is not restricted to the clergy or to the tiny minority in the missionary society. All are to share in spreading the good news that all who call upon the name of the Lord shall be delivered.

The missionary call and hope of deliverance are in a setting that includes blood, fire, smoke and darkness, all of which echo Judah's recent calamities as well as giving warning that the future holds not only good news but bad. This is not a contradiction. It is, in a nutshell, what the whole book and the whole Bible is about, namely that to the eye of faith, and with the help of the Holy Spirit, bad news is never the last word; it is mysteriously the herald of hope. Locusts, starvation and mayhem in Joel lead via lament to deliverance, peace and plenty. War tells of peace, crisis of salvation, destruction of prosperity. These verses, indeed the whole of Joel and the whole Bible, can be seen as commentaries on that supreme day of the Lord when God was crucified but which we call 'Good Friday'.

The day of the Lord: bad news *Joel 3:1–8*

All the major prophets and some of the 'minor' prophets prophesy against 'the nations'. Whether they had one clear reason for making these prophecies is uncertain. What is certain is the relevance of some of the constituent themes to our and every age. And what is equally certain is that we nowadays are culturally 'programmed' to resist their relevance. One task of the commentator, therefore, is to 'deprogramme' and then 'reprogramme'.

First, compare Joel chapter 3 with Matthew 25:31–46. Both tell of the day of the Lord's judgment when all the nations are present. Both tell of the day of reversal, of both good news and bad news, of just deserts, division and punishment. In both great numbers of the nations are made to suffer while God's people are greatly blessed. In the case of Joel we moderns are conditioned to hear little of worth. At the same time, parts of the Matthew excerpt have been made very popular by dint of selectivity and misreading. 'These my brethren' are of course the disciples. The nations are judged according to how they have treated the 'Church'. More or less exactly the same as in Joel. And, moreover, the punishment, often ignored, is harsher than Joel's because it is eternal.

Secondly, talk of 'paying back', retribution and just deserts does actually find a response in many of our own expectations if we look for it. We want the detective to find 'who done it'. We want the terrorist to be caught and punished, the child abuser himself to suffer, the rapist prevented from further rape. We are convinced that the oppressed should have their fortunes restored and the oppressors be made to pay. The cruel and callous should not be allowed to 'get away with it' and the perpetrators of all holocausts should be brought to book. Joel faced with the rape of Judah, child abuse, 'White' slavery and much else, presents the valley of Jehoshaphat (the Lord's judgment) as a source of hope and assurance. He faces a dispirited people and counters their despair with Churchillian confidence. He stirs up souls sunk into fatalism not with a mumbled 'pious' hope that all will come out in the wash, but with ringing declarations that right will triumph over wrong, that justice will have the last word. That the terrorist, the oppressor, the slave-trader and the despot will stand before the judge of all the world. This is beyond doubt because God is king of all the world. Therefore lift up your heads.

Does Joel help you better to understand Matthew 25:31–46?

Can you discern in your own 'bad news' the 'softening gleam' of good news?

Attention still centres on the ambiguous 'day of the Lord'. The day of decision and judgment approaches and the Lord summons the nations to attend. He is now the Supreme Commander of their forces, mobilizing their armies, strengthening their resolution and preparing their weapons, weapons which eventually will be turned against themselves. Ambiguity is everywhere (especially in verse 13), but in verses 14–15 all changes. Ambiguity has vanished. Once the nations are assembled in the valley, it becomes courtroom and execution chamber. The day of decision and judgment, division and separation has come.

So what do we have? An undercover God rejoicing in deception? Grossly unfair treatment of unsuspecting foreigners? Racism? Anti-anti-Semitism carried to extremes? First, we have 'mystery', which is different from a problem. Problems are for worrying about and maybe for solving. Real mystery, this Mystery, is our Reality, our Source and our God. This Mystery is the Way, the Truth and the Life (John 14:6), not a question. Secondly, we are shown God whom we already know as Lord of 'nature' and harvests, equally as Lord of history and the nations and their destinies. Moreover, this God is also Lord of justice and morality. And these are not isolated from nature and history but are bound with them in an indissoluble whole. In Joel's world there are no 'no-go' areas, no independent enclaves, no walled gardens. The word 'autonomy' doesn't exist. The Lord is God, Lord of all 'and ever more shall be so'.

God, who appears to be inconsistent, is, of course, the ultimate consistency, the real harmony. Why then the apparent racism, injustice and favouritism? Part of the answer is that, in dealing with our inconsistencies and sinful two-facedness, he is compelled sometimes to reflect it. In charge of everything, he finds himself responsible for hosts of warring factions.

Identified with the whole, he has at varying times and places to make special identifications. He must side with the good against the bad, with the kind against the cruel, with the oppressed against the oppressor, at the same time knowing that today's oppressed may be tomorrow's oppressors.

So, much of the ambiguity is in us. But not all. Some of it is because God knows how it will all end: in a cross where the ultimate ambiguity, the God-man, becomes sin and dies that sinners may have life. In a cross which also is the crucifixion of oppression, racism, rebellion, contradiction and all ambiguity and which promises the ultimate reversal of them and the enthronement of all their opposites.

All's well that ends well *Joel 3:16–21*

The book ends as a good prophecy should, with hope and promise. It can do this because the prophet is enabled to see the ultimate triumph of good somehow present even in the midst of disaster. He stands at the same time both in today and in that glorious secure tomorrow when the Lion's roar (Aslan's?) tells of assurance and peace. It comes with a fourfold message:

1. What strikes terror in the predator's heart is comfort to the cubs. God is Judah's refuge; God is a safe stronghold (v. 16).

2. All that has happened and is happening is somehow making known the good news that Judah's Lord is the one, true, universal, all-powerful Creator and Saviour. And that despite all appearances, evangelism and mission are taking place. God is his own apostle and interpreter.

3. The mockers have asked where Judah's God was to be found (2:17). It was a rhetorical question because they were convinced, as our culture is convinced, that he couldn't be found because he didn't exist. God's response is to give his home address. It is Zion, Jerusalem, Judah; a state where entry visas are not given to mockers (3:17).

4. Fear and famine have gone with the locusts, never to return. God now promises perpetual provision. There will be food for the body (v. 18), security from enemies (v. 19) and a kind of earthly eternity. And all guaranteed by God's presence; 'for the Lord dwells in Zion'.

In our world today we know destruction, threat, famine, insecurity and fear. We have our locusts, and some of them have nuclear warheads. We have our mockers, and some of the mocking is institutionalized in the culture, some lurks in the Church, and much of it inhabits our own thoughts. At Pentecost it was Joel who spoke through the apostle Peter when the Church was born (Acts 2:17–21). Joel can still speak to that same Church. He still speaks of the Spirit which can fall on every part of the Church, making dreams and visions realities. He still speaks of the God who is at home in the Church, the ever-present omnipotence who is our refuge and strength. He still speaks of God the provider, the one who defines our needs and then meets them. He still speaks to a hesitant Church and he says he is still the apostle and interpreter and that the mission will go forward. And Joel still prophesies more than he himself could hear about the refuge, peace and provision that lie beyond this earth.

In what ways do the assumptions of modern society blind us to God's word in Joel?

AMOS

During the eighth century BC there began to emerge in ancient Israel a remarkable group of people, whom we call the Classical Prophets. Amos was the first to appear (in about 760BC), but he was soon followed by others, Hosea, Isaiah and Micah. Although a southerner from Judah, Amos went to work in the northern Hebrew kingdom, which was called Israel. His message shares much with the other three great prophets of his century, but it is distinctive in containing the most sustained statement of God's righteous judgment upon his own sinful people. This is the book of divine justice and judgment *par excellence*; indeed, this austere message is hardly ever softened by words of mercy and hope, such as one finds in Hosea. Prominent among the sins condemned by Amos are social injustice (e.g. 8:4–6) and corrupt worship (e.g. 5:21ff). Israel's God is about to act to punish them, above all through conquest by foreign armies (e.g. 9:4). As we read the Book of Amos today, we naturally tend to highlight its moral challenge and to read it in large part as a call to repentance and a better life. It is worth noting, however, that in its original setting the book may have a rather more negative emphasis; disaster was about to strike and Amos explained why—the book could be described as a kind of epitaph for a dead (or at least dying) nation, richly deserving its fate.

One of the most interesting recent developments in biblical studies has been the application of the insights of sociology and economics to the study of the prophets. This can help us understand better the roles performed by prophets in ancient Israel; thus Amos can be presented as a figure on the margins of society challenging the forces of establishment which hold power at the centre of that society. If this sounds little more than saying in new words what we have known for a long time, there are also real challenges to our assumptions. For example, it has often been taken for granted that the Israel of Amos' day was enjoying an economic boom; however, some now question this and suggest that it had long been in decline.

The Book of Amos was probably mostly written (either by Amos himself or by disciples) shortly after his prophecies were delivered, and it gives us insights into a vital period in the formation of biblical faith. Indeed, as scholars become less confident about the early dating of many other parts of the Old Testament (including the Law), the real possibility is emerging that Amos may be among the earliest Old Testament writings available to us.

There is only one really hopeful section in the book, namely the last five verses, which look to better times in the future (9:11–15). This has often been assumed to be a footnote added long after the time of Amos. However, whether this is so or not, it is important to acknowledge that the finished book, as it was known by Jesus and St Paul, included these final verses which must not lightly be ignored. The final form of the book witnesses to the mercy and grace as well as to the justice of God. The Book of Amos is short, a book that can easily be read at a sitting (a real attraction to many of us!). However, it should be noted that it now forms part of a larger collection, that of the twelve 'minor' prophets (minor in length, that is, not in value). The importance of this literary setting is increasingly recognized, and it is worth reflecting on this too as one reads the Book of Amos.

Amos addressed an urgent word to a specific situation at a particular point in time, and he worked a very long time ago. And yet for all this, his book can be a rich resource for Christian theological and ethical reflection today. The very fact that each of the Old Testament prophets addressed a particular human situation can actually prove to contribute to the power of their words, making them more rather than less relevant today. Lessons for our own very different situations cannot be read off in any simplistic way, but if we take the original settings seriously we shall again and again be surprised by the challenges which are posed to our assumptions and values.

Further reading

B.W. Anderson, *The Eighth-Century Prophets*, Fortress Press, Philadelphia, 1978/SPCK, 1979

A.G. Auld, *Amos*, Old Testament Guides, JSOT Press, Sheffield, 1986

R.B. Coote, *Amos Among the Prophets: Composition and Theology*, Fortress Press, Philadelphia, 1981

J.L. Mays, *Amos*, SCM Press/Westminster Press, Philadelphia, 1969

J.A. Soggin, *The Prophet Amos*, SCM Press, 1987

Amos' origins

Amos 1:1–2

These verses serve to introduce us to the prophet Amos and the book which bears his name. Amos is described as being 'among the shepherds of Tekoa'. Tekoa was a small town in rural Judah, the southern Hebrew kingdom; it was towards the wilderness, some miles south-east of Bethlehem. It appears that Amos was from a farming background. Here we read that he was 'among the shepherds', whilst later we are told that he was a 'herdsman and a dresser of sycamore trees' (7:14). After experiencing a call from Yahweh to go and prophesy, he went to the northern Hebrew kingdom, Israel, where he worked in the royal shrine of Bethel (see 7:10–17).

Date. We are told here that he worked during the reigns of Uzziah, king of Judah (c. 783–742BC) and Jeroboam (the Second), king of Israel (c. 786–746BC). These kings enjoyed long and, it would seem, relatively prosperous reigns, during the period when the shadow of the conquering Assyrian empire began to fall upon the small nations of the area. A more specific reference to time is given as well: 'two years before the earthquake'. This seems to indicate an earthquake which took place in about 760BC (mentioned also in Zechariah 14:5), and we are probably to understand that Amos' ministry began two years before the earthquake. In addition to being a time-marker, the reference to the earthquake may also be a symbol of judgment; indeed, earthquake imagery seems to be used in this way elsewhere in the book (see 8:8; 9:5). It is possible that one of the concerns which motivated the work of Amos as it developed was to explain the anger of God which the earthquake seemed to express.

'The words which Amos saw'. Verse 1 describes the book which follows as containing 'the words which Amos saw'. This is a strange phrase, since we normally hear rather than see words, but it is found occasionally elsewhere (e.g. Isaiah 2:1). It reflects the important place of visions in this book (see 7:1–9; 8:1–3; 9:1–4). The words of Amos are said to concern 'Israel'—this could mean just the northern kingdom, to which he travelled to prophesy, but, since the kings of both territories are mentioned here, 'Israel' may have its broader sense of the whole people of Yahweh, southern as well as northern.

The nations condemned *Amos 1:3—2:8*

The Book of Amos is, above all else, a book of judgment. This section establishes that theme; for here we find a long sequence of oracles against the nations of the region. Damascus was the capital of Syria or Aram, to the north-east of Israel. Gaza (like Ashdod, Ashkelon and Ekron) was a city of the Philistines, who dwelt on the coastal plain to the south-west (today's Gaza Strip), whilst Tyre was a great trading port of Phoenicia, the area we would call the Lebanon. Edom, Ammon and Moab were three territories to the east of Israel, in the region we know as Jordan.

Israel too! The really surprising thing is that the sequence culminates in an oracle against Israel in 2:6–8. We may imagine that Amos' hearers were lapping up his condemnations of all their traditional enemies, and would have been shocked when he turned his fire upon them. Amos seems to have been fond of taking a traditional form (here the oracle against a foreign nation) and turning it on its head. The sequence introduces a theme which is to characterize the book as a whole, namely that of 'universalism', the idea that Yahweh is God over all nations. For this section credits the nations with moral responsibility (it is implied that they should know better than to commit the crimes they have); what is more, by adding Israel to the list, Amos appears to discount the particular claims of Israel to special status (see below on 9:7).

Social injustice. 2:6–8 make it clear that judgment upon Israel is imminent. We encounter for the first time here the theme of social injustice, one of Amos' major concerns and one of the main reasons cited for the coming judgment. The theme is found elsewhere in Amos (4:1; 5:10–12, 24; 6:4–6; 8:4–6) and is shared with the other eighth-century prophets. Clearly, Amos regarded the oppression of the poor as one of the most flagrant of Israel's sins. It may be that Israel under Jeroboam II was enjoying an economic boom (a kind of 'Indian Summer' before the final collapse of the nation), which had led to an opening up of the gap between rich and poor. An alternative possibility, though, is that a general economic decline had already begun to affect Israel back in the early ninth century, and that the gulf between rich and poor condemned by Amos was the result not of recent prosperity but of a long-term decline which bore particularly upon the needy.

Yahweh's favour rebuffed *Amos 2:9—3:2*

In 2:9–11 the prophet lists various gracious acts which Yahweh had accomplished for Israel: destroying the Amorites (a name for the native inhabitants of Canaan), leading Israel out of Egypt in the exodus and through the wilderness to the Promised Land, and inspiring prophets and Nazirites (men who followed a life of rigorous austerity; see Numbers 6:1–21). All of this might have been expected to elicit loyalty from Israel, but, no, they had merely responded with ingratitude. (In 4:6–11 we are told that Yahweh had also tried using punishments to encourage repentance, but that ploy had been equally unsuccessful.) We read in verse 12 that the Israelites had made the prophets and the Nazirites deviate from their callings. And so in verses 13–16 judgment is declared, in words which seem to speak of warfare and invasion. Did Amos already have Assyrian invasion in mind? 760BC may seem rather early for this prospect to be clear to him, but the language of invasion and exile is found at many points in the book (e.g. 5:5, 27; 6:7–8; 9:4)

Privilege brings responsibility. In 3:2 we encounter a remarkable word of judgment, which is introduced by a formula of great foreboding ('Hear this word . . .'). 'You only have I known of all the families of the earth': the reference is to the traditional doctrine of Israel's particular election by God (which was traced back as far as the call of Abraham, and exemplified above all in the exodus, mentioned explicitly in verse 1). But Amos draws a novel conclusion: 'therefore I will punish you for all your iniquities'. As elsewhere (see the sequence of chapters 1–2, and also 9:7), he takes a traditional form and inverts it. Israel's privilege means not indulgence but special demands, greater responsibility.

'How far do we live up to our responsibilities, both within our local situations and within the world as a whole?

Common sense *Amos 3:3–15*

In 3:3–6 we encounter a sequence of rhetorical questions, based on features of the natural world. They are all questions to which common sense suggests the obvious answer 'no, of course not'. This section encourages us to think in terms of cause and effect, and of each event having a rational explanation. What is the precise point of the sequence in verses 3–6? The 'pay-off' seems to come in the second half of verse 6: 'Does evil befall a city, unless the Lord has done it?' The disaster of Assyrian conquest is not meaningless chaos or the work of Assyrian gods, but the purposeful work of Yahweh himself. Perhaps implicit also is the idea that sin automatically leads to punishment. The next two verses (vv. 7–8) add two further thoughts in a similar style, with the same appeal to common sense. Surely God does nothing without telling his prophets and surely the prophet must communicate the word of God once heard.

Destruction deserved. In 3:9–11 we find further explicit reference to invasion. The nations are called upon to come and witness Israel's sin. It is clear that Egypt is one of the nations involved here; the other is less clear. The Hebrew text refers to Ashdod, one of the Philistine cities, but many scholars prefer at this point to follow the ancient Greek translation of Amos, which has Assyria. Because of Israel's many sins, its enemies will bring down its defences.

Hardly anything will remain. In verse 12 there appears an image from Amos' own professional background. As a shepherd might rescue a few bits of a sheep from a marauding lion's mouth, so the fate of Israel will be so grim that only a small residue will remain. The idea here is surely negative; there is no suggestion that a significant remnant will survive. In verses 13–15 the threat of judgment is made more specific; altars will be destroyed. Here, as elsewhere, the themes of corrupt worship and social injustice are twinned (see below on 5:21–24).

The reward of self-indulgence *Amos 4:1–13*

'Hear this word, you cows of Bashan, who are in the mountains of Samaria.' Strong language indeed. Amos condemns the self-indulgent women of Samaria, capital city of the northern kingdom, Israel. Isaiah rebuked the women of Jerusalem in similar terms and at much the same time (see Isaiah 3:16—4:1). The women of Samaria will he taken away with hooks, like real cattle—an image perhaps for deportation. Harmon is difficult to identify; it may refer to Mount Hermon, to the north of Israel.

'Come to Bethel, and transgress'. In verses 4 and 5 Amos again parodies a form which would have been familiar to his audience, this time the call to worship. 'Come to Bethel . . . and transgress.' The heavy irony of this is underlined by the words 'for so you love to do, O people of Israel!' Bethel is mentioned several times in Amos (3:14; 5:5–6; 7:10). Gilgal, a site near Jericho important since the time of the settlement (see Joshua 4), occurs in Amos only here and in 5:5.

'Prepare to meet your God, O Israel!' Verses 6–11 list all the punishments which Yahweh has already imposed in the hope of bringing his people back to him. Over and over, the refrain is repeated 'yet you did not return to me'. We may contrast 2:9–11, in which his mighty acts of favour are reviewed. Verse 10 notes that the pestilence which Yahweh had sent upon Israel was 'after the manner of Egypt', which serves to confirm the impression that this whole section recalls the plagues upon Egypt in the Exodus story (compare Exodus 7–12). We find also an echo of the Sodom and Gomorrah narrative (v. 11; compare Genesis 19). And there is more punishment to come, as we read in the awe-inspiring words of verse 12. 'Prepare to meet your God, O Israel!'

The chapter closes with the first of three brief hymn-like sections which punctuate the book of Amos (v. 13; see 5:8–9; 9:5–6). After references to Yahweh's creative activity, the declaration is made: 'the Lord, the God of hosts, is his name!' These three sections underline the

God-centred emphasis of the book of Amos, in sharp contrast to the self-centred abuses of worship and social order which he condemns.

Lament for a nation

Amos 5:1–27

'Fallen, no more to rise, is the virgin Israel.' Amos' beautiful words express a grim reality, that of the end of a nation. As verse 3 makes clear, precious little will be left of Israel (see 3:12). In verses 4 and 5 Yahweh appeals to his people: 'Seek me and live.' Gone is the note of sarcasm which we found in 4:4–5; here we meet an impassioned and deadly serious plea, with explicit reference to the prospect of exile. To the shrines mentioned in 4:4–5 is added this time Beersheba, a site in the south of Judah particularly associated with Isaac (see Genesis 26:23–33).

The second of Amos' three hymn-like sections follows in verses 8 and 9; this time the nature of Israel's fate is spelled out: 'so that destruction comes upon the fortress'. Verses 10–12 remind us of the grounds for judgment. They are followed by an isolated verse (5:13) which may well be the comment of a scribe trained in the 'Wisdom' tradition: 'He who is prudent will keep silent in such a time.'

When is it appropriate to speak a word of outspoken criticism, and when is it better to hold the tongue?

'Seek good and not evil'. Verse 14 ('Seek good, and not evil, that you may live') picks up the words of 5:4. The fullness of life is to be found in right relationship with God. Verse 15 goes on to spell out the implications of this in ethical terms: 'establish justice in the gate'. The second half of the verse adds a hopeful note: 'it may be that the LORD . . . will be gracious to the remnant of Joseph' ('Joseph' here is another name for the northern kingdom, Israel). This reference to a remnant certainly seems more positive than anything we found in 3:12 or 5:3. We seem here to have a hint of reprieve as a reward for repentance: this is uncharacteristic of Amos, and could possibly be a later addition (see below on 9:8, 11–15).

'Darkness, and not light'. 'Woe to you who desire the day of the Lord! (v. 18)—yet again, Amos redefines a traditional term. The background of the idea of the day of the Lord is much debated; suffice it to say that it was generally thought to be something to which to look forward. Amos here combats such false optimism in no uncertain terms.

Corrupt worship condemned. Verses 21–27 deal with one of Amos' major themes, the criticism of corrupt worship. This is cited as another major ground for the coming judgment. We have already met the theme, more briefly, at 2:8 and 4:4–5. There has been much discussion as to whether Amos and his prophetic contemporaries favoured the total abolition of Israel's system of sacrificial worship or rather called simply for its radical reform. It sometimes seems that abuse of the system is being rejected rather than the system itself. However, verse 25 (which implies that, in spite of the stories told in the books of Moses, Israel did not bring Yahweh sacrifices and offerings in the wilderness) could suggest that Amos is writing off these practices altogether. Be this as it may, there is no doubt where his own priorities lie: 'let justice roll down like waters, and righteousness like an everflowing stream' (v. 24). It is striking to note how the charges of corrupt worship and social injustice are coupled in Amos, not only here but also in 2:6–8 (compare 3:13–15). The same is true of the other eighth-century prophets (see Isaiah 1:11–17; Hosea 6:6; Micah 6:6–8). It is almost as though the worst thing of all in the eyes of these prophets was that self-centred and self-satisfied worship should go hand-in-hand with neglect and oppression of one's neighbour.

Are there any parallels between the abuses of worship which Amos condemns and our own worship?

Arrogance and self-deception *Amos 6:1–14*

'Woe to those who are at ease.' The complacent leaders of the northern and southern kingdoms alike are judged. They foolishly imagine themselves to be in charge of the most important of nations. They make arrogant comparisons with other territories: Calneh and Hamath were city-states to the north of Israel, and Gath was one of the Philistine cities on the coastal strip to the south-west. Israel's leaders 'put far away the evil day'; it would seem that they are less keen to see the day of the Lord, now that Amos has made them see what it would involve (see 5:18–20).

Idle indifference. A second woe follows in verse 4. The declaration of 'woes' is typical of the classical prophets (see Amos 5:18; Isaiah 5:8ff). The picture of ease is now painted in more detail. The powerful lie on beds of ivory: examples of ivory inlays have been found by archaeologists in Samaria (see 3:15). Like David they perform to the accompaniment of instruments (see 1 Samuel 16:23). This is a strikingly negative image of the great king, and of course Amos was quite ready to criticize the contemporary monarch too (7:11; see also Hosea 8:4). The country is going to ruin and yet its leaders are not distressed about the fate of 'Joseph' (see on 5:15).

Fitting punishment. In verse 7 the punishment is made clear: exile lies ahead, with the rich and idle going first—a fitting case of poetic justice! In the following verse, Yahweh reaffirms this sentence with an oath. Judgment is to be thorough, as is spelled out in verse 9. In 5:3 we read that the city that went forth a hundred shall have ten left; now we learn that if ten are left, they shall die. This disaster is evidently Yahweh's doing: it brings such awe and fear that one dare not mention God's name any more (v. 10), lest further wrath be called down upon Israel.

Justice turned into poison. Verse 12 recalls the rhetorical questions of 3:3–8. Israel's sin is as contrary to common sense as riding horses on rocks or ploughing the sea with oxen. Lo-debar and Karnaim (v. 13) appear to be the names of places taken by Israel from the Syrians during a recent resurgence of power. However, each word also seems to contain a pun, for Lo Dabar would mean 'a thing of naught' and Karnaim means 'horns', a common image of strength. By their minor victories, the Israelites fancy that they have vindicated their own strength. But they have another thing coming: Yahweh will raise up a nation against them (presumably Assyria). Defeat will be total, for Hamath (6:2) and the Brook of the Arabah seem intended to mark the northern and southern extremities of Israelite territory.

Locusts and fire *Amos 7:1–9; 8:1–3*

We now encounter a cluster of visions, which fulfil the promise of the first verse of the book. 'The words of Amos . . . which he *saw* concerning Israel.' It is surely significant that these visions of judgment frame the important narrative section (7:10–17) which we shall consider next. In Amos 7:1–6 we find two visions of judgment—the plague of locusts and the consuming fire. In response to each, Amos protests on behalf of Israel, 'O Lord God, forgive, I beseech thee! How can Jacob stand? He is so small!' Amos appears to feel a duty to intercede for his people: and indeed in each of these two cases Yahweh relents.

True judgment. However, with the third vision, that of the plumb-line (7:7–9), the pressure upon Israel is increased. Yahweh himself stands beside a wall, holding a plumb-line, a length of string with a weight on the end, used by builders as a way of checking that walls are straight and true. In this case, there is no appeal against the judgment of God and no relenting. 'I will rise against the house of Jeroboam with the sword', declares Yahweh. Jeroboam was a doubly significant name: not only was it the name of the contemporary king of the north, but also of the first ruler of that kingdom when it broke away from Judah after the death of Solomon (in about 920BC; see 1 Kings 12). The fourth vision (8:1–3), coming after the narrative passage, is again one of unrelieved judgment. The prophet sees a basket of summer fruit. The point of this depends on a pun in the original Hebrew, for the word for 'summer fruit' (*qayits*) sounds very like the word for 'end' (*qets*). 'The end has come upon my people Israel'; the fearful day of the Lord has arrived (see 5:18–20).

We may admire Amos' moral challenge, but can we today really believe in a God who creates wars and natural disasters to punish people? And if Assyrian invasion and earthquakes seem remote for many of us, how about the nuclear threat or Aids? Is God active in these?

A call to prophesy

Amos 7:10–17

This passage contains the closest thing we have in Amos to a call narrative. If it seems odd that it is not found at the start of the book (the obvious place, one might think; e.g. Jeremiah 1; Ezekiel 1–3), there is at least some kind of a parallel in Isaiah, whose call is recounted some chapters after the start of the book (Isaiah 6).

'I am no prophet'. Amos is active at the northern shrine of Bethel. He has declared that 'Jeroboam shall die by the sword, and Israel must go into exile away from his land' (v. 11). This provokes the charge that Amos has conspired against the king. In response to this, Amos comes out with the remarkable words: 'I am no prophet, nor a prophet's son; but I am a herdsman and a dresser of sycamore trees, and the Lord took me from following the flock and the Lord said to me, "Go, prophesy to my people Israel." ' Israel here could mean just the northern kingdom, but it is probable that the whole people of Yahweh, southern as well as northern, is intended. The precise meaning of Amos' words about himself has always been disputed. This is partly because there is no verb in the first statement (literally 'No prophet I, and no son of a prophet I'). It could mean 'I *was* no prophet originally', but most commentators favour the stronger sense 'I *am* no prophet'. Assuming this to be correct, what an amazing statement it is, coming from the man we often regard as the prophet *par excellence*! Striking too that he goes on to claim that 'The Lord said to me, "Go, prophesy." ' What are we to make of all this? It seems that Amos is dissociating himself from the general mass of paid, institutional prophets whose role was to give favourable oracles for the king and his shrine. He is claiming independence as an agent of Yahweh, called to speak the challenging word of God whatever it might cost him.

This narrative is in fact one of the foundations for the view that Amos marks the beginning of a new phase—that of independent, classical prophecy.

Amos plays down any idea of office ('I am no prophet'), and places all emphasis on the function of prophecy to which Yahweh has called him ('Go, prophesy to my people'). How far are we (whether lay or ordained) ready to sit loose to the trappings and privileges of office and listen for the demanding requirements of God?

'You who trample upon the needy' *Amos 8:4–14*

In verses 4–6 we return to the theme of the abuse of the poor. With an oath which recalls that of 6:8, Yahweh swears that he will not forget any of these cruel deeds (v. 7). In verse 8, judgment is described in terms which recall the earthquake (see on 1:1), and then, in the following verse, the range of natural imagery is broadened to take in that of eclipse: ' "On that day", says the Lord God, "I will make the sun go down at noon." ' We are reminded of the ominous question of 5:20, 'Is not the day of the Lord darkness, and not light?'. Songs will be turned into lamentation, as at 8:3.

No word. Earlier in the book (4:6–11), we read of all the punishments which Yahweh had sent, to no avail. As if all of this were not bad enough, verses 11–12 now add what appears to be an even worse punishment than lack of bread and water: a famine of hearing the words of the Lord. Seek where the people may, the word of the Lord is not to be found. The dreadful nature of this punishment becomes fully apparent when we recall how others in Israel could rejoice at the very accessibility of God's word: 'The word is very near you: it is in your mouth and in your heart, so that you can do it' (Deuteronomy 30:11–14).

All in vain. It is hardly surprising, then, that even fair virgins and young men (whom one would expect to be the most robust members of society) faint (v. 13). In verse 14 we read that those who have worshipped falsely shall fall and never rise again. Ashimah of Samaria may be the personal name of a goddess (perhaps taken over from the inhabitants of Hamath), but could simply mean the 'guilt' of Samaria. Two other place names are mentioned. Dan and Beersheba. Dan formed a pair with Bethel, these being the twin sanctuaries set up by Jeroboam I after his break with Judah (see 1 Kings 12:29). Pilgrimage to Beersheba, in the far south of Judah, has already been mentioned in 5:5. Dan and Beersheba are probably here, as elsewhere, cited as markers respectively of the far north and far south of Israelite territory (see 1 Samuel 3:20). The point is that, though the sinful Israelites may rush from shrine to shrine, all will be to no avail and destruction will inevitably follow.

Judgment upon the sanctuary

Amos 9:1–10

This chapter begins with another vision, not unlike those in the sequence found in chapters 7 and 8. Amos sees Yahweh standing beside (or even upon) the altar, presumably the one at Bethel. He commands the destruction of the sanctuary and all of the people (see also 3:14). There is to be no escape: verses 2–4 dramatically illustrate just how unavoidable the punishment is, and so underline the theme of judgment as we move towards the end of the book. This section is remarkably similar to Psalm 139, but with an important difference. In Psalm 139:8–10, we read 'If I ascend to heaven, thou art there! If I make my bed in Sheol, thou art there! If I take the wings of the morning and dwell in the uttermost parts of the sea, even there thy hand shall lead me, and thy right hand shall hold me'. Here in Amos, Yahweh is equally inescapable, but this is not good news but bad: 'I will set my eyes upon them for evil and not for good' (9:4). The people of Israel are in for a shock: though they hide at the bottom of the sea, Yahweh will command the serpent to bite them there, just as in 5:19 the serpent bites the man who finds refuge in a house. This dreadful message of judgment is driven home by the third and last of the hymn-like sections (vv. 5–6; see also 4:13; 5:8–9). The language used this time is the most dramatic of all; this is Yahweh, God of drought, earthquake and flood.

God of all. Amos 9:7 is a radical verse indeed. As before, Amos takes a basic tenet of faith (in this case the exodus tradition) and then treats it in a shockingly original way. Yahweh cares as much, it would seem, for the Philistines and the Syrians (arch-enemies of Israel for centuries) as for Israel. It is striking to compare 3:2. Amos' use of rhetoric is such that there he can make the point that Israel's special status qualifies it for special punishment, whereas here in 9:7 he can pull away all pretensions to special status! Here we see, at perhaps its most radical, Amos' universalism; for him, the whole world is the realm of God's activity. This insight led later prophets to affirm that there can be only one such God in the world and that his concern is ultimately not only to punish the nations or use them as his agents in punishing Israel, but also to draw them into the fullness of his salvation (see Isaiah 49:6).

In the last words of verse 8 we seem to have a glimmer of hope, uncharacteristic of Amos (see 5:15; 9:11–15). It may well be that these words have been added or at least amended by later scribes in Judah, aware that the southern kingdom had survived.

We have seen that Amos insists that his God is God of the whole world and that he has no favourites. Can we face the radical challenge which this poses to all our tendencies to narrowness and exclusivism?

A return to the good old days? *Amos 9:11–15*

This is the only really positive section in this book, which is otherwise so focused on judgment (see on 5:15 and 9:8). 'In that day' is a formula which often in the Old Testament introduces a vision of the future, whether of doom (Amos 8:9) or of hope (Isaiah 4:2). 'The booth of David that is fallen' probably refers to the royal house of Judah, which ended with the deportation to Babylon of the young king Jehoiachin, in 597BC, and of his uncle Zedekiah a decade later. This may suggest that we are dealing with an exilic addition to the book of Amos. A further indication of this may be found in the reference to possession of the remnant of Edom. It seems that Edom had taken advantage of Judah's misfortune at the hands of the Babylonians, and had thereby incurred the particular loathing of the Judaeans (see also Psalm 137:7). The reference to 'all the nations who are called by my name' is intriguing: the area covered by David's empire (which included Edom) is probably in mind. A return to the good old days, when Israel was itself a mighty power rather than under the control of foreign rulers!

Abundance and security. The book closes on a note of blessing, with a vision of plenty (verses 13–15; compare Jeremiah 31:10–14, 27–28; Ezekiel 34:25–31). The land will be more fruitful than ever before, and the people will never be exiled again. It is possible that these verses, like 11 and 12, were composed in Judah during the sixth century.

It may well be, then, that this passage is an addition to the book of Amos. We have occasionally suggested such a possibility elsewhere too. In ancient times, it was commonplace that books should be expanded somewhat, with changing circumstances—though the Book of Amos seems to be more of a single unit than most prophetic books. However, if this passage (9:11–15) is indeed additional, we should by no means automatically regard it as inferior. These verses are part of the text as we have it now, as Jesus knew it and as it has been read in synagogue and church for centuries. If not quite as old as the rest of the book, these verses of hope represent the experience and aspirations of ancient Israelites who had suffered much, and, as such, they demand our respect. The Book of Amos, as we now have it, affirms that our God is a God not only of justice but also of mercy.

OBADIAH

This is the shortest of the prophetic books, consisting of only one chapter. We cannot be certain of its date for the only evidence we have is indirect. Jerusalem, it seems, has suffered a catastrophe. It has been overrun by enemies and its suffering has been compounded by the treachery of Edom, its neighbouring nation (v. 11–14). The allusion here is probably to the destruction of Jerusalem by the Babylonians in 587BC at which time many of its inhabitants were deported. The detail of the description and the emotion it betrays suggest that the prophet himself may have been an eyewitness to these tragic events. For these reasons it has been suggested that the prophet's message belongs to the early years of exile. Against this, however, we have to set the circumstances described in verses 1 and 7 where Edom itself seems to be threatened by invasion by other nations. This would suggest that the book belongs rather to the latter part of the sixth century after the Israelites had returned from exile in Babylon in 538BC. This date would not, of course, exclude the possibility that the prophet had witnessed the conquest of Jerusalem in 587. By the early fifth century Edom as a nation was no more and had been displaced by nomadic Arab tribes.

Obadiah's words are both a protest at the treachery of Edom against its defenceless neighbour Israel and an assurance to this small nation in its struggle to survive that God is Lord of all nations. Against the overweening arrogance which acts in blatant disregard both of God and of humanity, Obadiah proclaims the 'day of the Lord', the ultimate time of God's reckoning (v. 15). But the faith proclaimed by the prophets was not simply a bolster for nationalism. It was a challenge to commitment to the holy God. Obadiah's words do not stand alone. They are to be understood as part of the celebration in worship of God's universal sovereignty and his demand for justice among all the nations. For Israel, too, comes under his judgment as

Amos makes clear (3:2; 9:7), and there is, moreover, salvation for other nations as the Book of Jonah declares. These, with Obadiah, are part of the 'Book of the Twelve'.

For further reading

J.H. Eaton, *Obadiah, Nahum, Habakkuk, Zephaniah*, Torch Bible Commentary, 1961

J.D.W. Watts, *The Books of Joel, Obadiah, Jonah, Nahum, Habakkuk and Zephaniah*, Cambridge Bible Commentary, 1975

For more detailed study

L.C. Allen, *The Books of Joel, Obadiah, Jonah and Micah*, The New International Commentary on the Old Testament, 1976

A brother's treachery *Obadiah 1–10*

Verse 1 sets the scene. Edom, a mountainous region south-east of Israel between the Dead Sea and the Gulf of Aqaba, is under threat of attack. The news has reached Judah, and the prophet has heard. But Obadiah is not unmindful of another perspective; beyond the human dimension is the Lord who works in history through the actions of nations and of kings (see Isaiah 10:5, 'Assyria, rod of my anger'; Jeremiah 27:6, 'Nebuchadnezzar, king of Babylon, my servant'). And so his opening words are momentous: 'Thus saith the Lord God'.

Edom had a special relationship with Israel. They were brother nations, in biblical tradition descended from the twin brothers Esau (Edom) and Jacob (Israel) (Genesis 25:24–26). But Edom's problem was pride, the kind of arrogance that sees itself secure and acts without mercy, reckoning without God. For Edom felt safe in its rocky fastnesses—'rose-red' Petra of today's tourist brochures, although dating from a later period, gives the 'feel'. But notice the mounting crescendo of the prophet's warning; though high as the eagle, or higher still like the stars (v. 4), they are not beyond God's reach (see Amos 9:2, in judgment; Psalm 139:8, in salvation). The message is underlined by its solemn closing words: 'oracle of the Lord' (v. 4).

The prophet's language is vivid. Worse than devastation left by thieves or looters who pick and choose their booty, more total than the harvesting of grapes where some fruit falls and is left behind (v. 5), is Edom's fate, deserted by those who had pledged loyalty, a breach of friendship beyond understanding in ancient reckoning (v. 7). Yet such was Edom's betrayal of Judah in its desperate plight when, in 587BC, Jerusalem fell to Babylon. Edom had been famed for its wisdom, but wisdom is more than intellectual astuteness. It includes moral obligation, and this is what Edom had violated.

Ruthlessness to refugees *Obadiah 11–14*

The enormity of Edom's treachery, its callous betrayal of a small nation, and 'your brother' at that (v. 12), in its fight for survival against the might of Babylon, moves the prophet with intense emotion. Israel's prophets were not automata, voicing messages which left them unmoved. To be a prophet was a costly task, a sacrificial calling, whether suffering in their people's suffering (Jeremiah 9:1) or standing with them under the judgment of God.

Notice the poignant repetition, multiple descriptions of distress, and accusation piled on accusation. Seven times in three verses we have the expression, 'the day of . . .' misfortune, ruin, calamity (three times, v. 13), distress (v. 12) matching distress (v. 14): there is pattern in the words. Then the accusations—they stood aloof, were no different from the cruel invaders (v. 11), gloated, rejoiced at Jerusalem's ruin, boasted (v. 12), took advantage of distress, gloated, looted (v. 13), and most tragically of all, cut off escape for the fugitives, betrayed the refugees (v. 14). For when Jerusalem fell and hope of saving the city had gone, Zedekiah with the pitiful remnants of his troops had tried to slip through the enemy lines (2 Kings 25:4). For this, the ultimate betrayal, Obadiah holds Edom responsible. The style of verses 12–14 is deliberately ironical, not a statement of a past event as in verses 11 and 15, but expressed as an eightfold plea to Edom, 'Do not gloat, boast, loot . . .' But the choice had already been made and the treachery was an ineradicable fact of history.

The prophet's language is vivid, leading some scholars to suggest that Obadiah was himself an eyewitness of Jerusalem's fall. Others, on the basis of the threat of imminent attack against Edom (vv. 1, 7), consider a date towards the end of the sixth century more likely.

For a description of the siege of Jerusalem, and the horrifying condition of its inhabitants, read 2 Kings 25:1–7.

The future is God's *Obadiah 15–21*

The prophet's thought moves on to a different plane in verse 15, beyond the immediate historical situation of the fate threatening Judah's old enemy Edom. He affirms courageously that God *is* a God of justice, sovereign over the affairs of nations, and evil does not go unpunished. The language is traditional. In Israelite thought the 'day of the Lord' meant the assertion of his kingship, when wrongs would be righted and his universal rule acknowledged. Too easily Israel distorted the idea, domesticating it for its own comfort (Amos 5:18). But they, too, were accountable to God, and so we find Obadiah's words against foreign nations counterbalanced by Joel's warnings to his own nation (see Joel 1:15; 2:1–2).

Judah itself, in the experience of exile, has tasted the cup of God's wrath (a common Old Testament metaphor for judgement), and so will the nations for their wickedness (v. 16). But with God there is always a future, not merely the past repeated but transformation, a new beginning for his people (v. 17). Yet inevitably justice for the victim means judgment on the oppressor. The metaphor of verse 18 is tragic, and solemn: 'the Lord *has spoken*' (for the power of the divine word see Jeremiah 23:29).

Verses 19–21 expand the promise of verse 17. From narrow restriction, the borders of Judah are to be enlarged, those exiled far from home resettled (Sepharad is possibly Sardis), and the Davidic monarchy restored (v. 21). Lastly come stirring words for a small, struggling community. This is the heart of Obadiah's message, borne out of faith in the limitless power of God: 'the kingly rule (rather than 'kingdom') shall be the Lord's'.

Obadiah addresses the perennial problems of complacent pride and ruthless cruelty. Where is God amid all the wretchedness of the world? He answers by reaffirming against all the odds that God's kingship is universal and unchallengable. And this king is just (Psalm 99:4). For Obadiah the evidence of God's saving action is possession of the land of Israel. The Christian's inheritance is of a different kind. Its possession involves no dispossession of others, no exclusion. It is for all.

It is easy to criticize Obadiah as narrowly nationalistic and materialistic. He speaks in Old Testament terms. But the confident faith against all the odds which undergirds his message demands attention and challenges us. God is in control, and human wickedness can never put a full stop to his saving purposes.

JONAH

It was not unusual in the ancient world for writers to fill in the gaps of history by writing what we would call historical fiction. There are many examples of this in Jewish literature.

The Book of Jonah is a work that fills in a gap. All that we know about the historical Jonah is what is recorded in 2 Kings 14:25. From this we may deduce that Jonah lived between 785 and 750 (the rough dates of Jeroboam II) and that he foretold victories for the king. If this foretelling of victories surprises us in view of the bad verdict passed on Jeroboam by 2 Kings 14:24, we must remember that Jeroboam belonged to the dynasty of Jehu, a dynasty that was established by prophets (2 Kings 9:1–15) and which suffered greatly at the hands of Syria before Jeroboam and his father Joash gained the upper hand against this northern enemy (2 Kings 13:22–25).

Jonah was known in Old Testament literature as a successful prophet, but that was all. Someone writing after the exile (fifth century BC) constructed around his character a highly artistic narrative with one of the most powerful messages in the whole of the Old Testament. Jonah in the story is a symbol of Israel and the drama is an exploration of the themes of mission avoided and mission accomplished in spite of the avoidance. God is presented as having a universal concern for the human race, and a foreign people is shown to be more receptive to his word than Israel itself.

No escape from God *Jonah 1:1–16*

The journey to Nineveh was an overland journey. It would probably go north-east via Damascus to Haran and then roughly east to Nineveh itself, a journey of about 700 miles. We are left by the writer to guess why Jonah did not want to carry out his mission. Was he frightened of the undoubted dangers of the long journey, did he expect simply to be ridiculed if and when he got to Nineveh and announced the judgment of the God of the insignificant country of Israel, or did he think that God had no business to be dealing with a nation other than Israel? Whatever the reason, he embarked in a ship that was probably bound for Crete—more or less the opposite direction from Nineveh.

The account of the storm and the reactions of Jonah and the sailors is full of deliberate contrasts. The Israelites were not a sea-going people, and it is thus to be expected that the sailors were non-Israelites. While the hardened sailors were terrified by the storm and toiled to lighten the ship, Jonah the non-sailor was fast asleep. Was he oblivious to what was happening because he was relieved at having escaped God's commission, confident that God could not get at him in a boat on the sea?

Old Testament tradition says otherwise, of course. There is no escape from God (Psalm 139:7–12) and he rules the raging seas (Psalm 107:23–31). Thus Jonah is forced to meet the crew, and the casting of lots marks him out as the reason for the storm. There is deliberate irony in the way Jonah describes his religion. He worships the God of heaven who made the sea and the dry land—yet he reckons that he can escape from this God whose power over sea and land he acknowledges in theory.

Jonah's willingness to be thrown out of the boat is not necessarily brave and unselfish. Presumably he expects to die, but at least this will finally absolve him from his mission to Nineveh. The passage ends with another contrast. Jonah, a prophet of God, is trying to turn his back on God. The heathen sailors pray sincerely and fervently to a God who is not strictly speaking theirs.

The psalm *Jonah 1:17—2:10*

Jonah's expectation that he would be freed by death from God's commission is not fulfilled. He is saved from death by being swallowed by the great fish. Now, for the first time in the story, he prays.

The psalm that occupies verses 2–9, while unique in the Old Testament, expresses thoughts that have parallels in many other psalms. The psalmist begins with the statement that God has heard his cry for help and has answered his prayers. There then follows an account of the psalmist's distress. Precisely what this was is not clear, whether sickness, or depression, or great danger. At any rate, the psalmist uses the imagery of seas and the pit to describe how he was in the grip of powers far too great for him, and so great as to put him out of reach of help from God. Yet against all expectations God did hear him, proving himself to be mightier than other so-called gods. Thus the psalmist will give thanks and praise, and acknowledge that deliverance comes from God alone.

It is easy to point out reasons why this psalm probably existed independently of Jonah and as such was taken and used by the writer. For example, the references to the temple, meaning the Jerusalem temple, do not fit well with a prophet who had served a northern king of Israel.

The purpose of the psalm. But the psalm has an important role in Jonah. It deliberately holds up the action of the story, marking in a literary way the passing of the time during which Jonah was in the belly of the fish. It also suggests a sort of conversion on the part of the prophet. It is not too literalistic to say that Jonah prayed the psalm *after* he had been in the fish for three days, and that the praying of the psalm was met by God instructing the fish to disgorge Jonah. In other words, Jonah was required to ponder the fact that he could not escape God's commission, and that God would not let him waste his life by opting out of it. When he had come to terms with this fact, he realized the mercy as well as the power of God. He was once again willing to be a servant.

Jonah's success *Jonah 3:1–10*

It is difficult to know, straight away, how seriously we are meant to take this part of the story. Jonah's preaching meets with phenomenal success. Without exception, the inhabitants of Nineveh accept the word of a prophet who comes from a people tiny and insignificant compared with Nineveh. In fact, in 734–721BC the Assyrian empire, of which Nineveh was the capital, brought to an end the existence of the northern kingdom Israel, perhaps within the lifetime of the historical Jonah. Further, Nineveh had its own gods, so why should it need or turn to the God of Israel?

Yet Jonah's preaching is so successful that even the king accepts the message and orders mourning as a sign of repentance not only for his subjects but for the animals also. Are we to take this seriously? The dramatic structure of the story demands that we do, for Jonah is a book that stresses the universal power and mercy of the God of Israel. The one who can call up the storm and then make the seas calm, and who can command a great fish to preserve the life of Jonah, must be taken seriously by the nations, however large or small.

The irony of the story. But when we take the story seriously, we see that it is ironic. We contrast, first of all, the readiness of the people of Nineveh to respond to God's message with the unwillingness of Jonah to proclaim that message in the first place. We also contrast the response of Nineveh with that of Israel, for whom Jonah is a symbol. The people of God had rejected and stoned the prophets that God sent to them. They had been no more willing to listen than Jonah had been prepared to speak.

Thus the chapter ends on a note of paradox. God sent his people into exile because they would not repent. The response that he hoped for from his own people was made in extravagant terms by a people who owed him nothing at all.

Jonah's real reason for not going *Jonah 4:1–11*

Only now does the writer answer the question that puzzled us initially: why did Jonah try to escape from his commission? It seems that the reason was theological. Jonah did not mind preaching the coming judgment of God as long as God inflicted the punishment. He felt cheated that God's mercy had accepted the repentance of the city, that these Assyrians, who were Israel's enemies, should be recipients of God's favour as well as Israel.

Consumed by a self-pity which argued that death was preferable to life, he sat down to watch whether God would destroy the city, grateful for the shelter provided by a plant. The removal of this shelter the following day and the summoning by God of an east wind brought different but renewed requests from Jonah that he should die. The writer of Jonah had almost certainly never been to Nineveh, but he was familiar with the east wind that occasionally blows in Israel. The prevailing winds come from the west and are cooled by the Mediterranean Sea. Those that come across the desert from the east are hot, sultry and dusty.

Even though he had not made the plant grow that had sheltered him, Jonah had appreciated it and had become fond of it. God asks Jonah to consider this point: if Jonah is sorry to have lost a plant which he did not make grow, is not God entitled to be sorry to lose many thousands of people and their animals whom he created? Was he not right to hope for their repentance and to show mercy when it was forthcoming? Did he not have a greater responsibility to be merciful to a people which, unlike Israel, could not tell left from right when it came to knowing God's will.

Two religions. *The Book of Jonah is concerned with two types of religion. In one, God is sincerely sought as a hope and security, but its followers gain a lot of their strength from the fact that they are a minority. While the rest of the world ignores or opposes God, the remnant is faithful to him, and deep down expects preferential treatment. It becomes offensive to this religion if it is apparent that God really does have a concern for all humankind, those who do not acknowledge him as well as those who do. It becomes difficult to accept as members of the club people who have done nothing to qualify for membership. The other type of religion in Jonah involves the imitation of God. This is a risky business when the God concerned does not seem to behave himself as humans would, above all, when his mercy is prepared to take risks where justice would carry out the sentence.*

The struggle in Israel . . . *The struggle between these two types of religion is at the heart of the Old Testament. A people is taken out of slavery in order to be a light to the nations, but believes firmly in its own privileges. The experience of exile and restoration (in Jonah probably represented by Jonah being swallowed by the fish and being disgorged) goes a long way towards deepening Israel's understanding of God's purposes; but it is still not enough. The pressures on the life of many Jews after the exile understandably increase their sense of isolation from the rest of the nations.*

. . . **and in the New Testament.** *The struggle is also found in the New Testament. In the story of the Prodigal Son (Luke 15:11–32) the elder brother represents those who want discipleship to give them special privileges. He can no more understand why the father should make such a fuss about the return of the lost son than Jonah can understand why God should want to pardon Nineveh.*

The struggle goes on in the Church, and we can be helped in it by the Book of Jonah. Probably no other book in the Bible links together so powerfully the mercy of God and his might as Creator. It is because he is Creator that his concern for his creatures is so great (Jonah 4:11). If we can begin to understand just this point, we may be helped to appreciate what is involved in the imitation of God and understand what it means to believe in God as Creator. We marvel at his mercy.

Let us pray for a faith that expects no privileges, which is grounded entirely in God's amazing graciousness to us, and which is equally gracious to all of God's creation.

MICAH

The Book of Micah is a neglected masterpiece within the Twelve Minor Prophets. It contains some of the most brutal language anywhere in the Bible in its denunciations of evil and injustice; it abounds in puns and word play. It is uncompromising and hard-hitting, to the point of forecasting the destruction of Jerusalem (over a hundred years before it happened!) with the implication that it would never be rebuilt.

One reason for its neglect may be the view of many commentators that material deriving genuinely from Micah can be found only in chapters 1–3. Who wants to study a book over half of which is anonymous? My own view is that material deriving from Micah can be found throughout the book; but I agree that, in its final form, the book is the work of, and reflects the outlook of, the post-exilic community in Judah. However, far from reducing the value of Micah as a whole, the post-exilic perspective adds a new dimension to it.

Micah lived in a small town in Judah during the reign of Hezekiah (727–698BC). It was a turbulent period, in which Judah and small neighbouring states were trying to resist the expansion of the Assyrian empire. In preparation for a major Assyrian invasion, which eventually occurred in 701, the area where Micah lived was militarized, and the state of emergency was made into an opportunity for powerful people in Jerusalem to rob and dispossess those who lived in the smaller towns of Judah. Micah spoke up powerfully against this action, condemning Jerusalem and its rulers, and looking forward to a time when God would provide his people with a ruler who would shepherd his people after the manner of David. Jeremiah 26:1–19 records that King Hezekiah turned in penitence to God on account of Micah's words.

The post-exilic community received words of Micah that said that Jerusalem would be destroyed and never rebuilt. But Jerusalem had been rebuilt; so the post-exilic community put his words in the context of their wider experience, adding immediately after his words about

Jerusalem's destruction the oracle that is found also in Isaiah 2, about the glory of Jerusalem in the latter days. Thus Micah reminds us that the truth is sometimes a combination of opposites: of individual insights declared uncompromisingly in a given situation, and the standpoint of a community with the benefit of hindsight and wider experience.

The comments are based on the Revised Standard Version (RSV).

Further reading

Micah, its problems and the major commentaries on it are admirably addressed in:

R. Mason, *Micah, Nahum, Obadiah*, Old Testament Guides, Sheffield, 1991

Judgment on Samaria and Jerusalem *Micah 1:1–7*

The title of the book puts Micah's prophetic activity in the period c. 750–700BC, although in reality it probably spanned no more than twenty years or so, from about 725 to 705. Micah can be said to have an anti-Jerusalem bias.

It is noteworthy, therefore, that he begins by describing God as coming in judgment not from the Jerusalem temple (Jerusalem is the cause of the sin of Judah, v. 5) but from his heavenly temple. The vivid description of mountains melting and of valleys cracking as God approaches has many parallels in the Old Testament.

Samaria's sin. The object of God's judgment is primarily Samaria, capital of the northern kingdom of Israel since its establishment by Omri in c. 870BC. Standing on a magnificent site with commanding views of the surrounding countryside, it withstood a siege of three years before finally falling to the Assyrians in 722/1BC. The reason for God's judgment is given in verse 7 as idolatry. The rulers of Samaria had turned from the worship of the God of Israel to the fertility religion of Canaan, with its images and the use of sacred prostitution. But Micah, as we shall see, was not particularly interested in religious practices. He was more concerned with justice and right dealing, and his criticism of Samaria's idols was more an indictment of the abuse of power which Canaanite religion could encourage.

Jerusalem, a high place! The RSV translation of verse 5 obscures an important point. Micah asks, 'What are the high places of Judah? Is it not Jerusalem?' In the Books of Kings, where the theology is that of Deuteronomy, Jerusalem is always regarded as the divinely chosen holy place, all others being 'high places' rejected by God. But Micah calls Jerusalem a high place! The opening passage thus warns us that we are in for some surprises.

The significance of where Micah lived *Micah 1:8–13*

Samaria had been a splendidly fortified city, and the northern kingdom of Israel had depended upon its army to defend it. It also had geographical advantages that the southern kingdom of Judah did not enjoy. Whereas access from the coastal plain to the heartland of Israel was impossible except along one or two easily defended routes, Judah had a soft underbelly in the lowlands, a transitional area between the coastal plain and the Judaean heartland which made access for a potential invader comparatively easy. It was in this area that Micah lived.

So far as we can tell, some time after the fall of Samaria in 722/1 BC, the area in which Micah lived began to be fortified against possible Assyrian attack. This involved putting military garrisons at strategic points along a crucial route that ran from north to south, from Bethshemesh to Lachish. If the presence of these garrisons was a reassurance to some, it was a burden to be borne by others, as the soldiers who were quartered there probably lived off the produce of the area.

Micah regarded the garrisons as a plundering of his people. The policy of trust in military might that had failed in the north was now being tried in the lowlands. In our passage, Micah warns the villagers of the area that the fortifications bring not security, but insecurity, and he warns them to be ready to cope with disaster when they are invaded.

Micah's striking language. The Hebrew of verses 10–15 contains a number of striking puns that cannot be easily reproduced in English. Some idea of their flavour can be conveyed by the following translation:

10b In Dustville, roll yourselves in the dust . . .

11b Do not go out, citizen of Out-town . . .

13a Harness the chariot to the horse, citizen of Horseville . . .

14c The homes of Deceitville are deceitful.

It is noteworthy that Lachish (verse 13) receives special mention, for this was the most strongly fortified city after Jerusalem, and the capital of the lowlands. The reference to Adullam is obscure (verse 15); but it may be a reference to David who, in Micah's view, had been a true shepherd of his people. This idea will recur in the important passage in chapter 5.

Abuse of power

Micah 2:1–11

This section falls into two parts, verses 1–5 and 6–11. In the first, Micah probably describes the actions of the local military rulers, who abuse their power by seizing lands and houses. Officially they do it in the name of security, but in reality they are feathering their own nests.

In verses 6–11 there is a highly artistic poem which opens with a triple pun and closes with a double pun on the verb 'to preach'. Micah's love of word-play is also evident here, as can be seen from the translation of verse 6: 'do not preach'—thus they preach—'one should not preach of such things'. We can suppose that the objectors to Micah's preaching are the powerful commanders who are criticized in verses 1–5. Micah, to them, is meddling in affairs that are none of his business, and should keep quiet.

He cannot be silent. But Micah's deeply held conviction is that no end, however important, can be so great as to justify ill-treating the very people who are supposed to be protected. Women and children are being driven from their homes, and people who go peacefully about their daily lives are abused (vv. 8–9).

As is often the case in Micah, the Hebrew is difficult to translate at a number of points. The RSV of verse 8a represents the very defenders of the people as in fact their enemies. Another possible rendering would be 'yesterday you were my people; today you are my enemy', indicating that the actions of the powerful had completely subverted the status of God's people from being his friends to being his enemies.

The passage concludes with a biting counter-attack. If he were telling lies or encouraging the people to drown their sorrows in drunkenness, Micah would be popular, and would be accepted by the influential as a prophet. But a prophet is not one who courts popularity, but one who often swims against the stream, in response to the prompting of God's Spirit.

Rulers denounced *Micah 3:1–4*

Chapter 3 is another highly artistic composition. It has three stanzas of roughly equal length, the first and third being introduced by the command 'hear!'. In the first stanza the heads and rulers are addressed, in the second the false prophets are condemned, and in the third stanza priests and prophets are added to the address to heads and rulers.

The striking thing about the beginning of the passage is that the heads and rulers of *Jacob* and *Israel* are addressed. It seems that Micah is either being deeply ironic, or he is trying to lull his hearers into false security before shocking them. Strictly speaking, the rulers of Jacob and Israel were the leaders of the northern kingdom. Was Micah therefore trying to mislead his listeners deliberately by making them suppose he was not talking about his own country? In that case, the shock would come in the third stanza, with the prophecy of the destruction of Jerusalem making it clear that it was indeed Judah that was being addressed. The other possibility is that, by calling the leaders of Judah the leaders of Israel, Micah was in effect saying that their cause was already hopeless, because Israel had ceased to exist after the fall of Samaria in 722/1 BC.

The brutality of Micah's language. The language of verses 3–4 is among the most brutal anywhere in the prophetic literature. The image is that of cannibalism. The powerful, in effect, skin their victims, and tear off the flesh to boil it in cauldrons. They break the bones of the victims to make more manageable the process of cramming the flesh into the cauldrons. If we find this language repulsive, then Micah has succeeded in what he wanted to say. For him, the sins of the rulers were as repulsive as cannibalism is to civilized people.

Zion no refuge *Micah 3:5–12*

Among the Psalms are several that contain what has been called 'Zion theology'. These are Psalms such as 2 and 24, which regard the hill of Zion in Jerusalem as the place of God's earthly dwelling, and which therefore see all human attempts to overthrow the Davidic king in Jerusalem as doomed to failure. The idea of 'the Lord in the midst of us' (v. 11) is part of Zion theology, and is met, for example in Psalm

46, in the refrain 'the Lord of hosts is with us; the God of Jacob is our refuge'.

Relationships distorted. Micah has scant regard for Zion theology. The conviction of 'the Lord in the midst of us' has, in his view, ceased to express Israel's obedient trust in God and has become instead a dangerous, almost magical, trust that makes the people believe that God will look after them whatever they do. For Micah, Zion is built with blood and Jerusalem with wrong (v. 10); that is to say, Micah does not look at the magnificent buildings in Jerusalem. He looks at human society and relationships in Jerusalem and sees there deceit, injustice and selfishness. Prophets make a living by being paid to say what people want them to say and judges give their verdict to whoever produces the biggest bribe. God will not tolerate this, and if a superstitious trust in the divine protection of Jerusalem leads them away from true faith in God, then he will remove that prop in order to make his people seek him anew.

The language which describes the desolation of Jerusalem seems to envisage no rebuilding of the city. In this, Micah differs from the later Ezekiel who has a vision of the temple restored, and also from the later editors of the Book of Micah. Micah apparently believes that God will do a new thing in which Jerusalem will *not* play an important role. Micah, in this way, attacks the most cherished symbol of God's presence in the Old Testament—the Jerusalem temple.

'Spears into pruning hooks' *Micah 4:1–5*

Look at Isaiah 2:2–4 and you will discover the Micah passage almost word for word as far as Micah 4:3. In fact, many scholars think that Micah 4:1–5 preserves the passage better than Isaiah 2:2–4, and that the end of the passage had been lost in the Isaiah version. At the same time, while a minority of scholars would argue that the prophet Isaiah may be responsible for this passage, almost none would claim Micah as the author.

The reason for this last point is quite simple. The passage goes against everything that Micah believed. He foresaw the destruction of Jerusalem and no rebuilding; this passage envisages a restored Jerusalem, as the centre of the world when God finally establishes his kingdom. It is clear that the editors of the Book of Micah added this passage, either taking it from Isaiah (which was then in a longer form) or taking it from a source used also by the editors of Isaiah.

Why and when did the editors add the passage? We can only guess. We know that the temple was destroyed in 587BC, some 120 years after Micah's prophecy. We know that it was rebuilt in 516BC, and that the community that lived in Jerusalem after that date came to believe that God had indeed punished, but had also restored the holy city. From their point of view, Micah had been right to prophesy Jerusalem's downfall; but he had not seen far or deeply enough into God's purposes. The poem about Jerusalem's exaltation was thus added to Micah in order to give his words new meaning. God might have judged Jerusalem; he had not totally abandoned it, and history proved this. This needed to be said.

However, today's passage is not merely about the rebuilding of a demolished city. It is a vision of the triumph of God's kingdom on earth, with Jerusalem as its capital. Whether or not Micah would have agreed with the image of a restored Jerusalem, he would surely have rejoiced to think of a world dominated by justice, peace, and security based upon mutual trust. He who lived in an agricultural area which was being militarized would surely have approved of the weapons of war being made into agricultural tools. And above all, he would have agreed that this was something that could only happen when the human race said in all seriousness, 'let us go . . . that he may teach us his ways, and that we may walk in his paths'.

Jerusalem besieged

Micah 4:9—5:1

This is another artistic poem, with three stanzas of unequal length, each introduced by the word 'now' (vv. 9, 11, 5:1). The situation implied in stanza one is that Jerusalem has been encircled by its enemies. The people in the city cry aloud in fear (vv. 9–10), yet they are asked, either in sincerity or irony, 'why do you cry aloud? Is there no king in you?' The remainder of the stanza (v. 10) declares that Jerusalem's citizens will become exiles in Babylon, but that God will redeem them from there.

The second stanza is reminiscent of Psalm 2 and of Isaiah 41:15–16. The Psalm tells of the nations gathered in vain against Jerusalem in an exercise that will fail because God's plan is greater than their plans. The same is found here in verses 11–12. Verse 13 is paralleled by the declaration in Isaiah 41:15–16 that God will make Israel into an instrument that will thresh and winnow her enemies. The third stanza, much shorter than the other two, returns to the picture of Jerusalem besieged and seems to imply the capture of the king in the words 'with a rod they strike . . . the ruler of Israel'.

As a whole, the passage is puzzling, especially in the way it juxtaposes the defeatist first and third stanzas and the triumphal second stanza.

Believing community and prophetic individual. It may be that we have an original poem of Micah which has been enlarged by the editors of the book in the light of their experience of Jerusalem's defeat and subsequent restoration. Micah may be responsible for stanzas one (with Assyria originally where we now have Babylon in verse 10?) and three, and the editors may have contributed stanza two. This suggestion may be disturbing to those whose view of the inspiration of the Bible is that God overpowered particular individuals to write the whole of the book traditionally ascribed to them. However, it is more realistic and exciting to accept that inspiration was a dynamic process in which the believing community put the Old Testament books into their final shape in the light of an experience of God that was larger than any one individual at any one time could have. We need prophetic individuals who go against the stream; but we also need the total experience of the believing community, the Church.

Not Jerusalem, but Bethlehem *Micah 5:2–6*

This passage is familiar to many, because it is quoted in the Epiphany story of the search of the wise men for the newly-born Jesus (Matthew 2:1–6). In the context of Micah it had a different meaning, and yet one which is not inconsistent with its use in the Gospel.

It is not impossible that, in the original form of the Book of Micah, this passage followed immediately after 3:12. As we saw previously, Micah did not envisage the rebuilding of Jerusalem; but neither did he believe that God's purposes had come to a complete stop. If 5:2 followed on from 3:12, Micah pointed to a new thing that God would do after he had carried out his sentence on Jerusalem. He would bring forth an ideal ruler from Bethlehem.

Although David is not mentioned in the passage, the language makes it clear that a second David will be raised up by God, and that he will be a shepherd, that is, a ruler who will protect all of the people (v. 4). Micah presumably has in mind the fact that David was king for a number of years over Judah and Israel before he made Jerusalem his capital, that he delivered the nation from the Philistines, and that he established peace. Micah thus looks for God to establish the house of David anew, but not in Jerusalem.

Micah's alternative view of Hezekiah. It is fascinating to compare this view with the theology of the Books of Kings. There, the king during most of Micah's ministry, Hezekiah, is one of only two kings who are praised unreservedly. Indeed, in 2 Kings 18:3 he is said to have followed the example of David. No doubt this is how things looked from the perspective of Jerusalem, where Hezekiah fortified the city and tried to stamp out rival shrines. From Micah's viewpoint things were different. During the reign of a king who is praised by the editors of Kings, Micah expected God to destroy Jerusalem and to raise up a new king of the Davidic line. But Hezekiah was not quite as bad as this may imply. The passage in Jeremiah 26:19 says that Micah's preaching caused Hezekiah to repent.

When did Micah expect the new king? Apparently during his lifetime, to counter the Assyrians. This is obscured in verses 5–6 by a post-Micah expansion of the text, which originally read:

And this shall be peace,
when the Assyrian comes into our land
and treads upon our soil;
he shall deliver us from the Assyrian
when he comes into our land
and treads within our border.

Concerning the timetable, Micah was wrong. But in the long term he was right. Matthew 2 sees the completion of Micah's insight in the birth of Jesus, the good shepherd and the prince of peace.

The noblest expression of Old Testament religion

Micah 6:1–8

This passage contains a verse that has long been regarded as the noblest definition of religion in the whole of the Old Testament:

'What does the Lord require of you but to do justice, and to love kindness, and to walk humbly with your God?' (v. 8). Furthermore, the passage seems to be saying that formal religious practices are less important than morally upright living. God is not one whose favour can be won by extravagant gifts. What is required is simple and straightforward, and within the reach of anyone. It does not need priests or temples.

Whether or not the passage comes from Micah himself, it certainly expresses his ideas. We have seen his hostility to Jerusalem, and his belief that its temple would be no more. We have seen his desire for justice and kindness and since, as a prophet, he was speaking in God's name, he was not simply a social reformer, but a man of deep, if non-conformist, religious faith, who walked humbly before God.

It has been a matter of debate for a very long time whether prophets such as Micah, Isaiah (in Isaiah 1:10–26), Amos (in Amos 5:21–25) and Jeremiah (in Jeremiah 7:21–23) really did envisage a religion of Israel without the temple sacrifices, or whether they were deliberately exaggerating their language in order to make people think more deeply about the formal religious side of their lives.

The fact is that, in the case of someone like Micah living in the provinces, we know little of the sort of religion that he practised. Did he come to the Jerusalem temple from time to time? Did he worship at a local 'high place'? Was his religion a spiritualized one of prayer, love and mercy? If it was the latter, and if he was, from the establishment point of view, a non-conformist, it is all to the good that we have his book. Powerful and centralized religious establishments do not have a monopoly of truth; and one of the exciting things about theology today is that it is being contributed to by non-establishment groups—women, the poor in South America, the oppressed in southern Africa, to name only some.

The evils of Samaria *Micah 6:9–16*

This passage is badly preserved in the Hebrew at some points, and is not easy to translate. This probably indicates that in essence it goes back to Micah, with one or two small additions. The most interesting thing about the passage is the mention of Omri and Ahab, two of the most powerful kings of the northern kingdom in the ninth century, 150 years before Micah's time. It may well be that Micah had no access to historical records about Omri and Ahab, even though Omri, in particular, is mentioned in texts outside of the Bible. Probably, Micah believed that the evils of Samaria owed their origins to Omri and Ahab, and it is to these evils that he refers.

Micah's complaint, which is God's complaint against Jerusalem (v. 9), is that the city has followed, not God's statutes, but those of Samaria. No doubt the people in Jerusalem who acquired wealth by dishonest means, whether by giving short measure (v. 11) or by relying on bribery or threats (v. 12), believed that there was no higher moral or ruling power of which they should take heed.

Wrong-doing and accountability. The Old Testament writers, Micah included, believed passionately that God is the one to whom a reckoning must be given, by great and small alike. Within this life, it is held, corrupt behaviour will result in loss of material blessing. 'You shall eat, but not be satisfied . . . you shall sow but not reap . . . you shall tread grapes, but not drink wine.' It is easy to describe this as simplistic, but is it? Are we not today beginning to suffer the effects of putting the unbridled acquisition of wealth before the proper stewardship of human and material resources? And we must remember that the Micah who warned of the consequences of ignoring justice and mercy was not a conformist, but an advocate, in religious matters, of the right to attack establishment religion. His example provides much food for thought.

Micah's farewell — *Micah 7:1–7*

This is the only passage in Micah in which the prophet seems to speak in the first person, and to give expression to his own deepest thoughts. The view taken in these notes is that the passage indeed comes from Micah, and that it formed the conclusion to the original book of Micah before it was expanded after the exile.

Up to now, Micah has been an observer, speaking to God's people in God's name; speaking in the third person. Now he has become a participator. He cannot, and does not, stand aloof from what is going on. The wrongdoings that he observes hurt him personally. Drawing upon an agricultural image familiar from his home, with its abundance of figs and vines, he likens himself to a hungry and a thirsty man, seeking food and drink from fruit trees and vines, and finding none because the harvest has lately stripped them bare (v. 1).

But his real hunger and thirst are for righteousness, and he finds none. There are no godly people left (v. 2). The powerful are as straight and upright as briars and thorns (v. 4). Friends cannot be trusted (v. 5), and families are so divided that home is where enemies are most likely to be found (v. 6). In this situation, only one thing gives hope, and that is trust that God can and will exert the sovereignty that alone can put things right. And this is no easy thing. It requires patience and courage: 'I will look to the Lord, I will wait for the God of my salvation' (v. 7). The history of advances in religion and in moral reforms has depended upon individuals whose sensitivity to justice and mercy was more developed than that of their contemporaries, who did not conform to the prevailing norms of self-seeking, and who were hurt by the wrongs done to the innocent. Whether Micah achieved anything for his generation we do not know. We have his book, however, and through it we hear his voice today.

The good shepherd *Micah 7:8–20*

The end of Micah's book is not by Micah himself but by the believing community. It rounds off the book beautifully and fittingly.

Verses 8–10 are the agonized cry of fallen Jerusalem: 'Rejoice not over me, O my enemy'. In falling, Jerusalem had learned to be penitent: 'I have sinned against him'. She has confidence that God will restore her, and that her enemies will be amazed; but she will be a different city because of her punishment.

Verses 11–13 are a cry to Jerusalem to rebuild her walls, and to expect to be the centre of the earth, as pictured also in 4:1–5. Verse 13 injects a sombre note, however. Not only Jerusalem, but the whole earth will be punished for misdeeds.

Verses 14–15 are a prayer to God that he will be a shepherd to his flock in a forest. Forests were the abode of wild animals fatal to sheep. Israel asks to be protected by God, and God promises to guide them, as he did when the people left Egypt and passed through the wilderness.

Verses 16–17 envisage the turning of the nations to God, a turning brought about when they see God once more shepherding his people. The attitude of the nations will be one of dread and fear. Israel, however, in spite of the experience of the exile, can still trust in a tender relationship with God. He will always have the last word and his greatest power is shown in forgiveness and mercy (v. 18).

True forgiveness. Micah has said much about the wrongdoing of God's people, and the judgment that will ensue. The last word of the book is one of the most sublime images in the whole Bible of God's power to forgive, and to mend what the human race has broken and distorted. 'Thou wilt cast all our sins into the depths of the sea.' What a pity that our modern contamination of the oceans robs these words of their original power to say that what God puts behind himself and behind us can no longer have power over our future.

Behind the Book of Micah is a struggle between the official representatives of religion and an outsider who speaks with the authority of independence. As far as we can tell, that struggle was won in the first place by the outsider. Hezekiah repented because of Micah's preaching and the people were spared. In the long run, it was official religion that won. Micah's book does not come to us in the form that he intended; it comes in an 'approved' version, in which the restoration and triumph of Jerusalem are envisaged.

This struggle and its resolution are pertinent to today. Some voices are urging that there be radical changes in the Church; others see it as their duty to preserve the Church unchanged. Both, in a sense, are right. Without non-conformist, prophetic figures the Church would become stagnant; but the weight of tradition must also have a modifying effect upon the voice of the individual.

This does not help us at any particular time to know what is right. It may encourage us, however, to pay more attention to prophetic voices knowing that they will not destroy God's Church but give new life to its weight of tradition. The Book of Micah is well worth re-reading from this point of view.

NAHUM

Despite the lapse of centuries many of the prophets speak with a voice we understand in the modern world. They cry out against injustice done to the helpless, the exploitation of the weak, and that self-satisfaction in worship which dishonours the holiness of God. The words of these prophets search our own motives and challenge our commitment. Their message is direct and meaningful. But the Book of Nahum is not one of these. It starts on a note of vengeance and its message sounds to us vindictive and nationalistic, gloating over its enemy Nineveh's defeat. What are we as Christians to make of it?

To see it in its historical context and to understand its function in ancient Israel's worship compels us to modify our first impressions. Nahum's words, couched in some of the most powerful poetry in the Old Testament, are probably to be dated shortly before the downfall of the brutal Assyrian empire. The ruthless treatment meted out to its conquered lands is the key to understanding the book of Nahum. It is a cry for help by a people desperate for relief from a powerful tyrant. And here immediately we sense a link with our own troubled world. Nahum's name means 'comfort', and in his affirmation of a God who is 'a stronghold in the day of trouble' (1:7) he brings comfort to the distressed. It is likely that his words were used in worship, first as a prayer for relief from suffering, then in later years as a testimony to God's saving action for the strengthening of faith in adversity.

Nineveh was the greatest of Assyria's cities, a rich and ancient city on the banks of the Tigris, in existence from about 5000BC. Although the prophet's language seems to imply that Nineveh has already fallen, this is no gloating over a conquered enemy. To speak as if future events had already happened is characteristic of the prophets as they affirm their confidence in God. This is genuinely predictive prophecy. But Nahum is a visionary as were many of the prophets. And as he cries out against the brutality of Assyria's oppressive regime his thoughts move on a wider plane, that of God's ultimate triumph over the cosmic evil which corrupts our world and sets nation against nation.

Nahum must not be read in isolation. It is part of 'the Book of the Twelve' (Hosea–Malachi) where Jonah tells of mercy for Nineveh, and where Israel are challenged about their own oppressive acts, and are equally accountable to God.

The notes are based on the Revised Standard Version.

Further reading

J.H. Eaton, *Obadiah, Nahum, Habakkuk, Zephaniah*, Torch Bible Commentary, 1961

R. Mason, *Micah, Nahum, Obadiah*, Old Testament Guides, 1991

J.D.W. Watts, *The Books of Joel, Obadiah, Jonah, Nahum, Habakkuk and Zephaniah*, Cambridge Bible Commentary, 1975

Rescue for the wretched

Nahum 1:1–15

There is an important hint in the title (v. 1) for the reading of the book. To ignore it is to risk misreading. What follows is 'vision', and to understand it purely on the historical level as simply a vindictive threat against Nineveh, Assyria's capital, is to miss its more profound significance. More is in the prophet's view than Nineveh's brutality, notorious though this was even in the ancient world. There is cosmic evil against which the Lord pits his might to avenge the wretched victims of oppression.

Nahum is a visionary and it is no surprise, then, to find in his words allusions to sinister forces which lurk behind historic Nineveh. The allusions are not spelt out but it is likely that he has in mind Ishtar, Nineveh's goddess of immorality and violence, and behind Ishtar God's primeval enemy the chaos monster (see the reference to 'Rahab' in Isaiah 51:9). This becomes more apparent in 2:5–7, but there are hints enough to justify this view already in 1:8 ('he will make a full end of her place/temple', so the Hebrew: see RSV footnote) and in verse 11: 'from you [feminine singular] has come forth the counsellor Belial', wickedness personified. Read from this perspective, verse 14 is directed not primarily against the wicked inhabitants of Nineveh, for the city's name is not mentioned, except in the title, until 2:8 (although inserted in the REB, for example, in 1:8, 11), but against Belial, the personification of wickedness, and this it is who is to be 'utterly cut off' (v. 15; the Hebrew verb is singular).

The chapter has three distinct sections: verses 2–8, the awesome presence of the avenging God; verses 9–11, a warning to God's enemies; verses 12–15, a promise for Judah (as also is v. 7 for all who trust the Lord).

The prophet starts with God. Four times (five in the Hebrew text) the sacred name Yahweh is repeated in verses 2–3. Asserting his unrivalled kingship (the meaning of 'jealous'), the avenging God, not powerless in the face of evil like some earthly rulers, acts to rescue the victims of oppression.

The rapid changes of person which confuse the reader (Judah is addressed in v. 13 and 15, Belial in v. 14) would be clarified for the first participants by the use of dramatic action in the course of worship.

The book is magnificent poetry, not to be dismissed lightly as 'a disgrace to the two religious communities of whose canonical Scriptures it forms . . . a part'. It is the affirmation against all the odds that the Lord acts in history and is not unmindful of those who flout the sovereign will of the God of justice.

Defeat for the destroyer *Nahum 2:1–12*

Chapter 1 ended with a joyful scene, a messenger running to tell good news: Belial (wickedness) is vanquished! Now Judah can express its thanks by celebrating its sacred festivals and fulfilling its commitments to the Lord.

In chapter 2 God's armies press the attack. Verse 1 is probably a reference to his actions in containing the enemy, 'he guards the ramparts, watches the road', rather than an ironical instruction to the adversary, Nineveh/Ishtar/Chaos. It thus forms a prelude to verse 2, a reminder that Yahweh's judgment is always and only the obverse of his saving action.

There is here the same intermingling of the historical and of that which is beyond history, a portrayal of Nineveh's downfall at the hands of the Babylonian armies and of the defeat of chaos by heavenly forces. The dramatic picture of fighting in the streets (vv. 3–4) is realistic in its detail: leather shields glistening, reddened for preservation, polished chariots flashing as the army charges. But the visionary prophet sees more than this. Here are echoes of Yahweh in battle against the forces of chaos (see Habakkuk 3:10–15; Isaiah 66:15). The target of the attack is Ishtar's temple (vv. 5–7), the 'sinister goddess' who, for this prophet, is 'the sum of opposition to God' (Eaton). The sluices are opened; in the flooded city buildings crumble, surely an echo of the deadly waters of chaos defeated by God (Psalm 93:4). Ishtar is led captive attended by her maids, the temple prostitutes (v. 7). Now at last Nineveh is named (v. 8), abandoned by its troops, filtering away like water flooding from a leaky pool. And there lies its wealth, pillaged from subject peoples, to be looted in its turn.

The scene of desolation is complete (v. 10). In a rhetorical question Nineveh is likened to a den abandoned by lions, a lair once of seeming security, of abundant sustenance from captured prey (vv. 11–12). The metaphor is significant. Ishtar is represented sometimes as mounted on a lion, or as herself a lioness; so, too the chaos monster is depicted as a lion.

How are the mighty fallen!

Reaping due reward *Nahum 2:13—3:19*

This chapter does not make pleasant reading. But we must be careful not to misread. The scene of devastation, the noise of battle, whips cracking, wheels rumbling, swords flashing, then the silence of death, 'heaps of corpses', are not God's doing but descriptive of Nineveh 'the blood-stained city, full of pillage' (v. 1). And its motivation, the insidious evil of the worship of Ishtar, goddess of sex and violence. And here the prophet looks beyond the wrong done to his own people Israel (see Amos 2:1). This is evil on a massive scale: Nineveh has betrayed nations and peoples (v. 4). Yet there is One with whom it she not reckoned, the Lord of hosts (v. 5). The description of her degradation (vv. 5–6) is loathsome, but she who degraded individuals by prostitution will herself suffer humiliation. The language of exposure, reflecting possibly a practice of the time, is not uncommon in the prophets (Jeremiah 13:26; Ezekiel 16:36f; Hosea 2:10). But there is no one to lament her, so hated and feared has she become (v. 7).

Then there is a lesson from history, straight from their own annals of triumph—and of brutality (vv. 8–10). Thebes, that great city on the Nile, for all its security, wealth and allies fell to Assyria in 663BC. So shall Nineveh fall. The fate of Thebes signals for Nahum not Assyrian might but 'the fragility of all human empire' (Eaton). Fortresses, troops, gates, all such security is in the end a sham (vv. 12–13). In a last desperate effort preparations are made to resist siege, and mud bricks are moulded for defence (v. 14). But though their forces are as multitudinous as locusts, and their ravages as devastating, they are as evanescent (v. 17). The metaphor changes: the sleep of death comes over them, the king is isolated, no healing, no lament. The last two words are the key to this fearful retribution. It is the outcome of 'evil unceasing' (*ra'ah tamid*; v. 19).

The descriptive poetry is magnificent and its challenge inescapable. Evil brings its own reward. Oppression works isolation for the oppressor; the din of violence issues in the stillness of death. The one who remains amid the wreckage of history is 'I, the Lord'.

On a profound level the message of Nahum is relevant to our world. The brutality of ancient Assyria against which the prophet protests is the outworking of a cosmic evil manifest wherever human rights are disregarded and the oppressor acts as if accountable to none. Nahum's portrayal of the avenging God shocks our sensibilities, but its real perspective is the despairing misery of the crushed and oppressed. True, we are to forgive our persecutors, but nowhere is the Christian bidden to go soft on evil and to make truce with oppression.

HABAKKUK

There may be many Christians who have never read the book of Habakkuk. For many it seems one of the more obscure corners of the collection of 'minor' (i.e. shorter) prophets, with which the Old Testament ends. Yet in New Testament times it was regarded as an important book. The community of the Dead Sea Scrolls produced an elaborate commentary on it, claiming that Habakkuk had predicted the coming of the Romans to Palestine. And it was from Habakkuk that Paul took the verse that was to be central to his ideas about 'justification by faith': 'The righteous shall live by his faith' (Habakkuk 2:4; see Romans 1:17; Galatians 3:11).

In fact the book, short as it is, touches on many central biblical themes. In 1:12–17 the prophet raises the question of divine justice in the face of undeserved human suffering, a theme we more often associate with Job. Like the other prophets, he condemns injustice in society, and especially the oppression of the weak by the strong—see 2:6–17. The next three verses (2:18–20) contrast the power of the God of Israel with the weakness of 'idols', in the style of 'Second Isaiah', the author of Isaiah 40–55 (see Isaiah 44:9–20). And chapter 3, which is a psalm that may go back before the time of Habakkuk himself, sets out an ideal of altruistic piety (3:17–18) which is also found in Daniel 3:16–18.

Who is Habakkuk? The book does not begin, as many prophetic books do, with information about when he lived. So we have only his own oracles on which to base any theory about his life and times. In 1:6 he refers to the 'Chaldeans'. This usually means the Babylonians, who sacked Jerusalem in the sixth century BC (in 598 and 587). If it has that meaning here, then Habakkuk must have been a contemporary of Jeremiah. His attacks on the king in 2:9–14 (whether this is the Babylonian king or king of Judah) are similar to Jeremiah's—

compare Jeremiah 22:13–19. Certainly he seems to have much in common with the prophets before the exile, of whom Jeremiah was the last.

But sometimes in the Old Testament Babylon and its people are little more than a symbol for any major power threatening Israel. From the sixth century until the time of the Romans the Jews faced many such powers, and the writer could even have Alexander the Great or one of his successors in mind: many of them were enemies to the people of Israel.

Because we do not really know when Habakkuk lived, we tend to read the book as a divinely inspired response to anything or anyone who threatens the existence of God's people. Thus we treat the book as rather unspecific. But if 'Babylon' is a symbol, then it may have been intended non-specifically, as a reflection on human history and God's involvement in it. Thus our lack of certainty about the book's origin may lead us to a true interpretation!

Further reading

J.H. Eaton, *Obadiah, Nahum, Habakkuk, Zephaniah*, Torch Bible Commentary, 1961

J.D.W. Watts, *The Books of Joel, Obadiah, Jonah, Nahum, Habakkuk and Zephaniah*, Cambridge Bible Commentary, 1975

The prophetic vision *Habakkuk 1:1–4*

At the beginning of his prophecy we see Habakkuk speaking to God in the name of all those for whom the state of society in Israel had become hard to tolerate because of injustice and oppressive government. Like the other prophets, Habakkuk sees around him a society in which 'righteousness and justice' have been 'perverted'.

'Righteousness and justice' is a catch-phrase in the prophets. It means a way of ordering human society so that might does not triumph over right, judges and public servants are honest and do not take bribes and the weak and helpless are protected against those who want to exploit them.

The plea for justice. The need for justice, in this sense, had been a constant theme in prophetic preaching since the days of Elijah, more than eight centuries before Jesus, and it was to be picked up by John the Baptist (see Luke, chapter 3). Habakkuk sees himself as the spokesman for those who are downtrodden and who suffer at the hands of unjust oppressors, and calls on God to intervene and help. As the people's representative he is quite prepared to speak plainly to God, asking him frankly why he has failed to act: 'how long am I to cry for help and not be heard?'

The modern world gives us examples of addiction to cruelty on both the international and the individual level, beyond the ancient prophet's worst nightmares. If we do not feel any sense of outrage and indignation that such things can happen in a world supposedly created and sustained by a good and living God, are we really taking either the world or God seriously?

Israel's enemies

Habakkuk 1:5–11

Apart from a brief period of real independence, under the kings David and Solomon in the tenth century BC, Israel was always more or less under the thumb of some greater empire. In the sixth century the Babylonians, whose power-base was in modern Iraq, conquered most of Palestine and Syria, and even made inroads into Egypt. For Israel's politicians and people this made the Babylonians (or 'Chaldeans' as the Old Testament calls them) the greatest of all possible enemies. But the prophets (especially Jeremiah) saw in their conquests not just human aggression, but the hand of God stretched out to punish his rebellious people.

God's instruments. Habakkuk captures the tension between these two ways of seeing the world-conquerors. They are 'a bitter and hasty nation'; they 'fly like an eagle', and 'terror of them goes before them'; they are 'guilty men, whose own might is their god'. Yet on the other hand it is God who is at work through them. Speaking now in the person of God, rather than of the people as he did in the opening section of this chapter, Habakkuk says that 'I' (that is, the God of Israel himself) 'am rousing the Chaldeans'. He is no doubt right to say that this is something that the people 'would not believe, even if told'. For them the difficulty was to believe that God could possibly use a pagan and godless nation to punish his very own people. For us it may be impossible to believe that God is involved at all in wars and political tensions. Most of us will part company with the Old Testament at this point. Nevertheless the prophets may be able to help us appreciate that God's work can sometimes be puzzling or contrary to appearances, and at least to realize that human political affairs, both national and international, are far from being a matter of indifference to him; though we may want to be far less confident that we can tell which side he is likely to be on, in the extreme complexities of world affairs, than the prophets were.

A question of God

Habakkuk 1:12–13

The paradox of God's decision to use the Chaldeans as his instrument in punishing Israel is brought to a sharp focus in these verses. It is God who has 'destined them to chastise'; yet God's character, as the people of Israel knew it, was such that he would not be expected to tolerate such an evil and bloodthirsty nation, who 'devour men more righteous than' themselves. The prophet is faced with the problem of how to reconcile the specific message God has given him to proclaim with what he believes to be true of God in general. He fails to see how one can be made to square with the other: he challenges God to explain himself.

The courage of faith. Christians sometimes talk as though it were blasphemous or improper to raise questions like these—that it shows a lack of true faith, or irreverence towards God. The Old Testament is more robust, and believes that if God is really God, he is quite capable of facing the most demanding questions we may put to him. A faith which closes its eyes and stops its ears when confronted with the real problems of human existence, or which thinks it already has all the answers, is not so much faith as self-deception.

Further questions

Habakkuk 1:14–17

For the moment, at least, the questioning continues. The great enemy which is about to destroy Israel is not merely cruel and remorseless, but also entirely indiscriminate in its destruction of other nations and their people, and thoroughly godless into the bargain. Seen in the perspective of God's intentions, they are no doubt meant to be an instrument of divine punishment on Israel, and perhaps on other nations too; but they themselves certainly did not see matters in that way. So far as they were concerned, foreign conquests were simply a perverted form of pleasure, and they enjoyed nothing better than capturing and destroying foreign cities and their inhabitants. It is all very well (says the prophet to God) to talk as though there is some great and solemn purpose behind our being pillaged by the Babylonians; I don't doubt that in your mind that is how it looks. But for those on the receiving end of this plan it is more like being a fish caught at random by a trawl-net or an angler's line. As far as the Babylonians themselves are concerned, killing us is just a day's sport; they certainly don't see the power and justice of *our* God at work in what they are doing. Indeed, for all practical purposes they don't worship any god at all: their own weapons are their gods, like a fisherman who virtually worships his own tackle, for whom angling is a kind of addiction.

The patient watchman *Habakkuk 2:1–4*

In his perplexity the prophet turns to God in the hope of some further vision, some new information about what the future holds for his people and for their enemies. Like Ezekiel (look at Ezekiel 3:17) Habakkuk sees himself as being like a watchman or look-out, standing on top of a tower to have a vantage-point from which he can see more of the divine plan than others, and will be able to let them know at once as soon as there is any fresh news. And God tells him that news is indeed on the way: a runner has been appointed to bring word to the prophet, and even though there may be a short delay before he arrives, the prophet must not despair, but wait in confidence.

A new message: strength in stillness. So far what he has heard has seemed puzzling: it has raised as many questions as it has solved. Now there is to be some new message, and the prophet will be the first to learn of it. By implication, we can expect it to be a message bringing some comfort and encouragement, some answer to the anxiety and distress of the prophet and his people. According to Habakkuk, however, a great deal is revealed about the people by the way that they await God's new word. To understand verse 4, we need to grasp a prophetic idea which is expressed most clearly by the prophet Isaiah, who prophesied in Jerusalem rather more than a hundred years before the Babylonians became a threat to Israel, around 740–700BC. This idea is that God can and will save his people from their enemies, but only if they do not try to overcome them by force of arms. The prophets were not pacifists, but they did believe that for a tiny nation such as Israel to attempt a military solution to the threat posed by the great empires of their day amounted to culpable stupidity, and that God could not be expected to protect them against their own folly if they insisted on going it alone. As Isaiah puts it (Isaiah 30:15), 'In stillness and in staying quiet, there lies your strength'. Habakkuk's message is essentially the same. If the nation is 'reckless', and tries to anticipate by force the deliverance that comes from God alone, it will totter and fall just as the prophet has already warned; what is needed is 'faith' or 'faithfulness', which means a quiet trust and confidence in God's power which does not rely on human help.

It is not clear how the prophets thought this message—which sounds like a call to the nation's leaders to pursue some kind of passive, non-aligned policy—was meant to be translated into concrete political and military realities; nor is it clear whether they thought that it could be applied to the individual faced with life's perplexities and threats. If we do want to find a word for ourselves as individuals in this best-known verse of Habakkuk, 'The righteous shall live by faith(fulness)', we can perhaps best see it as a call to endurance and perseverance in our trust of God to do what is best for us in the long term, whatever difficulties we may from time to time encounter.

The prophets were charged with acting as intermediaries between God and his people—praying for them to God, and telling them what God demanded of them and what he intended to do for them or with them. We might call the prophetic task a pastoral *vocation. The early Christians thought that in an important sense all the people of God were now prophets, filled with the Holy Spirit which had inspired the prophets who appear in the Old Testament as highly unusual, special people. How are Christians today meant to discharge their 'prophetic' calling?*

The plunderer destroyed *Habakkuk 2:5–8*

The rest of chapter 2 seems to provide some answers to the problems of chapter 1: how could God think it just to punish one group of sinners through the agency of another group that was still more sinful, and that did not even acknowledge him?

The solution to this puzzle, as we see it in the remainder of chapter 2, is watertight though hardly very consoling. The Babylonians will indeed sack Jerusalem; the prophet's earlier conviction that they were God's appointed agents for vengeance was no illusion. But the fact that God can use them in this role does not mean that he approved of them; they are useful to him, not dear to him. And so, when their mission against Israel is complete, they in turn will have to pay the price for their own inhumanity and capricious violence.

A precedent. Isaiah had said exactly the same about the Assyrians who had destroyed the old northern kingdom of Israel in 721 BC, leaving only the little southern kingdom, Judah, for the Babylonians to finish off. 'When the Lord has finished all that he means to do, he will punish the king of Assyria for this fruit of his pride' (see Isaiah 10:5–19). In just the same way, Habakkuk believes, the proud Babylonians will be overthrown in their turn.

The priority of justice. For what matters, in the minds of all the great prophets of Israel, is not that this or that nation should have the upper hand, but that God's justice should prevail. God does indeed care for his own people; he is far from indifferent to their suffering, and he does not love their enemies, even when those enemies become, temporarily, the instruments through which he checks his people's rebellion against his laws. But he cares more for justice, and he will see justice prevail, even if it means that he must endure seeing the world he has made lie in ruins. This is an uncomfortable message, and Christians have never believed that it can be the last word on the subject. But it is an authentic and central part of the prophetic witness.

Christians share with the ancient prophets a belief in a God of justice. But they also share the conviction that the same God loves and cares for us.

'Unless the Lord builds the house . . .' *Habakkuk 2:9–14*

We now come to some more short sayings beginning 'Woe betide . . .' Who is the object of God's anger, as expressed by the prophet? Is it the enemy—the Babylonians—or his own nation and its ruler, who (if the book comes from the sixth century) would be Jehoiakim (see 2 Kings 23:36—24:7)? Perhaps they are deliberately ambiguous. As we have just seen, God promises that when the enemy has completed its task as his instrument in punishing Israel, it too will be punished, and the most natural way of looking at these 'woes' is that they spell out in detail the crimes which make this promised punishment of the enemy every bit as just as the prior punishment of Israel at their hands. So perverse is it for a mere mortal man to kill and plunder in the pursuit of his own glory, rather than of God's, that the very stone and beams of his palace will cry out to him in horror—one of the Old Testament's most memorable pictures of human sin as an affront even to the inanimate world.

On the other hand, this condemnation of the Babylonian king may well be two-edged; for Jehoiakim himself, as we know from Jeremiah, had an obsession with building 'houses' (palaces) in the literal sense of the word. The king of Judah and the king of Babylon, then, are brothers beneath the skin; both are more interested in their own prestige than in the well-being of their subjects, let alone that of foreign nations. For God to punish first one, and then the other, is not a piece of arbitrary divine vindictiveness; both alike thoroughly deserve it. The Old Testament stands unequivocally against the misuse of power and status to obtain undeserved honour or to 'build' (we might say 'feather') 'one's own nest'.

Human vanity. Habakkuk's cries of 'woe' continue with a further condemnation of royal oppressiveness. Do they refer to Nebuchadnezzar, the king of Babylon, or to Jehoiakim, his own king? Undoubtedly the empire of the Babylonians was built with the 'blood' of thousands of subject peoples—which could hardly be said, without great exaggeration, of Jehoiakim's relatively modest building programmes. The territory of Judah—all that was left of the old dual kingdom of Israel and Judah—over which Jehoiakim reigned with such a show of magnificence had shrunk by this period to an area about as large as a medium-sized English county. Any sensible person could have seen, then, that the achievements of that Judaean king were 'a mere nothing'.

But to claim that this was an adequate description of *Babylonian* power required then, as it would require now, both a very cool head and a very brave heart. Those who have dreams of empire, still more those who know the reality of it, do not like to hear such a message.

The wine of God's anger *Habakkuk 2:15–17*

The Old Testament quite often uses the picture of a goblet of wine to stand for the fate that has to be accepted by a conquered nation, or for the anger of God that is poured out on a sinful nation or a sinful individual. Moreover, drunkenness struck the biblical authors as a particularly apt picture of the distracted and chaotic state that a newly-conquered nation would be in—staggering around with no sense of direction.

Making the punishment fit the crime. Here, then, Habakkuk almost certainly has in mind primarily the coming oppression of Israel, and other small nations, by the Babylonians. He sees them as conquering 'their companions'—the small countries with which they should have lived in mutual respect—not for any high motives, but out of pure malice and pleasure in other people's degradation, like a powerful host who forces his guests to get drunk because he enjoys seeing them behave indecently. God's response to such behaviour works on a principle very common in the prophets: he will make the punishment fit the crime. The Babylonians will be forced to drink from the goblet of God's own anger, and their own shame will far outweigh any pleasure they got from seeing others degraded. Even what they do to woods and animals (Lebanon was proverbial for its dense forests) will have its own punishment. Every aspect of the Babylonians' lust for power thus meets with just retribution.

Even here Habakkuk may be glancing out of the corner of his eye at his own king, Jehoiakim. Most of this saying does not fit the Judaean king, who could hardly be said to have oppressed the neighbouring countries. But he might well be accused of 'violence done to Lebanon', which is probably where he got the timber for the cedar palace that Jeremiah condemns (see the earlier comments on Habakkuk 2:9–11). Once again there is a measure of ambiguity, which may be deliberate. For the prophets, Israel is as guilty as other nations, and other nations are as guilty as Israel; God's just vengeance is no respecter of persons.

Unofficial religion *Habakkuk 2:18–20*

Maybe we are meant to be reminded by these verses that the gods on whom Israel's oppressors place so much reliance are in reality quite powerless to save them from the just punishment of God which has been predicted in the preceding sayings. But this passage may equally well be a fragment that had no original connection with its present context, and then it will have referred to the sin of idolatry as practised by God's own people, not just by their arch-enemy. Certainly the Israelites themselves practised forms of religion that were very far from the austere service of the one Creator God that the prophets demanded. Undoubtedly many people worshipped before 'wood', that is, sacred poles rather like our maypoles, which probably represented the old Palestinian goddess Asherah, and before 'dead stone'—pillars sacred to Baal.

The folly of idolatry. In any case, whether it is his fellow Israelites or their foreign enemies whom the prophet is condemning here, he uses a line of argument that became the stock Jewish approach to all religions involving physical symbols or statues of God or the gods. The argument is that it is not so much wicked as stupid and senseless to bow down before objects which you yourself have made. How can anyone think that a piece of wood, cut from the same tree of which other branches are used for cooking food, is a god deserving worship? Of course this really misrepresents what is going on when 'images' are used in worship, and is a rather 'unfair' argument. Images, icons, statues and the like are used as visual symbols through which the divine can be approached, and it is very doubtful whether anyone has ever literally committed 'idolatry' in the sense condemned by the prophets. Nevertheless the strong tradition that no physical object, however beautiful, can be an adequate way of portraying God has been absolutely crucial in Judaism, Christianity, and Islam; without it, the idea of a radical distinction between God and the created world, which is central to all three great religions, might never have been discovered. The positive point is made in the famous saying with which chapter 2 ends:

> *The Lord is in his holy temple: let all the earth be hushed in his presence.*

God is greater than all the things he has made, and the dark and empty sanctuary (the 'Holy of holies'), approached in silence, is a better symbol of his greatness than any 'idol', however lavish.

An ancient psalm *Habakkuk 3:1–8*

The third chapter of Habakkuk consists of a magnificent psalm, which many scholars think is much older than the time of the prophet—perhaps one of the oldest hymns in the Bible, going back into the eleventh or twelfth centuries BC. Whether or not this is so, it certainly forms a suitable climax to the book, and it deals in its own way with religious questions and problems that are surprisingly close to those raised by Habakkuk himself. Like a number of the Psalms, this poem begins by announcing that its subject is to be the mighty acts of God, his 'work' in the historical experience of his people. The ancient Israelites loved to recall all that God had done for them in the choice of Abraham and his family, the deliverance from Egypt at the hand of Moses, and the gift of a fertile land as their home.

Wrath and mercy. But the introduction to the 'Prayer of Habakkuk' tells us that we are going to hear about God's mighty deeds from a particular point of view. 'In the midst of the years thou didst make thyself known, *and in thy wrath thou didst remember mercy*.' The God of inexorable justice, whom Habakkuk proclaimed, is also a God who cares for his creation. Until now this theme has hardly been heard in the book. All the emphasis has been on God's vengeance, and the prophet has tried to convince his hearers that this vengeance is just and reasonable, whether it falls on Israel at the hands of their enemies, or on those enemies in their turn. As Paul was to put it, 'All have sinned, and fallen short of the glory of God' (Romans 3:23). But in this final chapter we see the other side of the coin: in his anger, God still remembers 'mercy'. This does not mean quite what we call mercy, but something nearer to 'commitment' or 'faithfulness to his promises'. In spite of all, God is in the end, beyond all reasonable hope, on the side of his people, and seeks their life, not their extinction. How this can be so, in the light of the stern warnings of the rest of the book, is obscure; yet by adding this psalm the compiler of the book makes it clear that vengeance without any room for forgiveness is not God's final word. The Old Testament bears abundant witness to God's care and concern for individuals, and contains many prayers which show how intimate and personal the Israelite worshipper's relationship with him could be: look, for example, at Psalm 42, or Psalm 63. But the Old Testament writers were in no doubt at all that this God was also awe-inspiring, even terrifying in his majestic power, and there are few passages that make this so clear as these verses of Habakkuk 3 (though Psalm 18 comes close to it).

> *God sides with his own people, but we have to beware of assuming too readily that we are that people.*

The divine warrior. God is here seen as living in 'Teman' or on 'Mount Paran'—in the desert south of Israel. God is seen as a God of the desert, just as he is in the Sinai stories. He is portrayed as a victorious general at the head of an army, making his way across the desert and sweeping away bedouin encampments ('Midian' and 'Cushan', peoples who lived in the Judaean wilderness) as he goes. The imagery of this passage has extremely ancient roots going back to the mythology of the Canaanites who inhabited Palestine before the Israelites ever settled there. 'Plague' and 'Pestilence' were the names of gods; and one of the great exploits of the Canaanite god who appears in the Old Testament as 'Baal' had been to overpower the great dragon or sea-serpent who symbolized all chaos and disorder in nature. In taking over these mythological themes and applying them to the God of Israel, the Israelites were claiming that it was none other than their own God, the God who had directed their history and who could be known in prayer and worship—private as well as corporate—who was the real victor over all the chaotic and godless forces that opposed them, whether these were natural disasters or powerful enemies. It was no doubt a comfort for people in Israel to feel that this awesome God was on their side in troubles; but the prophets were only spelling out something that is obvious in terrifying psalms like this when they stress that he is not the kind of God you can safely take for granted. To be his chosen people is not a very comfortable vocation.

Deliverance for Israel *Habakkuk 3:9–16*

The original Hebrew in this passage is obscure in places: not surprising, if it had already been handed down over a period of five or six hundred years even before it reached Habakkuk or the editors of his book. It seems a pity that the NEB translators have relegated to a note the most memorable picture of all: the sun raising its hands in horror at the sight of God striding over the desert (vv. 10–11). Terrifying as God's appearance is, he is coming (v. 13) to save his people, not to destroy them.

The Israelites who wrote this psalm were not thinking simply of an abstract description of how their God might generally be expected to act: they were thinking back to the national memory of how he had in fact acted in the course of Israel's history. God, as we saw in reading verses 1–2, had made himself known already, as one who in his wrath always remembered his commitment to his people. Though he had been ready enough to punish them, and would do so again if they deserved it, still in the last resort he was on their side and opposed to their enemies.

Virtue rewarded? *Habakkuk 3:17–19*

Ancient Israel seems mostly to have assumed that the person or nation that served God truly could be assured of a reward, and it seems seldom to have occurred to anyone that it would be somehow more virtuous not to expect one. Christians have sometimes felt superior to the people of the Old Testament for just this reason.

But this misunderstands the Old Testament. It is true that people in ancient Israel did not see much virtue in self-denial for its own sake: for them the world was to be enjoyed, because God had made it good, and it was only reasonable to expect that he would wish those who were loyal to him to receive a just reward in the form of prosperity and happiness. But if it came to a choice—it often did—between loyalty to God and immediate material advantage, there was no doubt which was to be chosen. And the choice is nowhere illustrated so memorably as in these concluding verses of the 'Prayer of Habakkuk'. Habakkuk's prophecies have made the vital point that God is on his people's side, but no one can simply assume that he or she is part of that people: the enemies of Israel are indeed hateful to God, but they can be found within the nation that calls itself by that name as well as among the Babylonian conquerors. The king of Judah is no more part of God's chosen people than the king of Babylon, if he blasphemes God by the way he lives.

Loyalty tested. Now we learn the other side of that truth: God is on his people's side, but that does not necessarily mean that they will enjoy instant success in all they do. Their loyalty to him may be tested by suffering; the harvest may fail, drought and famine may assail them, but throughout all this they must retain their allegiance to God. Anyone can see that there is something noble and worthy of respect in such an attitude, and the long history of the Jewish people under relentless and intolerable persecution provides endless examples of it.

Reading Habakkuk raises questions about God's justice and human justice. Can we, like the prophet, see the hand of God at work in political and military events, or in natural disaster? Even if we insist that God does stand behind the operation of both the natural order and the human world of international relations, can we go further and actually identify this happening or that as his 'work' (Habakkuk 3:2)? Why does the outcome of human affairs so often seem to be unjust, if God really does rule the world?

According to the prophets, one of the greatest affronts to God is presented by powerful nations that oppress and conquer their smaller neighbours, and by rulers who oppress their helpless subjects. It is not difficult to think of examples of both kinds in the modern world. Do Christians have a duty to speak 'prophetically' about such things? If so, what form should their protest take?

We have often noticed ways in which Habakkuk's message can be applicable to Christians individually—especially, perhaps, in presenting us with a particular idea of God, since the God he worshipped is clearly the same God that Christians believe in, though the aspects of God that are stressed in his prophecy may not be those we most naturally think of first. When we read Habakkuk, therefore, we may be reminded of truths about God that we sometimes neglect: his power, majesty, and relentless moral demands, his insistence on unswerving loyalty ('the righteous man will live by being faithful!'), and the terror he can inspire in those who oppose him.

ZEPHANIAH

The title of the book identifies the prophet by name, by ancestry and by date (v. 1), but further than this we have no information about Zephaniah. It is possible that he had an African ancestor, for his father's name is given as Cushi, and Cush was a name for Ethiopia. The listing of a prophet's ancestry in this way is unusual. The explanation may be that the Hezekiah mentioned was the king of that name who reigned from 715–687BC (see 2 Kings 18:1ff), but of this it is impossible to be certain. The date given for Zephaniah's ministry is the reign of Josiah (640–609BC). This king was famous for the religious reforms which he initiated. Added impetus was given to the movement for reform by the discovery of a law scroll (probably the nucleus of Deuteronomy) in the Jerusalem temple in 621BC. The account of the reforms and the finding of the scroll is given in 2 Kings 22–23. The nature of Zephaniah's denunciations against the impurity of religious life in Judah and Jerusalem suggests that his warnings belong to a time shortly before Josiah's reforms, probably about 630BC.

Zephaniah is much concerned with purity of worship but his horizons are not limited to Judah and Jerusalem, for the Lord's reign is universal, a note which resounds in the Psalms (e.g. 96:1; 98:4). The form of Zephaniah's message, much of which has the style of direct speech by God, together with the occasional echo of liturgical phrases (e.g. 1:7 and 3:5, the latter possibly quoting a hymn of praise) suggests that these words may have been designed for use in temple services.

Zephaniah speaks forthrightly about divine judgment but his message ends on a joyful note, for God is a God who works transformation in human lives and in this lies hope.

Further reading

J.H. Eaton, *Obadiah, Nahum, Habakkuk, Zephaniah*, Torch Commentary, 1961

R. Mason, *Zephaniah, Habakkuk, Joel*, Old Testament Guides, 1994

J.D.W. Watts, *Joel, Obadiah, Jonah, Nahum, Habakkuk and Zephaniah*, Cambridge Bible Commentary, 1975

Called to account

Zephaniah 1:1–18

The Book of Zephaniah shocks us with the blunt words of doom with which it opens: 'I will sweep the earth clean of all that is on it, says the Lord' (v. 2). Is this the vengeful Old Testament God of popular thinking, a total contrast to the loving God of the New Testament? That is a superficial verdict. Not only is judgment to be followed by salvation and joyful transformation (3:9–20), but the words must be understood in context. They were no less startling to their first hearers than to us, but certainly more meaningful and explicable. For Zephaniah is one of the prophets whose words were spoken in the setting of Israel's worship. Here at the yearly autumn festival, celebrating harvest and praying for next season's blessing, the prophet's word breaks in, shattering complacency. With his three-fold 'I will sweep away' (Hebrew *aseph*) he plays on the name of the festival *Asiph* (Ingathering, see Exodus 23:16).

Verse 4 narrows the focus to Judah and Jerusalem. The worshippers are guilty. Some had turned to astral deities (v. 5): some were 'hedging their bets', paying allegiance to Yahweh alongside Milcom, an Ammonite god (2 Kings 23:13), and so breaking the first commandment (Exodus 20:3). Others were simply ignoring the Lord, living their lives as if he did not exist (v. 6). Verse 7 brings us to the high point of the festival: silent before the Lord God! Yes, God is at hand, says the prophet, but coming for judgment, not for blessing. Then the political leaders are singled out. The references to foreign attire and dancing (vv. 8–9) are more sinister than they appear. They are part of pagan religious practices (see 2 Kings 10:22; Exodus 32:19). Next come the merchants and their commerce (vv. 10–11), and finally those who deny, not God's existence, but God's involvement with his world: 'the Lord will do nothing, good or bad', a remote, uncaring deity. Belief and commitment were no easier then than now.

The 'great day of the Lord' (v. 14) celebrated in the festival is in reality to be a time not of blessing but of doom (so Amos 5:18). God is no convenient ally to be taken up or neglected at will. He is the impartial judge of all the earth. And so in the midst of heedless celebration, Zephaniah turns the familiar and comfortable into the challenging and disturbing, a characteristic of the prophets.

Pride humiliated *Zephaniah 2:1–15*

Chapter 1 was entirely dark, full of foreboding. With this chapter a glimmer of hope flickers (v. 3), coming to full blaze in the latter part of chapter 3. But it starts, and continues, sombrely. Here is God's victorious warfare against all that opposes his rule, beginning with Jerusalem—which is for the prophet, as for Hereford Cathedral's *mappa mundi*, the centre of the world—then reaching out to the four points of the compass.

First, a dramatic plea to Jerusalem (vv. 1–2): take action before it is too late. The day of the Lord, the manifestation of his kingship celebrated yearly in the autumn festival, is, in the light of the world's sin, 'the day of the Lord's anger' (vv. 2–3). The poetry is impressive. The five lines of verses 2–3 all begin in Hebrew with the letter *b*, like a solemn drum beat: 'before (*beterem*) . . . before . . . before . . . seek (*baqqeshu*) . . . seek . . .'

Then come words of judgment against foreign nations, the Philistines to the (south) west (vv. 5–7), Moab and Ammon to the east (vv. 8–11), Ethiopia to the south (v. 12), Assyria to the north (vv. 13–15). These and similar oracles in other prophetic books (e.g. Isaiah 13–23; Jeremiah 46–51) are not simply nationalistic outbursts against other nations as though God was inevitably on Israel's side. They are affirming the universal reign of God (see Psalms 96, 97) before whose presence evil must be rooted out. The warning sounds as strongly against Judah, and indeed this takes precedence in the chapter, for upon those who claim special relationship with God lie special obligations. Only in humility and obedience is there hope (v. 3). For God is concerned with justice in the world. And here is a key thought of the chapter, that arrogance, *hubris* which fails to recognize human limitations and to acknowledge God's sovereignty, is the great obstacle to his just and gentle rule. Notice the words for 'boasting' and 'pride' in verses 8 and 10 and the description of Nineveh (v. 13), a city complacently secure, boasting of her solitary splendour, 'I am, and I alone', blind to God's authority in human affairs. How like Ezekiel's picture of Egypt's proud Pharaoh, 'My Nile is my own; I made it' (Ezekiel 29:3)!

The Lord's joy

Zephaniah 3:1—20

With chapter 3 Zephaniah comes full circle to where he began, with judgment on all oppression, on the self-willed who refuse to acknowledge God (vv. 1–2). This is not a vindictive God but one who defends the weak and oppressed. Jerusalem itself, says the prophet, is tyrannical, a city where people suffer. The leaders, political and religious, are guilty. This is poetry and each line of verses 3–4 begins dramatically: officials, judges, prophets, priests (so begin the lines in Hebrew). Then verse 5 breaks the sequence. There is another to be reckoned with—Yahweh, and *he* is just, dependable day in, day out.

But justice for the oppressed means judgment on the oppressor, and in verse 6 God speaks, rising from his throne to pronounce sentence, not out of petty jealousy (v. 8) but from his right to total allegiance (the first commandment, Exodus 20:3). 'Wait for me,' he says. The words are chilling, used familiarly of waiting for the Lord's salvation (Psalm 33:20), here in bitter irony.

Yet, if God is to be God, sin cannot have the last word. With one of those sudden inexplicable reversals found elsewhere in the prophets (e.g. Hosea 2:13–14) judgment becomes salvation. God takes the initiative. Hope lies not in human reformation but in divine transformation (v. 9). The disaster of the tower of Babel (Genesis 11:1–9) is reversed. The echoes are deliberate. Instead of confused speech, pure speech, instead of seeking a name for themselves, calling on the Lord's name, serving him 'shoulder to shoulder', instead of scattering, gathering (vv. 9–10). Even the Lord is pictured as singing! (v. 17). But there is a cost to it (vv. 11-12):

you shall no longer be haughty in my holy mountain.
I will leave in the midst of you a people humble and lowly.

Zephaniah shows us a God who is not to be trifled with. He is the living God, not humanity writ large. And having a right view of God means having a right view of ourselves, that we are accountable for our actions. We cannot sin with impunity, and we are not ultimately self-sufficient. We need resources beyond our own. Yet it is in our *transformation that the Lord finds* his *joy!*

HAGGAI AND ZECHARIAH

The Old Testament ends with three 'Minor Prophets', Haggai, Zechariah and Malachi, which point forward with increasing expectancy to the New. Haggai envisages a temple that no human craftsmen could build (2:6–9; see John 2:19–22). Zechariah sees the coming of a king to Jerusalem 'humble and riding on an ass' (9:9; see Matthew 21:5; John 12:15), and people mourning 'when they look on him whom they have pierced' (12:10; see John 19:37). Malachi foretells the coming of a messenger to 'prepare the way of the Lord' (3:1; see Mark 1:2; Luke 1:17, 76, etc.).

The second temple. A central theme in all three is the temple. This is because Haggai and Zechariah lived in Jerusalem at a time when the temple of Solomon, destroyed by the Babylonians two generations before, was being rebuilt (520–515BC). It was then that the 600 years of Jewish history known as the 'second temple period', during which Judaism and Christianity emerged, began. Some of the credit for the rebuilding of the temple must go to the two prophets (Ezra 3), but not all. At the time, Judah was part of the great Persian Empire and it was the new policy of the first Persian kings, such as Cyrus (Ezra 1:1–4; Isaiah 45:1) and Darius (Ezra 6), to encourage national aspirations by supporting institutions like the temple at Jerusalem.

Inspiration. So the role of our two prophets goes beyond setting the citizens of Jerusalem to work on the bricks and mortar of a new building. Within the new situation of peace and freedom they found themselves in, they use the building and all the traditions associated with it as a source of inspiration for people looking for the involvement of God, who sixty years ago seemed to have abandoned them, in their lives and their community. The key to these two books is to be found in this movement from modest historical reality in Haggai, to visions of a new age, not unlike parts of Daniel and Revelation, in the later chapters of Zechariah.

Further reading

R.J. Coggins, *Haggai, Zechariah, Malachi*, Old Testament Guides, Sheffield, 1987

D.R. Jones, *Haggai, Zechariah and Malachi*, Torch Commentary, 1982

P.R. Ackroyd, 'Haggai and Zechariah', in *Peake's Commentary on the Bible*, 1962

HAGGAI

Desperate situation

Haggai 1

The book begins with how things are. For some time the harvests have been poor. There has been a drought. People have tried everything, but to no avail. No one has 'job satisfaction'. The prophet puts this down to the fact that 'the house of the Lord' is lying in ruins. The people have been putting all their efforts into improving their own houses and refusing to contribute to the temple. He addresses his first prophecy to the city leaders, Zerubbabel the governor of Judah and Joshua the High Priest, and within a month (v. 15) work on the temple is under way.

Is a temple needed? There was at the time some anti-temple feeling in Jerusalem reflected in a passage like Isaiah 66:1–3—'Heaven is my throne and the earth is my footstool; what is the house which you would build for me?' One might compare the situation to that in countries where the poor live in squalid hovels right next to magnificent religious buildings. Where there is not enough to go round, is it not an affront to human dignity that the largest slice of the cake should go to the 'house of the Lord . . . for him to take pleasure in it' (v. 8)? It certainly would be if this was just the story of a successful appeal: one word from Haggai and everyone dropped what they were doing and began to work in the temple. Even if that is what happened at Jerusalem in the summer of 520BC (vv. 1 and 15), it is not the point of the book. It is about poverty, hunger, thirst, hardship, for which there was apparently no economic cure. What was missing was the presence of God, his 'glory' (v. 8), something that can be found in many forms, in music, in nature, in human love, but which, for the people of God, appears fully only in worship, 'in his holy temple'. When they realized this (that is what 'they feared before the Lord' in v. 12 means), their spirits were revived and they went about their business with a new sense of purpose. In the words of Solomon's Psalm: 'Unless the Lord builds the house, those who build it labour in vain' (Psalm 127).

A new age *Haggai 2:1–9*

The message of Haggai's second day of prophesying, which happened to be during the celebrations of the Feast of Booths (see Leviticus 23:39–43), says nothing of the actual building activities at all. It is about the 'spirit of God (that) abides among you' (v. 5) *in spite of the new temple*, not because of it. This takes us to the heart of Haggai's prophetic vision. Notice how he recalls the story of the exodus from Egypt rather than the story of the building of Solomon's temple, and the promise that God would dwell in their midst even in the wilderness (Exodus 25:8). The new temple was more like the flimsy booths in which the Israelites sheltered in the wilderness, than Solomon's temple, but it stands for God's glory and his power to protect.

Verse 4 perhaps recalls God's promise to Joshua at the end of the wilderness period (Joshua 1:5–6): 'As I was with Moses, so I will be with you. Be strong and of good courage . . .' As he was about to lead God's people into the Promised Land, so now they are about to enter a new age of peace and prosperity more glorious than the golden age of Solomon (1 Kings 6–10). This is not just the vision of a new temple. Heaven and earth are involved. Some of the signs and wonders that accompanied the exodus will herald the new age. Haggai also envisages a day when all the nations of the world will acknowledge God's power and return to him the silver and the gold he had lent them. Then the temple, filled with the treasures of the nations, even more splendid than Solomon's, will stand as a symbol of the Promised Land and the new Jerusalem towards which God's pilgrim people, 'a kingdom of priests and a holy nation' (Exodus 19:6), are journeying. The efforts of the threatened little community, struggling to rebuild and to survive, will be rewarded far beyond their wildest dreams.

Gift or gifts? The word translated 'treasures' in verse 7, literally 'desired things', was understood by early Christian interpreters to refer to the 'Desired One' and the coming of the Messiah to Jerusalem. Others apply it to the gifts of gold, frankincense and myrrh, brought from foreign nations by the magi to transform a humble stable into the dwelling-place of God.

Potent force *Haggai 2:10–23*

This passage begins with a curious discussion about holiness and uncleanness. Haggai asks the priests, What effect does the holiness of their temple sacrifices have on everyday life? The answer is, None. In other words, without some personal commitment or change of heart, rituals themselves are worthless. We can hear again the voice of the anti-temple tradition that goes back to Samuel (1 Samuel 15:22), Isaiah (1:11) and Amos (5:21–24). He then asks whether the same is true of uncleanness, and the answer is, No. If a priest touched you, no holiness was transmitted to you, you were unaffected. But if you came into contact with a leper or a dead body or some other source of uncleanness, the uncleanness was transmitted to you, and you became unclean too. So uncleanness was a more potent force than holiness. 'This people' in verse 14 refers to the citizens of Judah (as in chapter 1). So the uncleanness is the uncleanness of people who did not worship God at all, people who did not 'return to him' (v. 17)—and suffered the consequences. But all that has changed. From now on God will bless them, their fields, their vineyards, their orchards—and their temple.

God's servant. Haggai's last words are addressed to Zerubbabel alone (vv. 20–23). The prophecy recalls, on the one hand, the Song of Miriam where the horses and riders of Israel's enemies are thrown into the sea (Exodus 15:21), and on the other, the exaltation of the

Servant of the Lord in Isaiah (e.g. 42:1; 52:13; 53:12). This is a dream, like the vision of a new temple earlier in the chapter, that goes far beyond what actually happened to Zerubbabel. Haggai is looking beyond the frailty of a human institution. He sees the power of God (in the words of another biblical woman of faith) 'to put down the mighty from their thrones and exalt those of low degree' (Luke 1:52). The 'signet ring' is both a token of God's love for his servant (Song of Solomon 8:6), and a symbol of his authority over the world (Jeremiah 22:24).

ZECHARIAH

Behind the scenes

Zechariah 1:1–17

Zechariah's first day of prophesying was in the month before Haggai's last. After an introduction about hardened hearts becoming receptive, and how God is true to his word (vv. 1–6), Zechariah tells of his first vision. Angels or 'messengers of God' appear in all of the last three Minor Prophets (if we include Haggai 1:13), but are most prominent in Zechariah. In later writings they are named—e.g. Michael (Daniel 12:1)—but even in this earlier text some are distinguished by having various different tasks to perform. In this vision Zechariah sees a troop of angels on horseback, resting in the shade of a wooded valley. There was also an angel whose task was to explain to the prophet what was going on and to pray for his people in Judah. This is one of those glimpses into what goes on in heaven 'behind the scenes', as it were, like 1 Kings 22:19–23, Isaiah 6 and Job 1, where history is made. The leader of the angelic horsemen, 'a man riding upon a red horse', presents his troop as having just returned from patrolling the earth. They report that all is peaceful. This is perhaps a reference to the end of political unrest in the early years of the reign of King Darius, but also to the silent, desolate ruins of Jerusalem.

God's involvement. At this point in the vision Zechariah's angelic guide intervenes as other messengers of God have done (Isaiah 6:8, 11; Amos 7:2, 5)—'How long, O Lord?' God's 'gracious and comforting' answer is not given directly but we may imagine it was very similar to

Isaiah 40:1–2—'Comfort, comfort my people . . . speak tenderly to Jerusalem and cry to her that her warfare is ended and her iniquity is pardoned.' The angel then instructs Zechariah in what to say to his people. God is not distant or detached; he is passionately involved in the fate of his people. That is what 'jealousy', 'anger' and 'compassion' mean in verses 14 and 15. The powerful nations, in particular the Assyrians and the Babylonians, whom God commissioned to punish his people, have overstepped the mark. Now a new Jerusalem is to be built, with a new temple, and all the cities of Judah are to overflow with prosperity. God chooses the weak and with his help they will become strong.

Not forsaken *Zechariah 1:18—2:13*

This passage (all one chapter in the Hebrew text) develops the theme of God's choice of the weak. First, the prophet sees 'four horns', symbolizing, as they do in two of Daniel's visions as well (Daniel 7 and 8), the mighty nations that come from the four corners of the earth to oppress the poor, and 'four smiths' who have the power to overcome them. This is a dream that one day the skill to make weapons and armour is taken away from the nations of the world, and oppressive regimes are rendered powerless (1 Samuel 13:19–22).

Large vision. In the second vision another craftsman appears, this time a young architect on his way to draw plans for new Jerusalem, and another angel. Zechariah is instructed by the angels to intercept the young man and tell him that, in the first place, his plans are too small. What is more, the new Jerusalem will not need a wall because 'I will be to her a wall of fire round about, says the Lord'. Like Haggai's vision of the new temple, Zechariah's goes far beyond this world.

Verses 6–12 are a prophecy, still in the idiom of Isaiah (especially chapters 49–52), calling for a new start. God has sent his prophet Zechariah to tell the people that the time has come for them to return to their homeland and rebuild their lives there: 'Flee from the land of the north [that is, Babylon, place of exile] . . . Escape to Zion . . . Sing and rejoice, O daughter of Zion' God has not forsaken them: they are 'the apple of his eye'. Like Haggai (2:5) and St John of Patmos (Revelation 21:3), Zechariah sees the new age as a time when God will dwell among his people again, as he did in the wilderness (Exodus

25:8). Those who treated them unjustly will themselves be plundered and exploited. People from all over the world will join them on their jubilant journey home. Notice how the violent, aggressive language of oppression and revenge in verses 8 and 9 is accompanied by words of the utmost tenderness in verses 10 and 11, where God addresses his people as a woman, vulnerable but safe in God's home.

Call for silence. The concluding appeal for silence in God's presence reminds us that the place where God and the world meet more than anywhere is in worship. It is there that God's heavenly dwelling-place and earthly places of worship, like the temple, intersect: in the words of Solomon's prayer on the day he dedicated the temple, 'when they pray towards this place, hear thou in heaven thy dwelling place, and when thou hearest, forgive' (1 Kings 8:27–30).

The prophecies and visions of these two prophets, however bizarre or impossible they are, speak to our imaginations and tell us that with God's help we can achieve more than we ever thought possible. The situation that gave rise to them is all too familiar today: derelict buildings, homelessness, general discontent and a feeling of powerlessness. But these prophets see in the temple a symbol of God's involvement in the world. It is the place where heaven and earth intersect, where we have glimpses through the gates of heaven.

Transforming Spirit

Zechariah 3–4

The next two visions are about the temple, seen as a symbol of hope and new life. In the first, the High Priest Joshua is on trial at the gates of heaven, accused of injustice and disobedience, the sins that had led to the destruction of Jerusalem in the days of his grandfather. He stands before God, humiliated, his vestments covered with filth. Two angels debate his case, the one (called Satan) representing strict justice, the other compassion. Divine compassion prevails. Joshua is forgiven and charged with the task of looking after the new temple. This means caring for his people, and making it possible for them to come near the gates of heaven (v. 7). The re-establishment of the temple, its priests restored for all to see and wonder at (that is what 'men of good omen' means in v. 8), and the restoration of the Davidic king ('the Branch' as in 4:12–14, Isaiah 11:1 and Jeremiah 33:14–16), are not ends in themselves. 'In a single day', the Day of Atonement no doubt when the trumpet proclaimed liberty throughout the land (Leviticus 25:9–10), people will share what they possess with their neighbours, and peace and justice will reign (see Micah 4:3–4).

New power. In the second vision the prophet sees a seven-branched candlestick of gold like the one in the tabernacle (Exodus 25:31–40). His angelic interpreter explains that this stands for God, all-seeing, ever alert to the needs of the whole world (v. 10). Two olive branches, which symbolize his two messianic representatives, anointed like David with olive oil (1 Samuel 16:13; 2 Samuel 5:3), are on either side of the lamp. In verses 6–10 there is a prophecy about Zerubbabel, the Davidic leader. As in Haggai the purpose is to point beyond the feeble reality of a powerless human being and a modest temple building, to what weak, fallible human beings can achieve with God's help: 'not by might or by power, but by my Spirit, says the Lord of hosts' (v. 6). That Spirit can transform a small group of men and women with poor prospects and meagre resources into a force that can change the world. So in the figure of Zerubbabel, the anointed of the Lord, towering above his contemporaries, yet humbly engaged in building the new Jerusalem, plummet in hand, we have a way of thinking about Christ and his role in the salvation of the world.

> *Build up the Church as a place where believers experience the justice and compassion of God, and the world will soon be rescued from injustice and oppression.*

Way of life

Zechariah 8

The following six short prophecies about Zion are inspired, like much of Zechariah, by Isaiah, and focus on faithfulness, holiness, righteousness, salvation and other attributes of the new Jerusalem (see Isaiah 1:21–26; 2:2–4; 26:1–6; 65:17–25). The first is about the 'zeal of the Lord of hosts' (Isaiah 9:7; 37:32), that impatient urge that makes God suffer our pains and act on behalf of those he loves. He will come to Jerusalem, even as it is, unclean, in ruins, without hope, and his coming will make it into the faithful city it once was, built upon a holy mountain. He chooses to dwell among those he loves, whatever their failures or misfortunes. They will be able to grow old in peace and security and contentment, watching their children and grandchildren playing in the street. Even God will be amazed at the transformation (v. 6).

Security. The agreement to be loyal to one another in verse 8 is set in the context of three great biblical words. 'I will save you' is much more than 'rescue': it means giving you victory (Isaiah 37:35), security (26:1) and justice (43:12) as well. 'Faithfulness' suggests being firmly established, like a dynasty or a government (Isaiah 7:9). 'Righteousness' includes both justice for all (Isaiah 11:4 and 5) and victory (41:10).

In verses 14–17 God confides in his people, telling them about the anger and hate that had turned him against them. This is the faith that can see the hand of God in catastrophes as well as prosperity, in failure as well as success (Isaiah 45:7). In the words of Job: 'The Lord gives, the Lord takes away. Blessed be the name of the Lord' (Job 1:21). He then outlines the way they are to live in the new kingdom: it is to be a way of truth and peace, truth and compassion between individuals, truth and compassion in government. Verse 19 picks up the theme of fasting from 7:3. True fasting is feeding the hungry, housing the homeless and clothing the naked (Isaiah 58:6–7). Do that and all the fasts will turn into days of joy and happiness for everyone, days of real truth and peace.

Zechariah gives us visions of a new world where violence and greed are destroyed, and compassion rules.

Humble victory

Zechariah 9

Chapters 9–14 are different from 1–8. There are no dates, no angels, no references to Zerubbabel and Joshua or the rebuilding of the temple, no moral teaching. But the two parts need not be separated from one another. The violent defeat of Zion's oppressors, with the exaltation and triumphant return of the king to Jerusalem, takes up themes from Haggai 2 and Zechariah 1:16–17. The bitter intensity of the attack on the Phoenician cities to the north, especially Tyre (v. 4) and the Philistines to the west (vv. 5–7) has a long history going back to the stories of Samson and Delilah, Saul and David, and appears often in the prophets (Amos 1:6–8; Isaiah 23; Jeremiah 47; Ezekiel 26–28). It again denotes the intense involvement of God in the affairs of the world. Where there is oppression he will stamp it out ruthlessly, showing no mercy to the oppressors. The day of vengeance, when the trumpet sounds and justice will be seen to be done, and God enters the fray 'in the whirlwinds of the south' (v. 14), will be a day of blood and violence (compare Isaiah 63:3).

Freedom. But blood has another meaning in biblical language: 'because of the blood of my covenant with you, I will set your captives free' (v. 11). A covenant sealed by the shedding of blood (Exodus 24), is one that is not broken. Exiled Jews, bound to their God by the everlasting covenant rite of circumcision, and estranged Christians who are one with Christ in the blood of the new covenant, are 'prisoners of hope' (v. 12). Whatever their plight, wherever they are, God will not forget them. They will be restored, and their new life of hope will more than compensate for the old (v. 12).

A new age when all the powers of evil, embodied in the aggression and injustice of international politics, will be ruthlessly destroyed. Exiles and captives will return home.

Humble and weak. At the heart of this chapter is the picture of the Davidic king returning triumphantly to his city 'humble and riding on an ass' (v. 9). Ultimate victory goes to the humble and weak. Actually humiliation and degradation figure quite prominently in biblical pictures of the Lord's anointed. Psalm 22 is a well-known example, beginning with the words 'My God, my God why have you forsaken me . . . ?' Even the mighty Zerubbabel does not shrink from taking the plummet in his hand and joining the humble builders (Zechariah 4:10). It stands to reason that if God is willing to enter into our sufferings and struggles, like a woman in labour (Isaiah 42:14), his anointed cannot triumph until he too has known what it is to suffer: 'and being found in human form he humbled himself and became obedient unto death, even death on a cross. Therefore God has highly exalted him . . .' (Philippians 2:8–9).

God's society

Here the prophet tackles the problem of a nation let down by its leaders. They resort to all kinds of misguided activities (like those condemned in Deuteronomy 18:10–11) to find answers to questions only God can answer. They are like a flock of sheep without a shepherd (see Isaiah 53:6). The solution, as radical as any in the Bible, is to choose their own leaders from amongst themselves (vv. 3–5). People used to being under a ruling class or family need to be encouraged to take the lead themselves. That is what the prophet is doing here. He tells them that with God's help society is going to be turned upside down: they will be like 'mighty men in battle' while those that ride on horses will be brought down. They can provide their own rulers, their own weapons, their own cornerstone: 'The very stone which the builders rejected has become the head of the corner; this was the Lord's doing, and it is marvellous in our eyes' (Mark 12:10–11; Psalm 118:22–23). God will show them a mother's compassion. Under the new leadership divisions will be healed and the people will find new strength and hope in their unity. Everyone, young and old, will enjoy the new freedom (vv. 6–7).

There will be another exodus from the lands where they have been in exile. Verse 9 almost suggests it will be as though they have come back from the dead: 'with their children they shall live (or come to life) and return'. They pass safely through 'seas of distress' (not 'Egypt': see RSV footnote to v. 11). Their mighty oppressors, Egypt and Assyria, will be powerless to stop them, and they will be free. There will hardly be enough room in the land when they all come home (compare Isaiah 54:1–3).

The last verse sums it all up in two famous biblical phrases: they will be 'strong in the Lord' and they will 'walk in his name' (RSV 'glory' is not in the Hebrew text). This is a new society, based on a living faith, because it is God's society, created by him and founded on obedience to his laws of justice and righteousness. This is what 'walking in his name' means.

Amid all the exotic imagery the most remarkable theme is the role of ordinary people in the hoped-for 'new society'.

The prophet is now called to address a situation of injustice in his own country and, like a good shepherd, try to rescue his flock from neglect and exploitation. The people in power believe that their wealth is a gift from God ('Blessed be the Lord, I have become rich', v. 5), a reward no doubt for their righteousness, and are without a scrap of compassion for the sufferings of the poor: 'a flock doomed to slaughter'.

Staffs broken. In traditional prophetic style (1 Kings 22:11; Isaiah 20; Jeremiah 19; Ezekiel 12:1–7) the prophet sought to get his message across by performing symbolic actions. He had two staffs (or shepherd's crooks) and he made them into symbols of what he most wanted to achieve: 'Grace' (or rather 'Beauty') and 'Union'. In place of ugly scenes of injustice, he wanted peace and harmony; and in place of discord and division, he wanted cooperation and unity of purpose (Zechariah 3:10). He failed. Hideous injustice continued and so he symbolically broke his two staffs. God's people could no longer be 'a light to the nations', to show the world what the 'Grace' of his covenant meant (v. 10). The covenant was that 'out of Zion would go forth the law and the word of the Lord from Jerusalem' (Isaiah 2:3). Instead, there was injustice and oppression, and Israel is nothing but a bad influence on the nations. The breaking of the other staff 'Union' symbolized the break-up of God's people (v. 14). Israel would be torn apart again as on the day when King Solomon's golden age ended (1 Kings 11:30–35). Even God's 'holy nation', his 'kingdom of priests' (Exodus 19:6) can be destroyed by injustice.

Thirty pieces of silver. 'The good shepherd' would not expect a wage for his work. So here the disillusioned prophet shows his contempt for current attitudes towards wealth by getting them to pay him thirty pieces of silver, which is the price of an injured slave (Exodus 21:32). Then, like another disillusioned hireling from a more familiar story (Matthew 27:5) he threw the money away. There is no mention of any 'treasury' in the Hebrew text: 'to the potter' (RSV footnote) sounds like an idiom corresponding to English 'to the birds'.

Transformation *Zechariah 12:1—13:1*

After an introductory verse proclaiming God as Creator of heaven and earth and 'the human spirit', these final prophecies (chapters 12–14) begin with pictures of Jerusalem marvellously transformed from powerlessness to strength (see Isaiah 41:14–15; 52:1–2). First, it is to be like a 'cup of reeling' or 'trembling'. This means that, if it falls into the hands of an enemy, it will make him suffer and render him incapable of standing upright, as though he had drunk some toxic beverage. Next, it will be like a heavy stone, so heavy that if anyone tries to carry it off, he will injure his back. Lastly, if any army tries to attack it, they will mysteriously panic: horses will run about blindly, not knowing where they are, and their riders will behave like madmen. The little family of Judah will look on in amazement and experience new strength and hope.

The picture of victory in verses 7–9 takes up the same egalitarian theme as 10:3–5. The ordinary people of the peasant communities in the Judaean countryside are to be given the same status as the royal family and the wealthy citizens of Jerusalem. The weakest members of society will have special protection 'on that day', and will have the strength of David to stand up to Goliath (1 Samuel 17). Idealism increases still further in the picture of the family of David (which includes the Messiah, of course) leading the triumphal procession and looking like God and his angels—a picture recalling chapters 1–3 as well as Hebrews 1:1–4.

Shock horror. The climax is reached in verse 10. A new spirit of compassion and supplication will turn the people away from their obsession with wealth and success, to the recognition of the suffering they have caused. The clue to this striking verse, quoted in the Passion narrative (John 19:37), is to be found in 13:1. Just as healing and forgiveness were discovered in the sufferings of the Servant of the Lord in Isaiah 53, so here the shame and horror at what they have done shock them out of their complacency. A new possibility of forgiveness appears, like a fountain (13:1), and they are cleansed from sin and uncleanness. Their suffering victim, like the Servant in Isaiah 53, is not identified, but probably refers collectively to the nation, till now wounded and destroyed by greed, neglect and injustice (see Isaiah 1:5–6).

The Book of Zechariah ends with the most vivid and, at the same time, the most universal picture of 'the day of the Lord'. The last battle between the powers of good and evil is fought to a finish. God is universally acknowledged as king over the whole earth, and worshipped in perfect holiness in Jerusalem. It is to be compared to the apocalyptic visions of the end of the world in Daniel and Revelation, but again picks up many of its ideas and images from Isaiah (3:24–26; 40:3–5, 9–10; 65:17–25; 66:18–21). It begins with the siege and destruction of a defenceless Jerusalem. The armies of the world are attracted by the prospects of unopposed pillaging and rape. Then when all the principalities and powers of the world are gathered there, they are confronted by the power of God. An earthquake will open up a valley through the middle of the Mount of Olives. The whole land will become a plain, except for the new Jerusalem, standing secure on its holy mountain (v. 10). A terrible plague will break out in the camps of the invaders, and they will panic and start killing each other (vv. 12–15). The survivors will recognize the supremacy of God and come to Jerusalem to worship him once a year at the Feast of Booths. God reigns at last supreme over the whole earth.

Faith. In all this, one verse stands out, verse 9, where the kingship of God and his oneness are linked, as they are in Isaiah 44:6. Prayers for the coming of the kingdom (like the Lord's Prayer) are prayers for the victory of the one true God over all other powers. Hymns celebrating the kingship of God, after his defeat of the powers of chaos and injustice (Psalm 93, 97–99; Isaiah 43:15–21), are expressions of faith in his power to overcome evil. So verse 9 (along with Deuteronomy 6:4–5 and Mark 12:29) is a kind of creed: 'We believe in one God, who is king over all the earth.'

New Jerusalem. The temple regulations with which the book ends (vv. 20–21) remind us that the prophets Haggai and Zechariah were closely involved in the building of the second temple, and were themselves perhaps priests. They nicely round off their vision of a new Jerusalem, where impurity and materialism will be banished forever from the house of God (Mark 11:15–18).

MALACHI

The Book of Malachi presents a striking contrast to the preceding book of Zechariah. In place of the visions and powerful figurative language of Zechariah, Malachi is concerned with practical matters and with plain speaking. The book is generally regarded as anonymous. It is unlikely that Malachi is the prophet's name. It means in Hebrew 'my messenger' and is probably taken from 3:1, although the messenger there referred to is not the prophet. Nevertheless, to be God's messenger was the essence of a prophet's role.

Malachi's main concern is with the religious questions of worship, temple and priesthood, though, like the great eighth-century prophets, he does not ignore the fundamental importance of human relationships to a right relationship with God. One of the main themes of the book is 'faithfulness'—faithfulness to God and to one's fellow humans, not least to wives. Malachi is totally against divorce. It is the breaking of the solemn covenant of marriage (2:14).

The book is commonly assigned to the mid-fifth century BC, around the year 450. The reference to 'governor' in 1:8 suggests the post-exilic period when Judah no longer had a king but was under Persian control. This is the word used of Nehemiah who was appointed governor of Judah under the Persians in 445BC (Nehemiah 5:14). It is generally agreed that Malachi is to be dated a little earlier than Nehemiah's time since the sorry state of affairs described in the book shows no knowledge of the reforms of either Ezra or Nehemiah. However, it is difficult to be certain on this point as much of the history of fifth-century Judah is obscure.

The Old Testament ends with a pointer to the future. To this the New Testament responds: 'the time is fulfilled, and the kingdom of God is at hand; repent, and believe in the gospel.' Malachi 3:1 becomes the beginning of Mark's Gospel (1:2). The promised Elijah (Malachi 4:5) is identified as John the Baptist (Mark 9:11–13). The implications for the New Testament understanding of the person of Jesus are clear. He is not the Lord's forerunner but the Messiah (Mark 8:28–29).

For further reading

J.G. Baldwin, *Haggai, Zechariah, Malachi*, Tyndale Commentary

R.J. Coggins, *Haggai, Zechariah, Malachi*, Old Testament Guides, Sheffield

R.A. Mason, *Haggai, Zechariah, Malachi*, Cambridge Bible Commentary

Dishonourable worship *Malachi 1:1–14*

Malachi is a book full of questions, a book of controversy and argument between the Lord and his people. 'I have loved you' says the Lord (v. 2); not a new idea (see Deuteronomy 7:7–8; Hosea 11:1), but this time challenged by a dispirited people. Their days as an independent nation had gone with the exile. The community was small and impoverished, under a Persian governor (v. 8). And so the people retort: show us the evidence, prove your love. The proof, says the prophet, is not confined to the past, to God's dealings with their ancestor Jacob (Genesis 27–28; 32:22–32. What a trickster he was!). Israel has a future, and God is active.

For its enemy Edom the words are harsh (vv. 3–4). But this is no petty favouritism. Edom was a brother nation turned ruthless enemy at the time of Jerusalem's defeat by the Babylonians (Psalm 137:7). It becomes in the Old Testament a symbol for cruel treachery (Ezekiel 35:15; Joel 3:19–20). God is powerful 'beyond Israel's borders', righting wrongs and seeing justice done (v. 5). But if this gives comfort to Israel, what follows shatters their complacency. Israel's own priests, not Edom, are the target of the prophet's searing denunciation. For the great God (twenty-three times Malachi calls him 'the Lord of hosts') is belittled, and that in the very act of worship. The priests are argumentative and self-satisfied: 'How have we despised your name . . . polluted the altar?' (vv. 6–7). By replacing joyful worship with grudging obligation, giving God their left-overs, and boredom to boot!

Malachi seems much concerned with religious observances, less with social justice than his great predecessors (though see 3:5). But outward observance is symptomatic of inner commitment: theology affects daily living and belief shapes action. Better no offerings at all than unworthy ones (v. 10), a sentiment similar to Paul's in 1 Corinthians 11:27–29. Verse 11 is much discussed. Is it referring to worship by Jews living in Gentile nations (the diaspora) or to any sincere pagan worship? Psalm 50 suggests another possibility. The Psalmist, too, affirms God's universal rule 'from the rising of the sun to its setting' (v. 1), God's constant presence and power, and, in this context, questions the efficacy of animal sacrifice: 'Offer to God a sacrifice of thanksgiving' (vv. 7–15). Malachi's intention in verse 11 may be similar.

Keeping faith *Malachi 2:1–17*

Chapter 1 accused the priests of dishonouring God. But God does not lightly let his servants go. This chapter calls for a new start, 'Now, O priests . . .' Above all, it emphasizes the seriousness of sin and personal accountability.

Verse 3 is not just gratuitously offensive. It speaks figuratively of the loss of ritual purity and of consequent exclusion from priestly office. The choice is theirs, and it is a solemn one, for priesthood means both privilege and obligation, grounded, says the prophet, in an ancient covenant between God and their forebear Levi (see Deuteronomy 33:8–11). (Malachi incidentally, like Deuteronomy, classes priests and Levites together, in contrast to another view in the Old Testament which regards Levites as assistants to the priests—Numbers 18:1–3.) God wants this covenant to hold. But a covenant has two partners and imposes mutual obligation—the gift of 'life and peace' is to be matched by the response of reverence (v. 5).

Malachi's view of priesthood is high. The priest is 'the *messenger* of the Lord of hosts' (v. 7), a role more characteristic of prophets. Malachi is sometimes criticized as narrow in his emphasis on sacrifice, yet he sees instruction, not sacrifice, as the priesthood's primary task. But the priests betray their calling. The contrast between the ideal and the actual is poignant, not least in their bias to the rich (vv. 8–9).

Verses 10–17 seem to be addressed to the people generally. Now the prophet asks the questions. With one father Jacob (see 3:6; or is God meant?) and one God their Creator, why not keep faith with each other and with the covenant which God made at Sinai with their ancestors? The prophet does not spell out the covenant requirements. The people know them. It is not knowledge they lack but commitment, threatening the community's survival by foreign marriages which implicate them in pagan worship (see the solemn warnings in Exodus 34:16; Deuteronomy 7:3–4).

Yet the people are penitent, flooding the altar with tears (v. 13). Why doesn't God respond? Because human relationships are part and parcel of relationship with God. Breaking faith with their wives meant breaking faith with God (vv. 14–16).

Verse 17 reverts to the basic complaint of priests and people: God is remote, unconcerned, indifferent to morality. But this chapter has shown that morality is at the heart of worship, a view similar to Matthew 5:23–24.

Unchanging God — *Malachi 3:1—4:6*

The question at the end of chapter 2 is answered immediately. God *is* coming, and first to the place of worship. After the custom of Eastern monarchs, a messenger goes before the 'great king' (1:14), announcing his coming (compare Isaiah 40:3). The 'delight' of verse 1 contrasts dramatically with the reality. The remote, inactive God of the people's complaints comes in awesome, overpowering presence (v. 2). If worship is to be worthy, its leaders must suffer the pain of cleansing (vv. 3–4). Malachi (like Amos 5:18–20) radically reinterprets a popular hope.

To understand the verses that follow we must realize that this chapter is not a simple sequence. The prophet's thought darts to and fro with the solemn urgency of his message. Verse 5 is not the sequel to verse 4, but reverts to the querulous question (2:17), 'Where is the God of justice?' But justice (*mishpat*) means also judgment, and that against God's own people, against all who violate the integrity and liberty of others. Malachi's concern is clear. For him worship and ethics meet.

A new section begins with verse 6 (the word 'for' in RSV is misleading and better translated 'truly'). God has not changed (1:2) despite the sceptics' complaints. The broken relationship is not his doing: 'return . . . and I will return' (v. 7). But the people are uncomprehending. The failure of the priests means an untaught people (2:7–8). 'What need to return/repent?' they ask. They know not that they are robbing God, they the worshippers (v. 9).

Yet there is a way forward. Verses 10–12 bring both challenge and promise. Malachi is often criticized here for a mechanical, simplistic view of blessing. This is unlikely. His intention throughout is to expose the attitude which devalues commitment and diminishes God's sovereign freedom, binding him in automatic response to ritual action. Malachi's eschatological hope has an immediate and practical counterpart. Tithes are the necessary support of the Levites (Nehemiah 13:10–11 shows the sad results of non-payment), and where their task of teaching is fulfilled the outcome will be blessing. Then the community will be at last a *delight* to the Lord in whom they had, unworthily, professed to *delight* (3:1).

The complaints of the sceptics continue (vv. 13–15), but now other voices respond: God not only hears, he remembers (for the idea of a record, see Esther 2:23; 6:1) and takes action to claim his treasured possession (v. 17).

Malachi is an uncomfortable book. It shatters the complacency of those who would trifle with holy things, whose religion bolsters their ease and self-satisfaction, makes no demands and effects no transformation. It is a warning against the insidious externalizing of commitment, a reminder of how dead faith can become even for those who profess to worship the Lord, the king.

BIBLE READING NOTES FROM BRF

BRF publishes two regular series of Bible reading notes—*New Daylight* and *Guidelines.* These are published three times a year (in January, May and September).

New Daylight provides a pattern for daily Bible reading. Each day's reading contains a Bible passage (printed out in full, from the version chosen by the contributor), along with a brief commentary and explanation, and a suggestion for prayer, meditation or reflection. The sections of commentary often draw on and reflect the experiences of the contributors themselves and thus offer contemporary and personal insights into the readings. Sunday readings focus on the themes of prayer and Holy Communion.

Guidelines contains running commentary, with introductions and background information, arranged in weekly units. Each week's material is usually broken up into at least six sections. Readers can take as much or as little at a time as they wish. The whole 'week' can be used at a sitting, or split up into convenient parts: this flexible arrangement allows for one section to be used each weekday. A Bible will be needed. The last section of each week is usually called 'Guidelines' and has points for thought, meditation and prayer. A short list of books, to help with further reading, appears at the end of some contributions.

Both *New Daylight* and *Guidelines* may be obtained from your local SPCK bookshop or by subscription direct from BRF.

For more information about the notes and the full range of BRF publications, write to: BRF, Peter's Way, Sandy Lane West, OXFORD, OX4 5HG (Tel: 01865 748227)